D1141681

The New Sociological Imagination

The New Sociological Imagination

Steve Fuller

SAGE Publications
London ● Thousand Oaks ● New Delhi

© Steve Fuller 2006

First published 2006

Apart from any fair dealing for the purposes of research
or private study, or criticism or review, as permitted
under the Copyright, Designs and Patents Act, 1988, this
publication may be reproduced, stored or transmitted
in any form, or by any means, only with the prior
permission in writing of the publishers, or in the case of
reprographic reproduction, in accordance with the terms
of licences issued by the Copyright Licensing Agency.
Enquiries concerning reproduction outside those terms
should be sent to the publishers.

 SAGE Publications Ltd
1 Oliver's Yard
55 City Road
London EC1Y 1SP

SAGE Publications Inc.
2455 Teller Road
Thousand Oaks, California 91320

SAGE Publications India Pvt Ltd
B-42, Panchsheel Enclave
Post Box 4109
New Delhi 110 017

British Library Cataloguing in Publication data

A catalogue record for this book is available
from the British Library

ISBN-10 0 7619 4756 6   ISBN-13 978 0 7619 4756 1
ISBN-10 0 7619 4757 4 (pbk) ISBN-13 978 0 7619 4757 8

Library of Congress Control Number: 2005928700

Typeset by C&M Digitals (P) Ltd, Chennai, India
Printed in Great Britain by Athenaeum Press, Gateshead

Contents

Contents

Preface

Several years ago Sujatha Raman urged me to write a book explicitly dedicated to 'social theory', since it was clear that social theorists were no less parochial than any other speciality and were especially allergic to the sort of reflexive considerations introduced by the sociology of knowledge. Indeed, the ease with which social theory detaches its concerns from empirical sociology makes it a sitting duck for ideology critique. Little surprise, then, that social theory's rise as an autonomous field over the past quarter century has corresponded to ideology critique's terminal decline. In contrast, I have always believed that the most interesting social theory is never about theory *per se* but some empirical domain or pressing policy matter.

My opportunity to write this book came at the instigation of Chris Rojek, who had liked my review of Adorno's *Introduction of Sociology* that appeared in the Autumn 2000 issue of *The European Journal of Social Theory*. The original idea was for me to write a 21st century version of C. Wright Mills' 1959 classic, *The Sociological Imagination*. This book shares Mills' somewhat paranoid political sensibility, his broadly positivistic methodological sympathies, his allergy to trendy academic Newspeak (with structural-functionalism here replaced by postmodernism) and his conviction that social science is vital to confronting the (now very different) future that awaits us. A sense of just how much the world has changed since Mills' day can be gleaned by glancing at the terms and definitions listed in this book's Glossary, only about half of which he would recognize.

I have delivered parts of this book on various occasions over the past five years. However, in terms of presenting more-or-less the book's entirety, special thanks must first go to my students in two Warwick University MA courses,

Philosophy and Social Theory and Sociology of Modernity, and the graduate summer school at the University of Lund, Helsingborg, both held in 2004. Thanks to Anne Kovalainen and Pekka Selkunen, who invited me to present the annual Westermarck Lecture to the Finnish Sociological Association in 2002. A debt is also owed to Davydd Greenwood and Immanuel Wallerstein, who permitted me to develop my thoughts in the context of projects sponsored by, respectively, the Ford and Gulbenkian Foundations. Some of my past and present graduate students whose work has engaged me with relevant issues that I might have otherwise neglected include Ahmed Bouzid, Nigel Christian, Jim Collier, William Gisby, Kirk Junker, Joan Leach, Bill Lynch, Hugo Mendes, James Mittra, Govindan Parayil, Peter Schwartzman, Mark B. Smith, Milena Stateva, Maiko Watanabe. Others who have offered me insight and inspiration, as well as useful criticism, include Zainal Abidin, Alf Bång, Babette Babich, Randall Collins, Gerard Delanty, David Depew, Jean-Pierre Dupuy, Aditi Gowri, Paul Griffiths, Patrick Heelan, Meera Nanda, Greg Radick, Greg Ransom, Amanda Rees, Francis Remedios, Gene Rosa, Arnaud Sales, Zia Sardar, Skuli Sigurdsson, Nico Stehr, Roger Trigg, Stephen Turner, Anne Witz. Finally, this book is dedicated to my former partner, Stephanie Lawler, without whom I would have been much less human.

Introduction

My starting point is that sociology, as the flagship discipline of the social sciences, is suffering from an identity crisis. The crisis is epitomized by those both in and out of academia who wonder what the field adds that cannot be already gleaned from the humanities and/or the natural sciences. Even if this question lacked a serious intellectual basis, it would still have a firm institutional basis – especially when universities happily restructure departments in response to market pressures. It is much too easy to justify the existence of sociology simply by pointing to the availability of large research grants and student enrolments. For those solely concerned with maximizing demand, the next question is *not* how to bolster sociology but how to find more efficient means of meeting and increasing demand. Sociology is thus reduced to a disposable means to the maximization of policy-relevant research income and employer-friendly accredited degrees. Sociologists deserve a better grounding for a discipline of historically noble aspirations.

The central aspiration of sociology – and the social sciences more generally – has been to make good on the 18th century Enlightenment promise of creating a 'heaven on earth'. This vivid, perhaps even scary, turn of phrase refers to the systematic secularization and scientization of monotheism, which privileges human beings as created in the image and likeness of God. The aim, then, is to create a world in which humans exercise dominion over nature without exercising dominion over each other. *The New Sociological Imagination* is an updated attempt to articulate that ambition. Until the advent of the social sciences, both humanists and natural scientists have found this goal ridiculous. On the one hand, before the sociologically induced field of cultural studies, humanists have found only a minority of humans fit to exercise dominion, namely, the authors and authorized interpreters of the 'classics'. On the other hand, the history of the natural sciences can be told as a long struggle to erase whatever distinctions monotheistic societies have introduced to discriminate humans from non-humans – what Max Weber originally called the 'disenchantment of the world'.

We should not forget that what is often derided as the 'instrumentalist' and 'positivist' approach to science represented by Francis Bacon, Auguste Comte and, perhaps more controversially, sociology's Holy Trinity of Marx, Weber and Durkheim, treated the natural sciences as a means to overcome the prejudices of classical humanism in the name of a truly 'social science' that would have something to say *about, to* and *for* every human. Before reason was 'reduced' to an instrument that could be used by specific people to achieve specific ends, it had been largely presented as a divine possession that might be transmitted to humans as a gift. And before positivism paved the road to validity with sense data, explicit logic and verifiable procedures, truth was often delegated to divinely anointed experts, if it did not elude human comprehension altogether. In a time when the distinctiveness of humanity is itself at risk, it becomes important to stress the uniquely anthropocentric character of these movements that are too easily dismissed today.

To be sure, much harm has been done in the names of 'instrumentalism' and 'positivism' – but no more so than by the alternatives. While it would be hard to find a self-avowed positivist who supported Hitler, some hermeneuticians and deconstructionists at least went along for the ride. In any case, the promise of social science remains as long as these harms can be traced to humans in their various social arrangements who can be held responsible for their actions, from which future generations may learn. This is in stark contrast to envisaging that the ills of the world result from either an incorrigible and unaccountable deity or blind natural forces, including those inhabiting our own bodies. An unfortunate feature of our postmodern condition is that one quickly moves from admitting the difficulty of tracing both the causes and effects of human action to rejecting the task altogether, typically in a Nietzschean 'post-ethical' gesture. To the true social scientist this gesture is neither big nor clever but simply an abdication of responsibility for the decision-making contexts that challenge and define our common humanity.

In the pages that follow, the reader will note that I make much of one's attitude towards history. This is in keeping with my own project of *social epistemology*, a normative version of the sociology of knowledge that aims to use what is empirically known about organized inquiry to enlighten our present and empower our future (Fuller, 1988). There is a tendency, even among sociologists, to stereotype the sociology of knowledge as reducing complex patterns of thought to mere 'reflections' of their socio-historical settings, thereby rendering every argument self-serving. The basic problem with this caricature is that it conflates matters relating to one's sense of *location* and *destination* in history. If people's minds simply reflected their environments, there would be no need for the sociology of knowledge. Empiricism or perhaps phenomenology would do the trick. However, people are generally dissatisfied with where they find themselves and aspire to a better state. Beyond an interest in demystifying and usurping theological authority, this is what made the 'self-transcendent' character of religion so fascinating to the early social scientists. If our knowledge is the most coherent expression of our experience, then why don't we settle for less in life? Why don't we accept distress, disappointment, defeat and death more gracefully by justifying them as *facts* rather than turning them into *problems* for social policy and political action? Why have we longed to change the world and not simply cope with it? To me these are the questions that define the legitimacy of the social sciences, and the sociology of knowledge deserves credit for having consistently raised them.

My robust defence of humanity as the central project of the social sciences reflects my own precocious entry and advancement in academia. I arrived just as the project was beginning its downturn. The third quarter of the 20th century will be remembered for two tendencies that underscore the profundity of Alvin Gouldner's expression, 'welfare-warfare state': an unprecedented expansion in the capacities of various parts of the globe for widespread destruction, corresponding to an unprecedented redistribution of political and economic resources both within and across nations. In terms of *Realpolitik*, the two sides were alternative deterrence strategies – threats and bribes – in a world where large groups of people fundamentally distrusted each other. However, one of the original logical positivists, Otto Neurath, had proposed in the aftermath of the First World War that the redistributivist ethic associated with a wartime economy could be justified even without the sense of 'permanent emergency', a phrase from Bismarck's Germany that Daniel Bell later recast to capture the Cold War mentality (Proctor, 1991: Chapter 9). Indeed, after the Second World War, evidence emerged in the spread of welfare states that struck a balance between capitalist and socialist excesses, even in nations with strong libertarian traditions like the UK and USA. I chart and diagnose the decline of this sensibility in order to identify new vistas for a rejuvenated sense of 'society' and a science fit to study and minister to it. As of this writing there remains one significant site for the sensibility I seek more generally: the United Nations, which has tried to keep the world's focus on problems its states can tackle more effectively in unison than in opposition. Sachs (2005) is an excellent recent expression that even acknowledges a spiritual ancestor who also figures in these pages, the Marquis de Condorcet.

Readers expecting extended treatments of such scholastic staples as 'agency *versus* structure', 'micro *versus* macro' and 'constructivist *versus* realist', will be sorely disappointed. Most of these binaries lacked any salience in sociology before the 1970s and will do little to help address the discipline's 21st century predicament. This is simply because the binaries take for granted the legitimacy of sociology, a standpoint that may work with more impressionable undergraduates but is unlikely to persuade those familiar with contemporary intellectual currents. I develop this observation in Part One. Chapter 1 argues that the vividness of 'society' as a distinct domain of inquiry has gradually disappeared with the rise of neo-liberalism and postmodernism, which are roughly the political and philosophical sides of the same world-historic movement. In Chapter 2, I sketch the world we are on the verge of losing, one that joins the social sciences and socialism together in the project of turning *Homo sapiens* into proper human beings. Chapters 3 and 4 chart the rise and fall of socialism as the political vehicle for this project, drawing attention to the vexed role played by the biological character of humans in defining matters of welfare, especially since an increase in animal and more broadly ecological concerns has coincided with a contraction of the public funding base for human welfare. Chapter 5 highlights the overlooked contribution of the British sociological tradition to this discussion. Of the major national traditions, Britain's alone came to grips with Darwin in a way that boosted sociology's scientific and political relevance, the principal legacy of which is the welfare state. America's was the only other national tradition equally permeated by Darwinism, but its early sociologists took it in rather disparate scientific and political directions, as exemplified by the laissez-faire capitalism of William Graham Sumner, the populist eugenicism of Edward A. Ross, the symbolic interactionism of George Herbert Mead and the ecological segregationism of Robert Park (Hofstadter, 1955). Finally, Chapter 6 illustrates how contemporary sociological discourse obscures the issues raised in the previous five chapters.

Part Two considers the various ways biology has influenced and challenged the social sciences. Chapter 7 shows how certain biological views have been presupposed, sometimes tacitly and often analogically, by the main strands of the sociological tradition. Chapter 8 brings the matter up-to-date by identifying better and worse ways for social scientists to engage with human biology. The lesson here is that sociologists should stop deferring to the authority of biologists – both those who encourage and discourage us from incorporating their findings. Instead an independent sociological understanding of biological knowledge is required, especially given the rise of 'bioprospecting', a heady mix of molecular biology, medical concern and global capitalism. Chapter 9 introduces Peter Singer's attempt to replace Marx with Darwin as the scientific foundation of progressive politics in an era that has witnessed the reversal of socialism's fortunes. This is the point at which the alarm should sound for those interested in preserving the integrity of social science. The normative retreat from 'humanity' to 'human nature' to simply 'nature' entailed by Singer's 'Darwinian Left' is further developed in Chapter 10 by following the cross-species migration of the concept of 'sympathy' as a basis for moral concern.

Part Three projects this recent re-biologization of the social world on a larger world-historic canvas. Chapter 11 distils the issue into a clash of worldviews, albeit one that defies the current trend to define global tensions in terms of the West's difficulties with Islam. Indeed, I include Islam with the West as 'anthropic' cultures, the science in which is historically informed by monotheism, a phenomenon whose centrality to the sociological tradition is too often overlooked. However, the Darwinian Left marks a significant move in what I call a more 'karmic' direction, whereby the human is reabsorbed into natural history. Chapter 12 makes clear what is at stake, namely, the privileging of human beings as the locus of value in nature. 'Orientalism' and 'Occidentalism' refer to the complementary ways in which denizens of traditionally Christian and Muslim cultures demonize each other for having failed to respect that privilege. This point can both help us come to grips with '9/11' and alert us to the significance that over the past quarter century international development policy has shifted from the specific goal of alleviating human misery to a more diffuse global ecological agenda, in which humans play an important but somewhat diminished role. These matters are taken up in Chapter 13. Chapter 14 situates this shift as part of the revival of 'racial hygiene', a biosocial science now discredited because of its deep involvement in the Holocaust. Nevertheless, its sensibility remains in recent calls for biodiversity and the curtailment of human expansion. Arguing counterfactually, I propose that had the Nazis not embarked on the Holocaust, they might well have brought us closer to the 'paradise' advanced by today's ecological activists.

The book concludes by arguing that the Darwinian Left and the affiliated sciences of sociobiology and evolutionary psychology by no means spell the end of social science, since these would-be successor fields leave what it means to be human radically indeterminate. However, they do force us to consider the extent to which our humanity depends on our biology. Strong anti-biological currents may be found in traditions as disparate as philosophical rationalism and idealism, artificial intelligence and cyborg technosciences and, of course, the 'artificial person' (i.e. *universitas*, or 'corporation'), the legal category on the back of which the social sciences were first launched. Perhaps some combination of these currents can turn a re-imagined sociology into a reality for our times.

As this summary already makes clear, I take seriously the *prima facie* claim that the biological sciences can explain social life. In particular, I do not deny the presumptive basis for reducing sociology to biology, namely, that all social life, regardless of species, began from transactions among individuals whose identities rest on family membership. According to this logic, social formations that behave most like families (i.e. proto-racially) are most likely to survive. An example of this line of thought is that states fail because they 'artificially' try to maintain complex relations among individuals who bear no 'natural' relationship to each other. Thus, I am willing to entertain Richard Dawkins' 'selfish gene' view of modern evolutionary theory as the burden that social science needs to overcome to maintain its autonomy from the natural sciences. My response is to argue that what makes some animals 'human' is their participation in large-scale corporate projects that defy the gene's eye-view of the world, largely because they have managed to control their selection environment sufficiently to neutralize, and sometimes reverse, the effects of what Darwinists call 'natural selection'. These socially constructed categories of selection then become the primary sources of personal identity and the terms in which survival is redefined.

A rough-and-ready mark of the human is that people are more concerned with the transmission of their *ideas*, or even their *reputations*, across generations than their genes, or even knowledge of their family lineage. Indeed, that people, including academics outside the social sciences, normally find it difficult to accept that ideas have any material bases whatsoever offers an albeit perverse ray of hope. On the one hand, it helps to explain the perennial scepticism toward the sociology of knowledge; on the other, it equally explains the aversion throughout the ages to accept a fully biologistic understanding of the human condition.

There are three historic precedents for a distinctive counter-biological sense of 'social selection': *religious, academic* and *political*. First, the universalist aspiration of Christianity provided the basis on which Auguste Comte proposed sociology as a science aimed specifically at bringing certain animals (*Homo sapiens*) closer to divine salvation. The second and more down-to-earth precedent is the long-standing academic interest in independently examining candidates in terms of their personal achievement, which has tended to undercut any association between merit and origins. The third and most extensive precedent, which explains the perennial sociological fascination with Hobbes, has been the institution of citizenship as imposing obligations on individuals – such as voting, tax payment and military service – that compels them to engage in activities whose main beneficiaries range significantly beyond oneself and one's kin.

Finally, before embarking on the task before us, some remarks are in order about how – or, indeed, whether – the practice of sociology would need to be different in my 're-imagined' form. Certainly the word 'sociology' would recover its original normative force, as disciplinary practitioners see themselves contributing to the constitution of the societies they study, typically by raising subjects' collective self-consciousness. Such an account most naturally fits action-oriented research today, but I believe that even – and perhaps especially – more classically positivistic 'hypothetico-deductive' approaches to social research should be seen in this light. Much more important than sharply dividing science and politics is the idea that sociological claims are testable against their target populations. Here positivistic methods, which treat experimentation as the gold standard of research, offer two greatly underestimated virtues. The first is their concern with sharply distinguishing what the sociologist claims and what the subjects express or reveal about themselves. The other is their tendency to envisage subjects in situations somewhat alien from their natural surroundings. The former grounds both the inquirer's accountability and autonomy, thereby overcoming the temptation toward irresponsible ventriloquism, while the latter points to the capacity of subjects to become other and, ideally, more than they have been, thereby avoiding a complacent pessimism toward the prospects of change. This empowering and progressive side of positivism is neither much seen nor heralded anymore. However, as I shall now endeavour to show, it deserves to be recovered as part of the new sociological imagination.

PART ONE

DESPERATELY SEEKING SOCIOLOGY IN THE 21ST CENTURY

ONE

Tales of the Academic Undead

The Mysterious Disappearance of Society

We social scientists are the Academic undead who restlessly roam the earth dreaming of a world filled with 'social facts' that we mistake for the actual world we no longer quite inhabit. This hypothesis would certainly explain why we can't see ourselves reflected in general histories of science. It would also account for why those of us most protective of the title 'social scientist' – sociologists – are also most likely to drag any current issue back to a pastiche of Karl Marx, Max Weber and Émile Durkheim (and perhaps one or two others), whereby the understanding of European reality in the first decade of the dearly departed 20th century is treated not as a graveyard of defunct ideals but the matrix out of which all subsequent social understandings must emerge. Perhaps that is also why the 'critical' posture of social science typically feeds off the world as it is without saying much to its inhabitants about how it ought to be. A final sign of our Undead status might be the increasing success of humanists and natural scientists in forging a 'third culture' that reasserts a robust conception of *human nature* that is brandished at least as a crucifix, if not wielded as a dagger, in our recoiling faces (Brockman, 1995, www.edge.org).

Let's hope I have described no more than the nightmare of one living social scientist. But suppose we really are the Academic Undead. It would not be hard to identify a moment when our fate was sealed. Indeed, it may have been first announced in supermarket newstands across the UK on 3 October 1987, when *Women's Own* magazine published an interview with Prime Minister Margaret Thatcher. It contained the following notorious passage:

I think we've been through a period where too many people have been given to understand that if they have a problem, it's the government's job to cope with it. 'I have a problem, I'll get a grant.' 'I'm homeless, the government must house me.' They're casting their problem on society. And, you know, *there is no such thing as society*. There are individual men and women, and there are families. And no government can do anything except through people, and people must look to themselves first. It's our duty to look after ourselves and then, also to look after our neighbour. People have got the entitlements too much in mind, without the obligations. There's no such thing as entitlement, unless someone has first met an obligation.

This assertion unleashed a torrent of social scientific, social theoretic, and socialistic critique, not least the characteristically earnest Fabian Society pamphlet (no. 536), 'Does society exist?' Authored by Brian Barry, an analytic philosopher who was then Professor of Political Theory at the London School of Economics (LSE), the pamphlet dutifully weighed the arguments on both sides of the issue before concluding that, contrary to Mrs Thatcher's assertion, society does indeed exist. While Barry may have assuaged the fears of Labour Party operatives, little had he realized that Thatcher was anticipating what is nowadays, generally speaking, a rather respectable and self-styled 'progressive' view across the arts and sciences – not least in sociology, where the leading professor in the UK's leading department, and disciplinary chair for two iterations of the national 'Research Assessment Exercise', entitled his vision for the 21st century, *Sociology beyond Societies*, in which 'beyond' is meant more subtractively than additively (Urry, 2000).

I call this emergent sensibility, associated with the new 'third culture' and toward which even sociologists are gradually moving, *bioliberalism*. Bioliberalism consists of a politically devolved eugenics policy that encourages the *casualization of the human condition*, by which I mean the tendency to make it easier for humans to come in and out of existence, especially in terms that do not presume the human condition to be an unmitigated good. Bioliberalism is the biggest threat to the social sciences, as both a disciplinary and a political project: that is, *sociology* and *socialism*. The two italicized concepts are more intertwined than many wish to admit. Indeed, were another reason needed to believe that social scientists constitute the Academic Undead, it would be the ease with which we dissociate the incontrovertible decline of socialism from the sustainability of sociology as a field that retains an intuitive appeal to students and operational purchase on researchers.

My Gothic imagery is partly inspired by the Gulbenkian Commission on the future of the social sciences convened by the world-systems theorist Immanuel Wallerstein (1996). It concluded that the very idea of the social sciences – especially 'sociology' as the name for the general science of society – has outlived its usefulness. According to the Commission, sociology had made sense over the previous 150 years, with the ascendancy of nation-states in the Europeanized world increasingly concerned with integrating diverse peoples in terms of a set of sub-systems, each fulfilling an essential social function, to which the standard-issue sociology textbook dutifully assigned a chapter: Family, Education, Economy, Health, State, etc. Talcott Parsons' structural-functionalism marked the high watermark in this conception of sociology (Parsons, 1951).

However, the end of the Cold War has resulted in the decline of the 'welfare-warfare state', to recall Alvin Gouldner's (1970) resonant phrase for the entity upheld by Parsons that defined clear ideological loyalties, secured the country's physical borders and checked the flow of global capital. Unsurprisingly, as the 20th century came to a close, both empiricists and theorists drew increasing attention to the indeterminate and permeable boundaries of 'society', often in the spirit of heralding a 'postmodern' or 'non-modern' condition that replaces traditional hierarchical relations between 'macro' and 'micro' entities with a flat ontology of indefinitely extendable networks whose members need not even be human (Lyotard, 1983; Latour, 1993).

Of course, if sociology – or social science more generally – is currently in its death throes, then it must have come into being at some point. The parentage is certainly clear enough, even though the parents themselves were conjoined only in death. Although no one seriously questions the status of Durkheim and Weber as founding fathers, they were contemporaries in neighbouring countries who never took much interest in each other's work. Their mutual ignorance cannot be explained by some trade embargo between French and German academics, since each found colleagues in the other's country more interesting. The rather banal truth is that Weber and Durkheim simply thought they were doing different things. Theirs was a posthumous American-style shotgun wedding ministered by Parsons (1937).

To many Germans of Weber's generation, 'sociology' – with which Durkheim happily identified – still smacked of Auguste Comte, who had coined the term to promote social science and socialism as two sides of the same project, as Karl Marx did, in his own way, for the following generation (though without Comte's term or his obsessive concern to specify the programme's endpoint). German social scientists had struggled hard to keep themselves from being reduced to policy-driven researchers and classroom propagandists – and the word 'sociology' only served to muddy dangerous political waters (Proctor, 1991: Part 2).

A century later, sociology may be academically institutionalized, yet the mirror image of this problem arises on two fronts: on the one hand, eager-to-please 'evidence-based-policy' researchers and, on the other, true believers in 'identity politics'. For both, 'sociology' sounds pretentious, suggesting a rather grandiose conception of society above and beyond what (policy) clients or (student) constituents are willing to countenance. Yet, were they to view these matters from the grave, Durkheim and Weber could have finally agreed on the value of the term 'sociology' – if only to remind social researchers who closely identify with a specific clientele or a constituency that it is too easy to cater to market demand while the organized pursuit of social knowledge disintegrates, as interest in some aspects of social life attract attention at the expense of others of potentially equal import.

Durkheim's and Weber's contributions to the foundation of sociology appear Janus-faced because of the radically different visions of society they inferred from the respective fates of their countries in the Franco-Prussian War of 1870–1, which they both experienced as youngsters (cf. Baehr, 2002a: 20–5). France, one of Europe's oldest nation-states, had been humiliated in the war, which suggested its decline, even degeneration – as opposed to the vitality displayed by the recently unified Germany. Not surprisingly, then, Durkheim regarded 'society' as an organism whose ailments were explicable and treatable in medical terms, while Weber saw 'society' as an artificial configuration of individuals best understood through various legal and economic arrangements that enable them to do things they could not do on their own – such as turn Germany over the course of a generation into the powerhouse of Europe. Where Durkheim wanted norms that stabilized a potentially deteriorating situation, Weber sought norms that resolved power differences while expanding the parties' capacities for action. Thus, Durkheim positioned himself as keeper of the means of societal reproduction by teaching the next generation of French teachers, while Weber periodically offered himself as a political player, culminating in a role in drafting Germany's first republican constitution.

These alternative visions of society have been played out in the subsequent history of sociology. Epistemologically, Durkheim and Weber represent a 'top down' versus a 'bottom up' view of society, as might be expected of analysts who enter the scene of social action at different moments in the history of their respective countries – on the one hand, *in medias res*, and on the other, *ab initio*. The 1970s witnessed the scholastic entrenchment of the

Durkheim–Weber divide in ontological terms as 'structure' versus 'agency' (Giddens, 1979). An academically domesticated Karl Marx was inserted somewhat desperately into the breach as a possible basis for synthesis, given the 'agentic' (a.k.a. humanistic) bias of the early Marx and the 'structuralist' (a.k.a. economistic) bias of the later Marx (Bhaskar, 1979). (For a critique of this unfortunately enduring turn in social theory that props up Wallerstein's gloomy prognosis for the future of social science as a whole, see Fuller (1998a, b).)

Perhaps a death rattle from sociology's pedagogical trenches may be heard in courses relating to something called 'deviance', which retain their traditional popularity, though the word nowadays appears in scare quotes and researchers wince at the 'social problems' perspective from which the field arose. After all, deviance presupposes a strong sense of 'normativity', which after Michel Foucault has acquired a negative connotation that Durkheim would not have recognized. Instead of a Durkheimian focus on the sense of inclusiveness fostered by the public recognition of deviance from a common normative structure, the emphasis has now shifted to the deviants so excluded. Moreover, Foucault's historically based observations have been confirmed for the past quarter-century by micro-sociological studies, mostly by symbolic interactionists and ethnomethodologists. They have pointed to the ultimate unenforceability – or rather, arbitrary enforcement – of the norm-deviance binary. Thus, while sociology remains the preferred training ground for para-legal and para-medical professionals, students come out wanting to empower those traditionally dispossessed by the legal and medical systems.

Of course, this turn against systemic normativity has been 'progressive' in the obvious sense of conferring a renewed sense of agency on victims and patients, the criminal and the disabled (Rose, 1999). However, it has been a short-term benefit that needs to be measured against a long-term cost. This academic 'rage against the system' has come to be seen as an end in itself rather than a means to a larger end. Foucault and his fellow-travellers have had little feel for the dialectical character of history, according to which all putative ends are really means to some further ends. (This is what that recovering Hegelian and born again pragmatist, John Dewey, meant by 'instrumentalism', which was unfortunately lost on his more positivistic admirers.) Thus, the Foucaultians fixate on the second moment of a dialectic – the 'antithesis' – not realizing that it too is supposed to be superseded by a more comprehensive normative sensibility.

At risk, if not lost, in the Foucaultian demotion of dialectics is a rather deep Enlightenment idea – itself a secularization of the Christian salvation story – that was carried forward in the 19th and 20th centuries by followers of Hegel and especially Marx. It is that a norm that at first governs the practice of only a few can be extended to the many, overturning the default ('natural') tendencies of all concerned, thereby remaking the world for the greater benefit of everyone. In the past, the minority had dominated the majority by stabilizing their differences, typically by both legal and ideological means. Such was the nature of aristocracy. The Enlightenment proposed a more dynamic and even self-destructive sense of domination that has inspired the full range of left-leaning politics from liberal policies of expanding the electoral franchise to more explicitly socialist policies for redistributing wealth in a productive society. It is as joint recipients of this legacy that the fates of social science and socialism have been sealed together.

When, in the late 1970s, Foucaultian historiography and affiliated micro-sociologies were first regarded as joined in common cause against the Parsonian structural-functionalist sociology establishment, it was common to read the post-structuralist 'deconstruct' to mean the Marxist 'demystify'. In this context, the promiscuous use of words like 'critical' and 'reflexive' papered over what turned out to have been a profound difference in orientation. Originally, Foucault and friends were read as glorified troubleshooters who pinpointed how the Enlightenment had so far fallen short of its potential, which presumably could be remedied by better crafted legislation and administration. However, the Foucaultians truly came into their own in the 1980s, as faith in the welfare state, and socialist politics more generally, faded. Now their views were more likely to be seen in tandem with the emerging neo-liberal sensibility championed by that Thatcherite guru of political economy, Friedrich von Hayek. An important semantic marker of this transition is the regression from Kantian *autonomy* to Aristotelian *agency* to characterize the aspiration to self-determination by deviant groups. Whereas 'autonomy' implies the resistance and transcendence of natural tendencies (e.g. the temptation to sin, the submission to tradition), 'agency' implies the simple permission to express natural tendencies previously repressed (e.g. by the state).

Before Hayek accepted the chair at the LSE in 1932 from which he would sow the seeds of the neo-liberal counter-revolution, his mentor Ludwig von Mises had been the centre of an alternative Vienna Circle to the more famous one associated with the logical positivists and frequented by Ludwig Wittgenstein and Karl Popper (Hacohen, 2000: Chapter 5; Ebenstein, 2001: Chapter 5). These two Vienna Circles seeded the meta-scientific views of, respectively, the 'micro' and 'macro' perspectives in contemporary social science. Taking the latter first, the logical positivists were known in their heyday as the 'Red Vienna Circle' because its membership featured such card-carrying socialists as Otto Neurath and Rudolf Carnap, who held that societies could be modelled and regulated like closed physical systems, based on a few operationally defined, interacting variables (Reisch, 2005). The general equilibrium approach common to Parsonian structural-functionalism and Keynesian welfare economics drew epistemic sustenance from this perspective and, through Viennese émigrés like Paul Lazarsfeld, professionalized US social science in the Cold War era, mainly by the development of sophisticated quantitative methodology for relating individual and collective perceptions (Platt, 1996: Chapter 3). Thus, sociology became the science *of* and *for* the welfare state, the political rubric under which 'society' travelled. Perhaps the last original thinker in this tradition was James Coleman.

In contrast, the members of the Mises Circle wanted to turn the clock back to the 18th century Scottish Enlightenment, that is, when 'civil society' was still an object of natural history (as opposed to social engineering) and before nation-building became an expectation of statecraft. Eschewing all mathematical techniques, especially statistics, Mises' Vienna Circle held that no state planner could ever aggregate, let alone supersede, the collective experience of agents in a free market. They were highly critical of the Weimar Republic's tendency to see democratization in terms of mass mobilization, which in turn imputed a spurious cognitive superiority to organized groups over the phenomenology of situated individuals (cf. Peukert, 1993: Chapter 8).

Hayek aside, perhaps the most influential of this group was the international finance lawyer and amateur sociologist Alfred Schutz, whose own work came to be incorporated into the discipline's mainstream via the generalized invisible hand model of social order that continues to travel under the name of the 'social construction of reality' (Schutz, 1964; Berger and Luckmann, 1967). Indeed, the most faithful recent follower of this Viennese tradition has made the long – perhaps even unwitting – pilgrimage back from studying the distributed character of biomedical research to that of the financial markets where it all began (cf. Knorr-Cetina, 1999; Knorr-Cetina and Bruegger, 2002). Originally Schutz asserted what he called the 'social distribution of knowledge' in reaction to what he took to be the artificial collectivization of sentiment made possible by the emergence of tabloid newspapers and broadcast radio in the 1920s (Prendergast, 1986). Schutz was extending a point already found in Weber's later political writings, which would have the public recognize that the complexity of the modern world requires the 'professionalization' of politics, a consequence of which is that ordinary citizens would learn more but know less about how to operate in the political arena (Baehr, 1998: Chapters 3–4).

The balance sheet on Schutz's impact on the social sciences thus turns out to be rather mixed. On the one hand, as we shall see in Chapter 4, Schutz's critique of the pseudo-immediacy of mass communications can be deployed to mount an epistemic critique of today's anti-globalization movement. On the other hand, Schutz's market-driven fixation on 'intersubjectivity' (a.k.a. the price mechanism, through which buyers and sellers try to second-guess each other and then adjust their expectations accordingly) has helped to undermine the idea that individuals spontaneously possess a sociological sensibility transcendent of their daily interactions. I mean what the pragmatist George Herbert Mead called the 'generalized other' and the existentialist Jean-Paul Sartre dubbed the 'subject-we'. It is also what the classical sociologists held was responsible for large and 'heterogeneous' (often a euphemism for 'indifferent' or 'hostile') populations identifying equally with that most alienated of collective representations, 'God', who was then invested with the power of galvanizing the faithful into a collective agent with a unified sense of purpose. This spontaneous sociological sensibility underwrote the universalist projects unique to the human condition. However, thanks to Schutz and fellow-travellers, it is now fashionable to reduce the sociological to the intersubjective and to regard any irreducible residue as more disabling than enabling – a case of 'groupthink' rather than 'solidarity'.

Schutz's legacy is perhaps strongest today in Anthony Giddens, who has risen over the past two decades from prolific textbook writer to the architect of Tony Blair's 'third way' (itself an Orwellian re-working of an old phrase for the welfare state). Giddens' consistent scepticism about the prospects for organized movements of the sort traditionally represented by trade unions and class-based politics has led him to call for a shift in the political centre of gravity from 'welfare' to 'lifestyle' (Giddens, 1994; cf. Fuller, 1995). Schutz would smile. As Giddens has stressed from his earliest methodological writings, the 'reflexive' dimension of social life is not an invitation to greater public control at a higher level of social analysis, but merely a recognition that new levels of social reality often emerge as the unintended consequence of social interaction (Giddens, 1976). The only privilege enjoyed by sociologists is to be (usually) among the first to identify such new levels. They do not possess superior knowledge about where society will or should go, since social agents are themselves 'always already' social theorists. Indeed, Giddens' brand of reflexivity enables the social researcher to offload (or 'delegate', in Bruno Latour's Newspeak) personal responsibility for findings that could have just as easily come from her 'knowledgeable agents', had they been inclined to develop them. Thus, Giddens replaced 'theory' in the Marxist sense of a second-order epistemological critique with a less threatening Wittgensteinian first-order mapping of the lived social ontology, or 'lifeworld', a project comfortably nestled between Winch (1958) and Searle (1996). If, as György Lukács maintained, journalism is the commodification of spontaneity, perhaps then social theorizing in the Giddensian mode constitutes spontaneity's *reification*.

The above developments have subverted the social scientific imagination from opposing sides – that is, from the *humanities* and the *natural sciences*.

On the one hand, the demise of a robust sense of society has empowered humanistically trained researchers in cultural studies to divine latent 'identity politics', the Newspeak for normatively self-sufficient deviant groups. As the political fortunes of Marxist universalism declined on the world stage, the negative concept of *ideology*, which implied a self-serving sense of self-deception, was given a positive spin as *culture* in that diffuse yet 'empowering' sense that has enabled cultural studies to dominate much of sociology today. (It would be interesting to trace the replacement of 'ideology' by 'culture' in sociology textbooks over the past quarter-century, charting the discursive shifts of such transitional 'soft Marxist' theorists as Raymond Williams and Terry Eagleton.) Whereas sociologists had been needed to demystify and otherwise *counteract* ideology, they are now needed to 'give voice' and otherwise *reinforce* cultural identity. It is as if cultural studies practitioners had read Ibsen's *Wild Duck* as an object lesson in how *not* to do social science, with the 'life lie' that held together the Ekdal family amplified into the 'imagined communities' concocted by identity politicians over the past two centuries (Anderson, 1983).

On the other hand, more subtly – but I believe more profoundly – postmodernism has re-opened the door to reducing the normative to the 'normal' in the strict statistical sense familiar to the biomedical sciences, including experimental psychology, namely, the aggregation of spontaneously generated events that vary around a natural tendency, or mean. Foucault (1975) himself had already invited this interpretation in his main methodological work, *The Archaeology of Knowledge*, with his conception of texts as sites for registering the 'frequency' and 'distribution' of utterance. It is worth recalling that this work was a reflection on the method deployed in *The Order of Things*, which claimed to have shown that 'humanity' as an object sufficiently distinct to merit its own set of sciences – the 'human sciences' (which, for our purposes, is tantamount to the social sciences) – emerged only at the end of the 18th century and was rapidly disintegrating as the 20th century wore on (Foucault, 1970). Far from being an integrated entity, let alone one possessing an immutable essence, the 'human' was for Foucault a temporarily stable convergence of certain independent social and intellectual tendencies.

Lest the shifting sands of intellectual fashion be given too much credit for changing the world, ultimately underwriting the pincer attack on the social sciences from the humanities and the natural sciences was the retreat of state power over civil society, rather than any decisive set of empirical findings, let alone a philosophically inspired realization of the pernicious nature of binary oppositions. Nevertheless, this attack has put social science on the defensive, fighting a rearguard action to stave off a rather anonymous but no less looming sense of domination, or 'empire', to use the word now in vogue (Hardt and Negri, 2000). In this context, 'resistance' is put forward as a less ambitious replacement of 'revolution', the maintenance of spheres of order – 'holding the line', as it were – in a world otherwise engulfed in chaotic capitalist flows. In this respect, 'identity politics' has filled the ideo-logical vacuum left by the decline of nationalism (Castells, 1998). Although these new ideas tend to be exchanged in the currency of thermodynamics and other stochastic sciences, one could just as easily conjure up the image of the early Christian sects who persevered in the face of Satan's multifari-ous temptations, bolstered by vague millenarian hopes.

Scepticism about a distinct realm of social facts *sui generis* above and beyond the default patterns of history emerged as soon as Durkheim pub-lished his *Rules of the Sociological Method* in 1895 (Gane, 1988). Nevertheless, the objections raised by his main antagonist, Gabriel Tarde, receded from view as Durkheim began to institutionalize the discipline – that is, until the 1980s, when Tarde's stock rose to new heights, thanks to French *penseurs du jour* like Gilles Deleuze and lately Bruno Latour. Given Foucault's role as a foil to Durkheim, we should not be surprised to learn that Tarde was the chief statistician at the French Ministry of Justice, who regarded the inci-dence of crime as simply behaviour that deviated from a norm upheld by the state for its own purposes. Tarde attempted to portray Durkheim as an academic naïf in matters of policy who took the normative imperatives of the Third Republic too much at face value, which then led him to conflate scientific and political issues.

While Durkheim recognized the social function of deviance in shoring up a common identity among the non-deviant, he also believed that at least some forms of deviance could be rectified through appropriate state action that brought the default 'natural norm' into conformity with the prescribed 'artificial norm'. In this respect, Durkheim's political sensibility was 'social-ist', with the teaching of sociology serving as a vehicle for turning society into a whole much greater than the sum of its parts. In contrast, Tarde, the seasoned – perhaps cynical – civil servant viewed the state in more reactive and less expectant terms. For Tarde, the regular occurrence of deviance was sufficient to justify the state as a vehicle of containment (*not* transformation), at least until some abnormal individual or event succeeded in shifting the *de facto* norm, which in turn would cause the state to shift its policies accordingly. Thus, Tarde's state was just one of several adaptive agents, each behaving according to its own spontaneously generated tendencies. (For an updated version of this debate, where I play Durkheim to Latour's Tarde, see Barron, 2003.)

By now the tenor of my response to the claim that social scientists are the Academic Undead should be clear: Our opponents are trying to turn back the clock, largely through systematically self-induced amnesia that enables them to accept the world as it is in these post-socialist, neo-liberal times. The distinctiveness of the strategy is noteworthy. By way of contrast, consider George Santayana's famous observation that those who forget history are condemned to repeat it (Santayana, 1905: 84). The comment was originally made in defence of the idea that entire societies undergo a life cycle comparable to that of each individual. Thus, for him historical amnesia was an expression of social senescence, something he accepted in the spirit of Epicurean fatalism: forgetting, however regrettable, is inevitable and – more importantly – uncontrollable. Santayana clearly had not envisaged the Ministry of Truth in George Orwell's *1984*, which through the concerted rewriting of history would turn this natural tendency to Big Brother's advantage. Yet, the torrent of academic texts propagated to captive classroom audiences, repeatedly announcing a 'postmodern', 'post-social' or even 'post-human' condition, amounts to just that – what used to be called, with Hitler and Stalin in mind, 'The Big Lie'.

So, when Latour (1993) boldly pronounces, 'We have never been modern', he is converting present-day disappointment and, above all, impatience into one big and long mistake that should not have been committed in the first place. Our own shortcomings are thus offloaded – or perhaps I should have said 'delegated' – to our wicked and/or incompetent ancestors. Latour would have us return to just before some major theorists and politicians invented the social sciences as the standard-bearers of modernity. Indeed, his great leap backward would return us to the moment when the market first asserted itself against traditional forms of social life – the 'great transformation' in European history – in response to which both social science and socialism came into being (Polanyi, 1944). In the process, the distinctly *aspirational* character of social scientific knowledge comes to be dismissed as a nightmare from which we – or at least those of us in the land of the living – are now awakening.

The fundamental intuition common to the founders of socialism as a political movement and social science as an autonomous body of knowledge is that *humanity is a project in the making*, one achieved by organizing a certain kind of animal in a certain range of ways. Our genetic makeup and default behavioural patterns provide *only* the raw material out of which 'human beings' may be politically and scientifically constructed. This is the primary normative meaning of 'society' in the modern sense, an Enlightenment legacy of which the nation-state and its agencies – not least universities – have been the main legal executors. However, the aspiration to become human need not be realized by *Homo sapiens*. History has thrown up many ways of retarding and even pre-empting what still ought to be called the 'socialist' project. Indeed, the postmodern revival of the quasi-pejorative 'utopian' to capture the aspirational nature of the human project suggests that failure is inevitable. Lest we capitulate too willingly to this judgement, let us now survey what is at stake.

TWO

The Social Sciences at Risk

A Brief History of the Stakes

In the broad sweep of history, the rise of the social sciences marks an important stage in the secularization of the monotheistic religious perspective represented by Judaism, Christianity, and Islam. The 14th century Muslim scholar, Ibn Khaldun, had produced the earliest attempt at laws of historical change that displayed the modern social scientific aspiration of systematically interrelating political, cultural, economic, and even ecological factors. Of special relevance is the unique position of humans in relation to the Divine Creator, in whose 'image and likeness' *Homo sapiens* is said to have been created. The two implied theological traits – the separateness of humans from other animals and the equality of all humans in the eyes of God – have anchored subsequent discussion about the distinctiveness of the social sciences from the other two great bodies of academic knowledge, the natural sciences and the humanities. On the one hand, the natural sciences traditionally have presupposed that everything can be studied in terms of their 'external relations' with other things, without considering their 'inner life' (or soul). On the other hand, the humanities traditionally have presupposed a strong hierarchy of merit among individual members of *Homo sapiens*, with categories like 'genius' and 'classic' playing significant evaluative and even explanatory roles.

Here we should recall the deep historic links between the natural sciences and the humanities that belie loose talk of a 'two cultures' conflict. Both have been classically concerned with a sense of reality that transcends the contingencies of place and time. This has been tied to a sense of knowing that is largely contemplative and sometimes even disempowering, especially when reality is identified with whatever resists deliberate attempts at change. On the one hand, the natural sciences arose from two observation-based disciplines, natural history and astronomy, whose objects – organic species and celestial bodies – were thought to have existed forever. On the other hand, there has always been popular talk of social reforms as 'going against human nature', and even the original philosopher of culture, Johann Gottfried von Herder, spoke of society as imposing a 'second nature'. When it comes to the human condition, the two great academic cultures prefer to study humanity without having to mingle with flesh-and-blood human beings in their entirety. Thus, evolutionary psychologists nowadays infer what makes us who we are from the remains of our Stone Age ancestors (including their DNA), whereas humanists continue to focus on artefacts of a more recent and literate age.

Those who doubt the historic complicity of the humanities and the natural sciences against an independent social scientific standpoint should consider the career of Charles Murray, an American devotee of the Mises Circle who co-authored the notorious anti-welfarist best seller, *The Bell Curve* (Herrnstein and Murray, 1994). He argued that Black academic performance stopped improving beyond a certain level of welfare expenditure. Given his prior libertarian reputation, Murray was interpreted as simply advocating the end of state-sponsored welfare programmes. In fact, he was mainly concerned that Blacks were judged against a purely intellectual standard of achievement that may not elicit their 'natural', more physically based talents. (For an intellectually sophisticated defence of a *state-based* education policy that respects 'difference' in this sense, see Conant, 1959.) In other words, Murray cast the defenders of welfare policies as trying to force Blacks to be like themselves, that is, something other than Blacks are – or can be.

In today's Newspeak, Murray respected (and reified) 'diversity'. He is no more (and no less) racist than Aristotle, to whom one should always turn for understanding the legitimation of this subtle humanities–natural sciences alliance. Murray's latest book, *Human Accomplishment*, drives the point home (Murray, 2003). Here he argues that our level of (intellectual) accomplishment is bound to decline with population expansion, simply because the standard of lasting achievement is ultimately dictated by some non-human sense of 'reality'. It is easy to see how this 'insight' could reactivate eugenic culling. Too bad Murray failed to deal with Randall Collins' (1998) sociologically sensitive argument that the historic constancy in the size of intellectual elites simply reflects the constancy of the collective attention span – and nothing more metaphysically luminous about the attended objects.

In contrast, the social sciences adhere to the maxim that the best way to study human beings is to interact with them, typically by getting them to do and say things that they might *not* do otherwise. This profoundly simple idea, common to experiments and ethnographies, has also inspired the triumphs and disasters that punctuate the history of modern politics. As I have argued, it has required an increasingly controversial assumption: *All human beings – whatever their individual achievements, competences, status or health – are equally significant members of society, whose strength ultimately lies in what they can do together.*

The social sciences came into their own during the 18th century European Enlightenment, when political theorists began to argue for a more integral connection between a state and its inhabitants than had been previously urged – by, say, Plato, Machiavelli, and Hobbes. In particular, a ruler should not simply keep the peace by keeping people at a safe – physical and social – distance from each other. The ruler also had to provide for their *welfare*. Statecraft thus had to go beyond the usual threats and deceptions, since rulers were now expected, as Adam Smith would say, to increase the wealth of their nations. This historic change of attitude had three important consequences. First, it led to a managerial conception of the state, in which economic matters acquired a public significance that had been previously left in the hands of private households and corporations. Second, it fostered a more discriminating sense of citizenship as 'contribution to society', especially for purposes of raising and distributing revenue. Finally, it led to the systematic collection of data about people's lives, culminating in a hardening of social categories (into classes and even races), which were then projected backward as having been implicit throughout history.

Social science and socialism were born joined at the hip – specifically in France in the 1820s, courtesy of Count Saint-Simon and especially his understudy, Auguste Comte, who coined both 'positivism' and 'sociology'. Given the multiple definitions that are often attached to positivism, it is worth observing two senses in which the natural sciences might be seen as the basis for the social sciences. One, due to Francis Bacon, simply involves the application of natural science theories and methods to social phenomena – a fairly straightforward case of what might be called 'reductionism' or 'scientism'. However, Comte's own view presupposes a more reflexive attitude toward the history of science: as the natural sciences have extended their sphere of applicability, they have also learnt more about how scientific inquiry itself works. Thus, a second-order discipline, called 'methodology' and later 'philosophy of science', is a by-product of scientific progress, which then feeds back to steer the subsequent course of science. Sociology – as the historically final science – is also the one with the capacity to comprehend all that has gone before it as a coherent point-of-view that can then be used to govern society. Broadly speaking, it was this Comtean image of social science that enabled its development to be aligned with the growth of the nation-state in the 19th and 20th centuries. (It is also the vision of social science that my own project of social epistemology seeks to uphold: cf. Fuller, 1988.)

Generally speaking, social scientists have provided a layer of mediation between the governors and the governed in complex democracies – especially with respect to those of the governed whose opinions the governors do not trust. Of course, the governors need to know what their various constituencies think, but it is not clear that putting government policies to a direct test, such as an election, will result in an outcome that is either favourable to the governors or faithful to the beliefs and interests of the governed. Thus, social scientists armed with surveys, focus groups, and participant-observation techniques have given voice to the people without directly inserting them into the policy-making process. A government that wishes to keep its options open will find frequent and decisive elections inconvenient, not least because it then must accept the legitimacy of the outcome, even if it goes against what the government would want or expect. However, once social scientists deliver public opinion as 'data' to policymakers who are allergic to direct accountability, the data function as a vaccine – that is, inoculation against further charges of accountability. Thus, policymakers say that the people have been heard and their views are taken 'under advisement'.

The capture of public opinion as data defers the need for an immediate government response: analysis and interpretation must come first! This conclusion unites the most earnest social scientist and the most cynical policymaker. For social scientists, the drive to empirical work has often been motivated by the perception that there are norms already in place in society that escape what the government wants to impose. For policymakers, however, once these norms are revealed, they enable greater control of the potentially recalcitrant subjects. Moreover, at a reflexive level, the social scientist is herself subject to a similar sort of capture. The policymaker refuses to interfere with the social scientist in her work, just as the social scientist refuses to interfere with her subjects in their day-to-day business. In both cases, autonomy enables greater instrumentality because just as the subjects do not interfere with the social scientific account of their activities, social scientists (as 'value-free' inquirers) do not interfere with the political use of their research. In response to this arguably cynical manipulation of both public opinion and social science, social activists and even some social scientists have promoted 'consensus conferences' and 'citizen juries' as intermediary bodies whose decisions are (ideally) binding on government policy (Fuller, 2003b).

The distinctiveness of the social sciences may be summed up in two words used to characterize the objects of their inquiry: *meaning* and *welfare*. The former captures what marks the social sciences from the natural sciences, the latter what marks it from the humanities. Both words have been invoked to call into question the status of a species-based *human nature*. The distinctiveness of meaning attributions points to irreducible differences in personal histories, whereas the concept of welfare presupposes that humanity can collectively transcend the fatalism implied in our mortality as individuals.

On the one hand, the appeal to meaning has served to remind would-be reformers that effective social change requires recognizing that individuals already have standpoints that inform their actions – and it is only by starting from these standpoints that they can be persuaded to do otherwise. Once this position is taken seriously, the electoral enfranchisement of every adult is rendered plausible. On the other, the appeal to welfare has inspired the creation of political units, nation-states, designed to infuse a sense of social solidarity among biologically unrelated individuals (i.e. 'citizens') by providing them with health, education and even minimal subsistence in return for political participation – most notably at elections and in war. Thus, the first professor of sociology, Émile Durkheim, used his discipline as a vehicle for promoting the idea of a welfare state in France (under the rubric of *Solidarisme*), an idea he had picked up from Germany, where it had been a Bismarckian innovation used to consolidate a politically bounded space united by language but divided by regional and class interests.

From their inception, the social sciences have had their conceptual foundations threatened by both the humanities and the natural sciences. On the one hand, the natural sciences have tried to reduce the semantic character of consciousness to a complex form of animal sensation; on the other, the humanities have tried to reduce welfare to an artifice designed to cheat fate. The attack had already begun by the late 19th century, as the Darwinian focus on differential reproductive success as the key to evolution provided a natural scientific interpretation of fate – as 'survival' – that humanists had previously lacked. The standard social science response to this pincer attack has been to convert what natural scientists and humanists see as *brute facts* into *social problems*, which are the proper subject matter of the social sciences. What might be otherwise regarded as irreversible features of the human condition, with which we can do no better than 'cope', were thus treated as challenges we might overcome by systematic inquiry and collective action.

Indeed, Darwin's staunchest contemporary defender, Thomas Henry Huxley, held precisely this view – that an 'evolutionary ethics' of the sort promoted by Herbert Spencer is a non-starter because humanity is distinguished by its *organized resistance* to natural selection. Huxley meant the various ways in which humans have transformed the natural environment to enable the flourishing of those who, from a strictly biological standpoint, are by no means the fittest. In his 1893 Romanes Lecture, Huxley memorably claimed that the human condition was not about 'survival of the fittest' but 'the fitting of as many as can survive'. We shall explore this sensibility in more detail in Part Three. Huxley's own field of medicine comes most readily to mind, especially its modern concern with prolonging life rather than simply letting nature take its course. But also included here are legal arrangements, in which succession to a corporate post or institutionalized role is prescribed on the basis of examination or election – that is, *not* family lineage. It is significant that the historically leading institutions in Western society – from the church and the university to the state and the firm – have progressed by *discarding* whatever links their membership may have initially had to kinship, the point at which biological factors normally gain a foothold in explaining and determining the human realm.

However, the social sciences have been in steady decline since the late 1970s. We have already alluded to several concurrent tendencies that point in this general direction. After initial gains, the political projects historically associated with the social sciences – socialism and the welfare state, not to mention international development policy – fell short of expectations. All of these projects shared the ambition of redistributing effort and income to enable humanity to become a whole greater than the sum of its parts. To be sure, the gap between the rich and the poor had begun to close, when compared to the previous century of European imperial expansion (Wheen, 2004: Chapter 10). Nevertheless, progress was painfully slow and costly. Thus ensued what Marxists call 'the fiscal crisis of the state', which in the 1980s led to the curtailment of welfarist initiatives and the toppling of socialist regimes worldwide. Also cut were the social science research programmes devoted to identifying and overcoming systemic social problems. The devolution of state powers to the private sector has been accompanied by a revival of Aristotelian arguments about the 'unnaturalness' of large social units (e.g. nation-states) and unlimited human expansion, resulting in a re-valorization of families and markets as 'natural' forms of social life. However, this traditionally right-wing message is now aligned with recent 'progressive' sciences of sociobiology, evolutionary psychology, and behavioural genetics.

The normative side of this shift is most evident in the conversion of 'Red' to 'Green' in the politics of self-avowed progressive thinkers and politicians. Thus, the older focus on the alleviation of specifically human misery has shifted to care for the environment at large. At a superficial level, this shift marks an increase in ambition. However, at a deeper level, it marks an admission of defeat, as policy goals are now defined primarily in terms of human self-restraint, such as birth control and pollution reduction. The ultimate goal appears to be not welfare maximization, but suffering minimization. Moreover, the criteria for success are more abstractly specified and hence potentially less controversial: Politics is made easier if one needs to achieve a certain carbon emissions standard – which can be accomplished by whatever means – than a certain level of minimum income, which clearly would require some form of economic redistribution. Not surprisingly, recent years have witnessed the rise of *corporate environmentalism*, whereby labour exploitation is rendered compatible with clean environments (Hoffman, 1997).

Lurking behind this 'greening' of the political left is the most funda-mental challenge facing the future of the social sciences: *Are humans always the privileged members of society?* The question arises once we consider that the Neo-Darwinian synthesis of Mendelian genetics and evolutionary biol-ogy does not privilege *Homo sapiens* above other animals. Because animals share 90+% of their genes, species turn out to be convenient taxonomic schemes, not natural kinds. From a strictly Neo-Darwinian perspective, even commonsensical appeals to a 'human nature' that sharply distinguishes us from the 'brutes' is little more than a myth. Of course, the myth lives on in the normative use still made by Noam Chomsky and Jürgen Habermas of our allegedly species-unique linguistic capacities. Nevertheless, 'species egal-itarianism' has expanded beyond Peter Singer's 'animal liberation' move-ment, as greater comparative research into humans and other animals tends to minimize the traditional differences between them. The more we study animals, it seems, the smarter they become, on the basis of which they then acquire greater normative significance.

At the same time, there has been a return to fatalism in the humanities, which – unwittingly perhaps – corroborates the same tendency. It is not quite a return to the original Greco-Roman paganism (though Charles Murray comes close), but it does share the same element of what Heidegger called our 'thrownness' into a world not of our own making. Thus, 'abjection' has acquired a significance that Marxists had previously reserved for the oppo-site movement, 'projection'. This newfound fatalism has been especially influential in French postmodern thought. It is ultimately explainable as a reaction to the decline of the Soviet Union, which had been the original basis of Jean-Paul Sartre's effusive claims about the prospects for collective action transforming the world for the betterment of humanity. More explicitly, the reaction follows the work of Roland Barthes, Michel Foucault, and Jacques Derrida on the death of what was variously called the 'subject', the 'author' or simply 'man'. It is a sensibility born of Nietzsche's 'Death of God' thesis, fuelled by the perceived failure of humanism, as the final moment in the Christian world-view, to prevent the atrocities of the 20th century, especially the two world wars. A measure of its influence is that many now are comfortable with Heidegger's assertion that language 'speaks us', rather than the other way round, when language was said to be definitive of *Homo sapiens*.

Moreover, contrary to the claims of Sokal and Bricmont (1998), there is now a generation of postmodernists who, regardless of their deficiencies in detailed understanding, are sufficiently enthusiastic about scientific matters to extol, under the rubric of 'political ecology', the virtues of selectively including (and hence excluding) a variety of humans, animals and even machines in the name of some advanced 'hybrid' collective order (Whiteside, 2002). Such 'cyborg worlds', the popular name for these heterogeneous regimes, are potential candidates for what scientifically straight ecologists call 'maximally inclusive fitness landscapes'. As we shall see in the final chapter, they have some disturbing precedents in the history of totalitarian politics, not least the origins of California-style 'clean environments' in the science of racial hygiene that peaked in Nazi Germany. We live in a time when an unprecedented openness to the inclusion of non-human members in the social order is combined with a heightened sensitivity to the difference between 'normal' and 'pathological' members – especially within *Homo sapiens* – such that the contraception, abortion, and euthanasia of (potential) members of our species have been accorded an unprecedented moral respectability among the *bien pensant*. Of course, the devolution of state authority has rendered the drive to eradicate such 'pathological' formations less direct than in the heyday of Nazi eugenics, from which it only follows that it is harder to recognize for what it is. The overall effect is a 'back to nature' movement of the most scientifically informed and ethically comprehensive kind – including not least the facilitation of our re-incorporation into nature in death. This is what I called the 'casualization of the human condition', the signature attitude of *bioliberalism*.

THREE

Socialism as the Elusive Synthesis at the Heart of Social Science

Before the fall of the Soviet Union in 1989, socialists could claim they had done a better job of uniting theory and practice than capitalists. Socialists had generally succeeded in raising the welfare of the bottom end of their societies, typically at the cost of lowering it at the top end. And that is exactly as the socialists would have wanted it. For, even if not all socialists held the rich personally responsible for the plight of the poor, all were in agreement that the rich constituted a structural obstacle in overcoming mass poverty. In contrast, capitalists have found it more difficult to square their own theory and practice. In theory, everyone should flourish with the liberalization of markets. Yet, in practice, even when the poor increased their income, it was never enough to catch up with the increases in wealth made by the rich. The result was an intensification of existing class divisions, or 'relative deprivation', which capitalist theorists could only attempt to explain away by invoking such *ad hoc* factors as the lack of a work ethic among the poor or the unpredictability of markets.

Back then capitalists found themselves on the defensive precisely because they agreed with the socialists on the entitlement of all human beings to equal opportunity. (The socialists of course desired additional forms of equality.) Capitalism does not imply contempt for the poor in the way socialism implies contempt for the rich. Both capitalists and socialists concurred that the right political economy would enable everyone to function as full-fledged members of society. Thus, the increasing political and economic disparities in advanced capitalist societies – especially the United States – suggested that capitalism's grounding theory was fatally wrong.

I certainly remember my mother, my original Jesuit teachers (some of whom had a hand in burning 'draft cards' in the Vietnam War) and the more radical, typically untenured, academics at Columbia claiming that Marx was correct at least in his general claim that once capitalist societies turned socialist, they would never look back. The welfare state was then seen as facilitating socialist reforms in countries with atavistically strong capitalist traditions, not (as today) providing a temporary safeguard in nations that have yet to master the laws of the market. As it turned out, a mere quarter-century's worth of political experience (roughly from the late 1940s to the late 1970s) was pumped up into proof that Marx had discovered the basic law of social progress (Wheen, 2004: Chapter 10). Perhaps unsurprisingly it took even less time to demonstrate, with equal conclusiveness, that Marx had been wrong all along.

To be sure, US sociology departments were already paving the way for the post-Marxist 're-liberalization' of the social order. The link between 'socialism' and 'social science' was treated as a mere accident of spelling when I was an undergraduate majoring in sociology at Columbia in the late 1970s. Back then, under the historiographical influence of Raymond Aron and Robert Nisbet, sociology was said to have emerged as a reaction to the French Revolution of 1789, which in the name of Reason had tried to replace, in one fell swoop, centuries of traditional order with a planned society. Sociology, at its best (so said my teachers), realized that this Enlightenment utopia was really a totalitarian nightmare in disguise, which would always fail to contain the paradoxical yet resilient character of human nature, as expressed in so-called 'organic' institutions like the family and the church. (From a strictly legal standpoint, one to which the original German sociologists were especially sensitive, these two institutions had radically different bases – the family being involuntary and the church voluntary. Nevertheless, that fact did not trouble the Cold Warriors, who focused on the anti-statism common to the two institutions.)

In the Cold War genealogy, the arch French diplomatic observer of Jacksonian America, Alexis de Tocqueville, figured as a founding father of the discipline, whereas his avid correspondent and Auguste Comte's British publicist, John Stuart Mill, did not. The exclusion of Mill from sociology had been relatively recent. As late as 1950, he was the second most cited figure in British sociology (Halsey, 2004: 175). To be sure, Mill did himself no favours to flat-footed future historians when he deliberately eschewed Comte's coinage of 'sociology' because of its barbarous mix of Latin and Greek roots. Mill's preferred word was the consistently Greek 'ethology', which literally means 'moral science' and was at first translated into German as *Geisteswissenschaft* by Wilhelm Dilthey but then re-invented as a 20th century German word for the holistic science of biological adaptation championed by Konrad Lorenz. At this point, Mill's influence was completely dissipated. An interesting counterfactual history of sociology could be told, had Mill not been so precious about etymology, itself a hangover from having been force-fed the classical languages at an early age by his father.

The crucial intellectual difference between de Tocqueville and Mill is that the former anticipated the Cold War's sense that democracy forces a trade-off between liberty and equality, whereas the latter held to the more 'socialist' idea that the two virtues could be jointly maximized by the rational redistribution of excess wealth. If one wishes to recover Mill in this context, a good place to begin is *the law of diminishing marginal utility*, the fundamental principle of welfare economics, which began life very much inspired by the idea of humanity as a normative project but eventually became a naturalistic account of how humans 'always already' behave (Proctor, 1991: 185–7).

For Mill, if someone possesses a sufficient amount of a good, the over-all welfare of society would be increased by transferring whatever more that person receives to someone who lacks a sufficient amount of the good. The basic idea is that the resulting compression of the difference in goods (i.e. the tendency toward equality) would be generously offset by the additional freedom that the transfer's beneficiary would gain to satisfy her wants (i.e. the tendency toward liberty). Mill interpreted this principle as a policy injunction to redistribute income to correct the injustices caused by artificial restrictions on the free flow of goods and services, which inhibited individuals from exercising their freedom to contribute as much as possible to the commonwealth. Generations of legal enforcement had made such injustices appear 'natural', sometimes even justified as products of 'fate'.

However, the science of economics formally broke with political economy when William Stanley Jevons successfully contested Mill's interpretation of the law of diminishing marginal utility in the third quarter of the 19th century. Jevons held that the principle is meant to *represent* – not correct – nature, behaving exactly like a physical law. The appropriate use for the principle, then, is not to decide on policies for correcting injustices but to identify the frame of reference from which it can be seen as *already* operating – the invisible hand's implicit reach. This reinterpretation came to be identified (somewhat misleadingly) with the 'positivist' turn that increasingly marked the history of economics – in particular, a focus on formal models of idealized closed systems (*à la* Newtonian mechanics) and pan-glossian explanations for the distribution of resources in actual societies: the political urge to redistribute wealth was thus permanently kept in check by the scientific search for hidden redistributions happening elsewhere in the economy. In terms of a familiar philosophical dichotomy, whereas Mill would move the 'is' closer to the 'ought', Jevons was inclined to find the 'ought' implicit in the 'is'. The former's weapon of choice for closing the is–ought gap was *policy*, the latter's *research*. This shift in perspective enabled positivism to lose its spirit, while preserving its letter.

Consider the difference in social standing between Mill and Jevons, whose arguments overlapped in the 1860s. Mill was among the most politically visible of the utilitarians – or 'philosophical radicals', as these original think-tankers styled themselves. He was a Liberal Member of Parliament in the Gladstone era, where he promoted the idea that imperialism was the best vehicle for extending freedom across the globe. Mill had no qualms about paving the straightest path to achieving the project of humanity, once the basic principles had been determined – as he believed they already had. He would be shocked to learn of the fallen state of social science today, whereby research is actually conducted to ascertain people's attitudes prior to – not to mention independent of – the implementation of specific social policies. Mill's ghost would ask: Why not simply first provide tax relief to encourage enlightened private sector agencies to conduct some social experiments, with the state carefully monitoring the consequences, with an eye to fine-tuning policy? Assuming a general acceptance of a utilitarian understanding of the human condition, this question would define the context for empirical social research, with voting simulating an attitude survey for state-wide social experiments.

In contrast, Jevons, the UK's first professor of economics, was keen to establish his discipline as 'value-free' – that is to say, valid regardless of who happens to be in power. In a society expanding its electoral franchise, the surest path to scientificity, then, is not to second-guess, let alone pre-empt, the opinions of the populace. Thus, for Jevons, judgements of value are ultimately subjective – that is to say, not something on which economists can pronounce – at least without having consulted the subjects in question. From Mill's high-minded Victorian perspective, it may look like that someone with only £1000 would benefit more from £100 transferred from the person with £100,000. But without further investigation, wouldn't this judgement simply rest on Mill's imposition of his own values? Could we not easily imagine a wealthy capitalist who values each additional £100 equally, perhaps because his or her identity is bound up with the very process of wealth creation? Why then should this person be coerced – say, via taxation – to support people who, had they the wherewithal, would have already provided sufficiently for themselves?

As it turns out, a paradox bearing Jevons' name is the bane of ecologists and others who believe, like Mill, in the ultimate satiability of human wants. Jevons (2001) showed that, for British manufacturers, an increase in the efficiency of coal use actually increases overall coal use, for the same reason (I suppose) that the availability of low-calorie foods encourages people to eat more. In other words, without potentially objectionable levels of state intervention, it is unlikely that more opportunities for consumption will sufficiently diminish the marginal utility of those able to take advantage of the situation. Such people will simply derive new benefits from consuming more. In this respect, the idea of productivity as an efficiency measure separable from a sheer increase in production proves elusive in practice: One can never produce enough because others can always be made to want more (York et al., 2003). According to the Jevonian argument on its face, the redistribution of wealth is inevitably coercive and may even do violence to the propensity toward growth. Had he not already existed, Karl Marx would have had to be created in the 1860s to stem the tide of this argument.

Of course, Jevons did not see himself as *trying* to benefit the rich at the expense of the poor. Rather, like Charles Murray and today's bioliberal pundits, Jevons thought he was reporting on default patterns of human behaviour. Indeed, today's postmodern purveyors of identity politics, who aspire to a 'separate but equal' multiculturalism, say much the same thing but appear more politically radical because they are writing after an additional 150 years of what has been arguably state-enforced repression of difference in the name of Durkheimian normativity. Yet, in the end, both the bioliberals and the identity politicians believe a clear break between the state and civil society would enable spontaneous forms of self-expression, what economists after Paul Samuelson call 'revealed preferences'. Perhaps the only substantive difference between the postmodernists and the bioliberals is that the former believe in the spontaneous aggregation of self-expression along sociologically salient lines. But at least the bioliberals have the courage of their convictions, ensuring that 'Nature' takes responsibility for discriminating between who deserves to live and die. The 19th century precedent is one of the false fathers of social science, Herbert Spencer, a man who fancied the term 'sociology' but who always meant the natural history of social life.

Notwithstanding the recent rewritings of the history of sociology that render Mill invisible, it is difficult to deny that the fortunes of socialism and social science have risen and fallen together. Thus, I assume that sociology emerged from reflections on the Industrial Revolution in late 18th and early 19th century Britain. Instead of the planned society, the implicit foe of the nascent sociological discipline was the emergent capitalist form of life that threatened to level the hard-won difference between civilized society and brute animal existence. Depending on the Enlightenment philosopher one chooses, this difference had been won in classical Athens or republican Rome but, in any case, had regressed in the Middle Ages when a Plato-inspired hereditary hierarchy was used to protect Christianity from the threat of Islam, which claimed to be its spiritual successor by promising a genuine brotherhood of humanity equal under Allah. However, for the Enlightenment wits, this threat was rebuffed by what, since the end of the Second World War, has been called the 'Scientific Revolution', the process whereby Christianity was allegedly liberated (i.e. secularized) of its feudal residue.

The twinned fates of socialism and social science is not so very different from the relationship between, say, the ecology movement and environmental science, despite in each case the latter's efforts to distance themselves from the former. (What differentiates the eco-twins from the socio-twins, of course, is that political-scientific support for the eco-twins is ascendant.) In the case of both social science and environmental science, the key issue is the *autonomy* of this body of knowledge from more established forms of humanistic and natural scientific knowledge. After all, Margaret Thatcher never denied the existence of human beings or even of such self-organizing social units as families. Similarly, she did not deny that we have animal natures and live in a physical environment. However, it is clear that she would have the normative and policy concerns that have distinguished the social (and environmental) sciences subsumed under more traditional socio-epistemic formations. And with the help of unwittingly obliging intellectuals, that is indeed happening.

Traditionally two opposing strategies have been deployed to preclude *all* members of *Homo sapiens* from fully participating in the project of humanity. The one portrays socialism as too ambitious, the other as too parochial. The first involves specifying a clear hierarchy within *Homo sapiens* that makes it unlikely that all of its members can ever be equal participants. This strategy was historically associated with humanistically inclined conservatives who nostalgically recalled a feudal order more stable than it ever was. The second involves the reverse motion of flattening the distinction between *Homo sapiens* and other animals, such that the concept of humanity loses its metaphysical grounding and moral priority. Thus, depending on their ability to respond to the demands of the environment, some people will turn out to be of greater value than others – and, indeed, some animals may turn out to be of greater value than some humans. This view has been characteristic of naturalistic liberals who by the end of the 19th century came to regard Darwin's natural selection as a generalization of Adam Smith's invisible hand. We shall see that the early 21st century scrambles these allegiances somewhat, but the upshot still crowds out the prospects for realizing the project of humanity.

The US lawyer-activist Jeremy Rifkin has seen half the story. In what he calls the 'age of biology', Rifkin (2001) rightly observes an ideological realignment, with social conservatives and the ecological left combined in opposition to the utilitarian view of life associated with biotechnology that is shared by the free market liberals and what remains of the Marxists. Rifkin regards this realignment as new, yet in fact it marks a return to the ideological state of play during the Industrial Revolution before the rise of socialism. The early 19th century debate was even couched as an anti- *versus* pro-growth argument, as it is today – only with the factory, not the laboratory, functioning as the lightning rod for people's hopes and fears. Back then protectors of the land and developers of industry occupied clear ideological positions that were mutually exclusive and jointly exhaustive. They were called Tories (Conservatives) and Whigs (Liberals), and their corresponding forms of knowledge were later immortalized by Matthew Arnold as the 'cultured' (humanists) and the 'philistine' (natural scientists) at a time when Britain was still innocent of social science (Lepenies, 1988). At that time, the Tories were the paternalistic protectors of the inveterate poor, while the Whigs regarded poverty as a retarded state of enterprise from which the poor had to be released.

Nowadays the two groups are defined as Ecologists and Neo-Liberals, respectively, and their spheres of concern have somewhat expanded. Ecologists extend their paternalism across species, while Neo-Liberals believe that the state inhibits everyone's – not merely the poor's – enterprising spirit. The ideological space marked by this pre- and post-socialist world is captured in Table 3.1. I should immediately say that the 19th century has not fully disappeared from the 21st century – at least not in Britain. In terms of Table 3.1, Conservatives and Ecologists are at loggerheads over whether fox hunting should remain legal. Here the livelihood of humans in the rural regions are played off against a concern for fox welfare. Similarly, Neo-Liberals and Liberals lock horns over whether an indefinite growth policy is likely to maximize welfare in the long run.

One key difference between the 19th and the 21st century expressions of this matrix is the exact nature of the thing that the opposing ideologues wish either to protect or to free. In the 19th century, that thing was *labour power*. Conservatives wanted to restrict labour both physically (namely the ability of individuals to move house to find work) and conceptually (namely family and guild prerogatives on the intergenerational transmission of property, trade, and craft). In contrast, Liberals promised freedom along both

Table 3.1   *The political landscape before and after socialism*

	Protectionist	Emancipationist
Anthropocentric	19th century Conservatism	21st century Neo-Liberalism
Species egalitarian	21st century Ecologism	19th century Liberalism

dimensions: on the one hand, Liberals wanted to sever people's hereditary ties to the land that legally inhibited the construction of factories and people living near these places of work; on the other, they wanted to dissociate labour from a specific human embodiment, which effectively reduced labour to a form of what Marx called 'variable capital' that was ultimately replaceable by the 'fixed capital' of technology.

In the 21st century, the object of ecological protection and neo-liberal emancipation is *genetic potential* (Fuller, 2002a: Chapters 2–3). Thus, ecologists campaign for a global intellectual property regime that prohibits 'bioprospectors' from appropriating the genetic potential of indigenous peoples and the patenting of animal and plant species. Meanwhile, neo-liberals envisage the aim of intellectual property legislation as simply the removal of barriers from people freely trading – and being held responsible for – their genetic potential as they would anything else in their possession. Moreover, the neo-liberals follow the practice of past liberals of foreseeing the replacement of the natural with the artificial, as the traded organic material is eventually superseded by synthetic biochemical versions that produce the same effects at less cost and risk.

What had yet to exist in the early 19th century – and what is disappearing in the early 21st century – are the various shades of red that used to cut such a dashing figure across the political landscape of Europe as socialist and social democratic parties, as well as their distinctive forms of knowledge. To be sure, these parties continue to exist, if only by virtue of organizational inertia – an ironic twist to the fate of the social democrats recounted in Roberto Michels' 1911 classic, *Political Parties*. Yet, as has become especially clear in the UK and Northern Europe, the old socialist parties are subject to strong countervailing forces from the ecologists and the neo-liberals. A more muted version of this tension can be even found within the US Democratic Party (for example, the strength of the recent presidential candidacies of the ecologically minded Ralph Nader and the neo-liberal Ross Perot).

We tend to forget that one of socialism's achievements was to wed a broadly utilitarian, pro-science and pro-industry policy perspective to an overarching sense of responsibility for all of humanity, especially its most vulnerable members. It essentially completed the secularization of Christianity promised by the Enlightenment (MacIntyre, 1994). This movement started with the 'religion of humanity' of the Marquis de Condorcet and Auguste Comte, extended through the various socialist movements of the last 200 years, and was most successfully realized in the heyday of the welfare state in the third quarter of the 20th century. As Hegel and Marx might have it, the genius of socialism was to generate an egalitarian political ethic from a dialectical synthesis of the two countervailing forms of inegalitarianism that came to be consolidated by the end of the 18th century: conservative paternalism and liberal voluntarism. For the first time, a form of politics took seriously the idea – at least as a regulative ideal of collective action – that all people belonged equally to *Homo sapiens*.

Socialism's inegalitarian roots remain latent in the Marxist motto: 'From each according to their ability (the liberal credo) to each according to their need' (the conservative credo). Marxists imagined that a spontaneously mutually beneficial division of labour would eventuate in a classless society. But what if we do not yet live in 'society degree zero' (the revolutionary moment) and classes are already in existence? In the 19th century, conservatives could see in the Marxist slogan the need to reproduce dependency relations, whereas liberals could read it as a call for the free exchange of goods and services. Both conservatives and liberals imagined that a legally sanctioned system of stratification would result in either case, be it based on ascription or achievement. Moreover, each not only justified their own position but also demonized that of their opponents, as in Charles Dickens' fictional portrait of the heartless British liberal, Thomas Gradgrind, in *Hard Times* and Bram Stoker's satirization of the parasitic Austro-Hungarian aristocrat, Count Dracula. The difference between these two forms of inegalitarianism are illustrated in Table 3.2.

The conservative strategy was to reproduce the current social order, no matter the opportunity costs, whereas the liberals wanted to invest current wealth most efficiently, no matter the social dislocation that resulted. For British liberals, the Poor Laws, which devoted 80% of local taxes to providing the poor with a modicum of food and shelter, could be better spent on roads and other capital investments to attract industry, thereby creating jobs that would enable the poor to provide for themselves by contributing to the nation's overall wealth. In contrast, the conservatives believed that the cost of maintaining a secure life was a stable hierarchy, which implied the perpetual reproduction of feudal dependency relations between the rich and the poor. To destabilize this hierarchy would be to incur untold damage, including unnecessary death. But for the liberals the far greater cost of stability was that the poor were never given the opportunity to rise to their

Table 3.2   *The two inegalitarian sources of modern socialism*

	Conservative Paternalism	Liberal Voluntarism
Legacy to socialism	State ensures that the able provide for the needy	State ensures that the needy become able
Vision of aristocrats	Hereditary protectors of tradition	Wasters of unearned advantage
Vision of bourgeoisie	Mercenary destroyers of tradition	Investors in earned advantage
Vision of poor	Vulnerable wards	Financial burden
Legal precedent	Poor laws	Enclosure laws
Economic policy	Minimum wage	Tax incentives
Welfare strategy	Social insurance	Mass education
Source of original equality	Fitness to fate	Innate capacity
Source of ultimate inequality	Natural hierarchy	Individual merit
Fictional devil ('demonized other')	Thomas Gradgrind ('Penny pincher')	Count Dracula ('Blood sucker')
Real devil	Jeremy Bentham	Oscar Wilde

appropriate level of merit (or die, if they prove incapable of adapting to the needs of the market), which impeded the overall productivity of society. Liberal political economists regarded the amount of unused inherited land as the ultimate symbol of this squandered potential.

Thus, the liberals began to query how class divisions were drawn: why sheer property ownership rather than earned income or merit? What is touted as the 'individualism' of liberal political philosophy is simply the real-ization that class divisions are conventional, if only because everyone is endowed with the same innate capacities but differ in their opportunities to employ those capacities. Liberals aspired to a world in which people could dispose of their capacities just as landowners could of their property: Ideally, you would be judged by what you did with your 'possessions' in this extended sense, in a free environment. As we shall see, this perspective has come to be reinvented as we acquire greater knowledge of specifically biological capacities. In any case, liberals agreed with conservatives on the need for some sort of principle of cumulative advantage but disagreed on its basis. In particular, what was an appropriate principle of *inheritance*? Legal theories of succession presupposed rather ancient biological views about the passage of competence across generations of family members that created grounds for a son's entitlement to manage his father's estate or assume his trade (for example, primogeniture). It was this common concern with the transmis-sion of accumulated advantage – what Richard Dawkins (1982) has reno-vated as the 'extended phenotype' – that would come to distinguish both liberals and conservatives from socialists most clearly.

FOUR

The Problem of Inheritance and Socialism's Ultimate Retreat to Naturalism

The question of inheritance – the inter-generational transmission of property – was central to the establishment of sociology in Germany, France, and the United States. The concept of welfare was meant to capture a collective inheritance to which each member of society contributed and from which each benefited, though – as Marx stressed – *not* according to some default biologically based principle. In the final quarter of the 19th century, all three nation-states transformed the legal basis for incorporating individuals into the social order: Germany consolidated, France secularized, and the USA expanded. The first president of the German Sociological Association, Ferdinand Tönnies, christened sociology's founding distinction, *Gemeinschaft* ('community') and *Gesellschaft* ('society'), as respectively the conservative and the liberal pole out of which this newly integrated conception of society was forged. A legal scholar by training, Tönnies regarded this conception as the culmination of a medieval innovation in Roman law, to which I earlier alluded.

Until the 12th century, Roman law recognized two general categories of social life – the two to which Thatcher's declaration of the non-existence of society would return us. In the 'natural' mode, property was transmitted through the family (*gens*), an equation of biological reproduction and social succession. But there was also an 'artificial' mode for temporary associations (*socius*), such as joint-stock companies and crusades, which were project-centred and ceased to exist once the project was completed and its profits were distributed to the project's partners. The *Gemeinschaft/Gesellschaft* distinction is grounded in this contrast, which also persists in folk understandings of biologically acquired traits as somehow more basic and durable than socially acquired ones. Missing from these two categories was an artificial social entity entitled to perpetual legal protection because its ends transcend those of any or all of its members at a given place and time. This entity – *universitas*, normally translated as 'corporation' – was thus brought into being (Berman, 1983). It is the source of the paradigmatic objects of social science research. Originally populated by guilds, churches, monasteries, cities and, of course, universities, this realm of *universitas* gradually came to include still larger corporate entities like nation-states and business firms, the constitution of which was central to the sociology of Max Weber.

Considerable significance has been justly invested in the *universitas* as a distinctive expression of humanity. The presence of this legal category testifies to a conception of society that is irreducible to either suprahuman fate or infrahuman drives – that is, the domains of theology or biology. In this respect, Condorcet and Hegel were only two of the more famous proto-sociologists who identified the 'universal state' with humanity rendered self-conscious. This identification was based not on some misbegotten chauvinism about the French Republic or the German Reich, but on the sheer logic of the concept of *universitas*. Not surprisingly, Toennies had earned his scholarly reputation as the German translator of Thomas Hobbes, who was among the first to exploit this logic for some politically interesting purposes.

Hobbes saw the potential of the *universitas* for self-improvement through the normative regulation of its members. Specifically, he recognized that this process would require the *redistribution* of properties from natural individuals to the artificial corporate person licensed as a *universitas*. For Hobbes, the fear and force that divide individuals in the state of nature would be alienated and concentrated in his version of *universitas*, the Leviathan state, whose absolute power would then enable the individuals to engage in sustained peaceful associations that would have the long-term consequence of fostering civilization, from which subsequent generations might benefit. The socialist ideals realized in the welfare state may be seen as having carried this logic one step further, as income redistribution aimed to remove the class divisions that emerge unintentionally from the advantage accumulated in post-Leviathan civil associations, which effectively created a 'civilized' version of the state of nature, as Marx perhaps most vividly recognized. In his more Communist moods, Marx seemed to believe that the proletarian revolution would devolve the Hobbesian sovereign back to the people, who armed with self-consciousness and modern modes of production, would be able to lead a secure and peaceful existence. However, short of that utopian outcome, the threat of the Internal Revenue Service ends up sublimating the generalized threat originally posed by the Leviathan.

No one ever denied that the redistribution of property (understood as both abstract qualities and concrete holdings) entails what economists call 'transaction costs' – that is, the costs involved in bringing about the redistribution. But how can one ensure that these costs are borne equitably and in ways that do not overwhelm the transactions they are designed to sustain? A neat feature of the Hobbesian solution – one long associated with Machiavelli – is that a credible threat of force is self-economizing (Botwinick, 1990). In other words, the threat works to the extent that it does not need to be acted upon, because prospective targets anticipate its bloody consequences; hence they take pains to avoid conditions that would result in those consequences. Of course, the threat needs to be credible in the first place, which is why Hobbes emphasized the absoluteness of the sovereign's power. Anything short of a complete monopoly of force would invite challenges that would divide the sovereign's energies between securing the conditions for redistribution and the actual redistribution. A normatively desirable redistribution of property may still result – but perhaps with a fraction of the original population. To be sure, this has been an acceptable price to pay for saving Humanity from the more recalcitrant elements of *Homo sapiens* – at least according to the revolutionary founders of the first French Republic. Others have been less sure.

In the final quarter of the 19th century, the first professional association of social scientists, the German *Verein für Sozialpolitik*, addressed this problem by proposing a minimal welfare state as the price the rich should pay for tolerating rapid social and economic change without generating civil unrest (Rueschemeyer and van Rossum, 1996). In this way, Germany could make a peaceful internal transition to its emergent status as a global imperial player. In the form of Bismarck's social security insurance scheme, conservative paternalism thus made its formal contribution to the realization of socialist ideals, since what had originated as a concession came to be a rallying point for Germany's nascent Social Democratic Party. Nevertheless, Bismarck's scheme did serve to immunize Germany from a Marxist proletarian revolution, whose potential resemblance to the first French Republic frightened partisans on all sides. Moreover, as long as the welfare state provided only the minimum – and not the optimum – for the maintenance of social life, there was little chance that the poor would ever have sufficient leisure to mount a credible organized challenge to the rich. In this respect, Bismarck's welfare state was designed to supplement Ricardo's 'iron law of wages', whereby workers are 'rationally' paid just enough to keep them coming to work the next day.

Whereas the conservatives unwittingly paved the way to socialism in their attempt to maintain order in the face of rapid change and rising aspirations, the liberal-inspired promise of greater overall productivity through greater cross-class mobility eventually won the political argument to create more robust welfare states. This argument, popular among Fabian socialists in Britain, was presented as a self-reinforcing 'virtuous circle': The wealth of society as a whole is promoted by everyone doing what they can do best, which means that everyone needs to be given the opportunity to demonstrate what they can do, which in turn will result in greater wealth for society as a whole. This shift in welfare orientation from the past to the future presupposed a different justification for progressive taxation. Whereas Bismarck's welfare initiatives mainly had the rich reward the poor for work well done in keeping them rich, the Fabian welfare state would have the rich make speculative investments on those most likely to maintain or increase their wealth in the future. Accordingly, the welfare state's attention shifted to 'front-loaded' expenditures in preventive medicine and educational access.

Although the Fabians' more generous sense of welfare came to define 'first world' nations by the third quarter of the 20th century, the strategy has always faced two countervailing forces that have tempted policymakers to return to the biological roots of inheritance: the persistence with which the rich try to reclaim their tax burden and the delay with which welfare beneficiaries improve their life chances. Both potentially wreak havoc on party political campaigns by implicitly raising the question of redistribution's transaction costs. It was against this background of impatience that *eugenics* promised, so to speak, *socialism on the cheap* (Allen, 1998).

The two people most responsible for advancing eugenics as an academically respectable basis for policy in the Anglophone world – Francis Galton and Karl Pearson – were self-styled 'scientific socialists' of the late 19th century (namely before Marxists cornered the market on the expression). For Galton and Pearson, the *laissez faire* policies of a so-called Social Darwinist like Herbert Spencer were sociologically naïve because they underestimated the extent to which a single illustrious progenitor could enable successive generations of unproductive offspring to occupy powerful positions. Here the eugenicists took specific aim at the British House of Lords. In a eugenic utopia, election to the upper legislative chamber would be rationalized by examining entire family histories to see which lineages demonstrated consistency or improvement in accomplishment across generations. Moreover, on that basis, the eugenicist could expedite the forces of natural selection by providing incentives to increase the reproductive tendencies of the more illustrious lineages and to decrease those of the less illustrious ones.

It is worth pointing out that in the 20th century eugenics has been pursued under at least three different conceptions of the genetic transmission of socially salient traits (Radick, 2005). First, Galton, Pearson and their fellow 'biometricians' in the Anglophone world imagined that each individual carries the traits of *all* previous ancestors, albeit in inverse proportion to the distance in generations from the individual's parents. In contrast, eugenicists who strictly adhered to Gregor Mendel's account of inheritance – the current scientific basis for genetics – were associated with the German science of 'racial hygiene', whereby *only* the individual's parents matter in determining her genetic constitution (Proctor, 1988). However, most ordinary jobbing eugenicists belonged to a third group, notoriously represented by Stalin's agricultural minister and self-styled 'dialectical biologist' Trefim Lysenko. They followed early 19th century biologist Jean-Baptiste Lamarck in holding that an individual's genetic constitution is sufficiently malleable that at least some trace of one's life experience can be transmitted to offspring. This – the doctrine of the inheritance of acquired characteristics – remained popular among those like Spencer whose commitment to evolution was independent of Darwinism. They never managed to shake off the anthropomorphic idea that individuals can directly contribute to the self-improvement of the species.

It is worth noting that the Lamarckian option was kept alive in the 20th century by more than Marxist dogma: Early in the century, the US developmental psychologist, James Mark Baldwin proposed to simulate Lamarck in Darwinian terms by claiming that selective advantage is conferred on those who can most easily learn what they are taught (Richards, 1987: Chapter 10). From this perspective, training does not so much impose a new order on individual bodies (and then their genes) as trigger genetic tendencies that are already more pronounced in some members of a population than others. The offspring of those so genetically advantaged thus come to the fore of society, thereby simulating a Lamarckian sense of progress.

Hanging in the balance of the three conceptions of eugenics is the kind of state intervention in default human reproductive patterns that is scientifically licensed. For example, the biometricians expected that traits from long forgotten ancestors would eventually re-emerge. Thus, they were keen on compiling actuarial tables and promoting preventive medicine to anticipate – and where possible pre-empt through sterilization, contraception and abortion – the recurrence of what they regarded as evolutionary throwbacks. As a eugenics policy, biometrics was, at once, epistemically more invasive and ontologically less violent than the Nazis who adhered to the Mendelian position in the hope that simply segregating or even eliminating people of Jewish parentage would eradicate Jewishness altogether. No additional questions need be asked, once the parents are known. In contrast, the Neo-Lamarckians supported the systematic restructuring of learning environments – the home, the school or the workplace – in the name of improving the conditions under which socially advantageous reproduction can occur. Welfare state social policy initiatives of urban renewal, education and health reform were typically informed by some combination of biometric and Neo-Lamarckian sensibilities.

In any case, the 20th century was largely a story of eugenics run amok. To nations faced with an influx of immigrants and mounting costs for public health and education, eugenics promised an easy way out – indeed, at an increasing number of points in the reproductive process, as knowledge of genetic causal mechanisms progressed (King, 1999). Early in the century, changes could be induced in reproductive patterns only by either modest incentives (for example, tax breaks, income subsidies) or brute force (for example, sterilization, genocide): the one insufficiently compelling and the other too repellent. However, today's eugenicists – now travelling under the guise of 'genetic counsellors' – can intervene at several intermediate stages, including amniocentesis and genetic screening, which are more likely to appeal to a broad moral consensus.

Moreover, following a landmark ruling by the French Supreme Court, there is now legal precedent for presuming that one has a 'right' not to have been born if those causally proximate to the birth could have reasonably anticipated that he or she would lead a seriously disadvantaged life (Henley, 2002). The noteworthy feature of this judgement, which was soon applied in other related cases, is its presumption, *à la* Thatcher, that society as such shoulders no special burden for the fate of its members. The Court ruled that the genetic abnormalities called 'disabilities' are not *prima facie* opportunities for socio-legal innovation, as, say, animal rights activists routinely urge on behalf of their intellectually sub-human constituency. Rather, disabilities are pure liabilities, but ones for which only the disabled person's parents and doctors are responsible. An intervention by the French Parliament has subsequently restricted the ruling to grant parents limited rights to sue for medical negligence in the case of disabled births. But the first step has been taken.

The French court ruling takes us a long way from the strong welfarist perspective of John Rawls' (1971) 'veil of ignorance', which justified substantial redistribution of wealth on the grounds that if one's own place in society is uncertain, then it is best to allocate resources so that even the worst social position is not so bad. Indeed, for some political philosophers, our increased ability to anticipate the differential outcomes of the genetic lottery provides sufficient grounds for rolling back Rawls altogether. Hillel Steiner (1998) has swung so far back to libertarianism that he would generalize the French ruling and have tort law absorb most of the state's claims to collectivize and redistribute benefits and harms. Steiner envisages a world in which a basic knowledge of genetic science and one's own genetic constitution would become integral to citizen education, for which individuals would then be held accountable as a normal part of self-management. For the feminist legal theorist, Roxanne Mykitiuk (2003), this emerging bioliberal regime is simply another step in the march of the post-Keynesian state. Thus, policymakers imagine that as we acquire a more fine-grained understanding of the relationship between our genes and our traits, the state can safely retreat to the regulatory margins of the market, ensuring that biomedical products and techniques do what is claimed of them. It is then up to the consumer, provided with such information, to make a decision and suffer the consequences.

Ronald Dworkin (2000) has tried to update Rawls to make a case for socialized insurance against genetic risk, a strategy endorsed by the UK's leading cancer research charity as a basis for public reinvestment in the National Health Service, despite current Labour government policy to devolve healthcare to the private sector (Meek, 2002). This reinvention of the welfare state turns on an elementary point of genetic science. Suppose we assume a fixed species or common gene pool – admittedly a 'closed system' that is placed increasingly under strain with progress in biotechnology. Nevertheless, in that ideal case, genetics demonstrates *both* the commonality of possible life chances (namely genotypes) *and* the arbitrariness of the particular life chances that are realized in individuals (namely phenotypes). Even given clear genetic markers for traits that are agreed to be 'disabilities', the only way to prevent those disabilities from ever arising at all would be to prevent the birth of anyone carrying the relevant markers – even given the unlikelihood that any of the aborted would have led a disabled life. The prenatal terminations proliferated by this approach are called 'false positives' by statisticians and 'errors on the side of caution' (on a mass scale) by everyone else. As a general policy for preempting undesirable outcomes, it adumbrates an intolerably risk-averse society. (For example, the relatively common Down's syndrome figured in some of the landmark French cases.) Yet, this policy is proposed as a post-welfarist 'paradise' embraced by not only neo-liberals but also ecologists, who invoke the 'precautionary principle' to similar effect.

There is a serious rhetorical difficulty with expressing the implications of bioliberalism's devolved eugenic sensibility. The contrast between the welfare state and bioliberalism is typically presented in terms of attitudes toward *risk*: the former supposedly aims to minimize risk, while the latter aims at least to accept risk, if not exactly to maximize it. However, given the ease with which bioliberals pre-empt negative life chances, this way of putting the matter is paradoxical. Although Rawls himself encouraged the view that individuals are naturally risk-averse, the redistributionist strategies of the welfare state actually aim to *collectivize* risk. In other words, the state enables the reorganization of people so that they are capable of taking *more* risks than they would or could as individuals. As either Spencer or Galton would have seen from their different perspectives, the welfare state's redistribution of resources artificially extends the selection environment to allow for the survival of otherwise unfit individuals – presumably because of the anticipated long-term benefit that such individuals would provide for the rest of society. In cases of subsidized education and healthcare to ambitious and clever children from poor homes, the social benefits are palpable within a couple of decades. However, the benefits derived from special educational and health facilities for the disabled depend on more extended notions of humanity and greater patience with consequences (Barnes and Mercer, 2003: Chapter 6).

Martha Nussbaum (2001) suggests that the policy imagination is recharged by the periodic adoption of what Max Weber would have called a 're-enchanted' view toward so-called 'monstrous births', which, rather than problems to be avoided or liabilities to be minimized, are symbolic events from which we learn something deep about what it means to be one of 'us'. Yet, the nature of this 'depth' is far from mysterious. It simply requires interpreting the monstrous birth as an occasion to extend the definition of the human rather than to have the birth excluded for failing to conform to the current definition. (The anthropology of Mary Douglas and the philosophy of science of Imre Lakatos provide interesting precedents for this line of thought: see Bloor, 1979; Fuller and Collier, 2004: Chapters 5, 7.) Historically speaking, such an attitude has been integral to the distinctive push of Western scientific medicine to regard death – like war, so said Jacques Chirac – as always an admission of failure. The unconditional commitment to the prolonging of human life, no matter the cost, or even the consquences for those whose lives are prolonged, is a secular descendant of the monotheistic concern for the weak and infirm members of *Homo sapiens*. In these most vulnerable parties – at least according to Judaism, Christianity, and Islam – lies the human stripped of its worldly power to a form that only God could recognize as 'His' own.

While it is convenient to argue that the concrete failures of socialism and social science explain the great ideological leap backward to bioliberalism, an important part of the explanation lies in the diffusion of political interest from the specifically human to a more generic sense of life. This reflects more than the cultural impact of Neo-Darwinism on contemporary political and ethical intuitions. It also reflects a profound change in political economy. The original defenders of animal rights were urban dwellers like Epicurus, Lucretius, Montaigne, and Bentham, who held no special brief for protecting the natural environment. Indeed, their pro-animal thinking was part of a general strategy of rescuing all sentient beings from captivity in 'the state of nature' (Plender, 2001). For them, as for Linnaeus, Lord Monboddo, and Lamarck, the highest compliment one could pay an animal was to say that it was fit for human company. Animal rights came to be absorbed into a general ecological ethic only with the decline of agriculture as a mode of production. Thus, by the time Peter Singer (1981) came to speak of 'expanding the circle' of moral responsibility, he ultimately had the entire planet in his sights – that is the preservation of animal habitats, not simply the incorporation of animals into human society.

I cannot say exactly when animal rights came to be associated with a specifically anti-humanistic sensibility that places greater value on wild over domestic animal existence. Nevertheless, the assimilation of animal rights to a global ecological ethic has served to lower *both* the criteria for an adequate human existence (namely to the minimization of suffering) *and* the tolerance for individual humans who fail to meet those criteria (namely the disabled, the infirm, perhaps even the unwanted). In other words, an extension of rights to animals in general has been accompanied by a restriction of rights to specific classes of humans. As we shall see in Chapter 10, this development may be seen as a scientific version of La Rochefoucauld's maxim, 'Familiarity breeds contempt'. In effect, animals receive the benefit of the doubt in a global ecological ethic simply because less is known about them.

A reified version of this judgement has been central to the Aristotelian tradition: Animals are morally neutral in a way that humans are not because the former always realize their lower potential, whereas the latter often do not realize their higher potential. Here the uniquely human capacity for free will plays an operative role. Admittedly, disabled humans are not personally responsible for their failure to realize their potential, but that does not prevent their lives from being valued less when compared to that of able-bodied humans. In light of this lingering Aristotelian sensibility, an unintended long-term value of conducting more research into animals may be that greater familiarity with the grades of animal life will enable similarly nuanced judgements of animals, including perhaps making them also liable for their own unrealized potential. These matters will come to a head as legislation is introduced to extend to animals formal legal protection, political representation and medical insurance.

We have seen the concept of welfare dissipated in two respects. On the one hand, ecologists have wanted to 'expand the moral circle' to cover animal welfare. In a post-socialist period when tax bases are often shrinking, this policy invariably involves spreading welfare provision more thinly among humans. It has resulted in more explicit discussions of tradeoffs in legal coverage and even 'triage' in healthcare. On the other hand, neo-liberals want simply to withdraw state involvement from all but the most basic welfare provision, converting individual tax burdens into added spending power that may be used as individuals see fit.

New developments in genomic-based biotechnology offer comfort to both the ecological and the neo-liberal views of welfare provision. On the one hand, the ontology underlying the new biotechnology stresses a 90%+ genetic overlap between humans and other animals, creating a presumptive parity of interests and rights. On the other hand, the research agenda of the new biotechnology is oriented toward the identification of specific abnormalities in specific strands of DNA, which ultimately would enable each individual to have a comprehensive understanding of her genetic strengths and weaknesses, so that she can make an 'informed choice' about the degree and kind of healthcare she is likely to need. For a sense of political contrast, an 'old socialist' would read the '90%+' figure as grounds for encouraging xenotransplantation, gene therapy, and animal experimentation – all in aid of maximizing the use of animals to promote human welfare. Moreover, rather than focusing on the uniqueness of each person's DNA, the old socialist would note that they are combinations of elements drawn by chance from a common genetic pool.

A sign that both the ecologists and the neo-liberals have evacuated the ground previously held by the red parties is that the welfare of the most vulnerable members of human society is largely abandoned as an explicit policymaking goal – though both continue to argue that the poor and disabled might benefit indirectly, such as by trickle-down economics or even some 'mercy killing' (especially if the minimization of suffering is taken to be an overriding value). Indeed, there is a tendency for both ecologists and neo-liberals to speak as if the fundamental problems of poverty and immiseration that gave rise to the labour movement and socialist parties have been already more-or-less solved – much as it is often claimed that certain previously widespread diseases like smallpox and polio have now been eradicated. But both sides of the analogy turn out to be empirically flawed and maybe even conceptually confused, if they assume that social progress, once made, is irreversible and hence worthy of benign neglect.

For their part, sociologists have done relatively little to illuminate this rather strange *pre-emptive futurism* that characterizes contemporary post-welfarist politics, even as the gap between the rich and the poor both within and between countries has increased over the past quarter century (Wheen, 2004: Chapter 10). Instead, sociologists have fixated on the generalized exposure to risk that the devolution of the welfare state has wrought, and the self-organizing 'lifestyle politics' that have emerged in its wake. It would seem that with the decline of the welfare state has come a phenomenolo-gization of the sociological sensibility, as if the ontology of social structures dissolves right alongside the devolution of state power. I refer here, of course, to the so-called 'risk society' thesis introduced by Ulrich Beck (1992) and popularized in the guise of 'ontological insecurity' by Anthony Giddens (1990). However, this is not quite phenomenology as Alfred Schutz under-stood it – nor is it politics as anyone normally understands it.

At the dawn of the mass media, Schutz (1964) famously argued that radio gave listeners a false sense of immediacy of events happening far beyond their everyday life experiences, which might embolden them into political intervention. (He was worried about fascist propaganda galvanizing the petty bourgeoisie to disrupt the political order.) If we replace 'radio' with 'internet', Schutz's reservations would seem to apply to the lifestyle politics associated with, say, the anti-globalization movement. This change of media enables the anti-globalizationists to control the means of know-ledge production to a substantial extent, while at the same time it enables them to autonomize their activities from ordinary politics. What is notice-ably lacking from this movement – especially when compared with the old labour movement – is sustained engagement with the people on whose behalf the demonstrations are made. Protestors tend not to be members of the classes represented but well-educated, well-meaning people who – by virtue of age, disposable income, or employment situation – can easily trans-port themselves to the first-world sites where global political and economic oppressors happen to congregate. The actual oppressed are typically too busy working in third-world sweatshops or fearful of local political reprisals to demonstrate for themselves.

To some extent, this lack of sustained engagement already had prece-dents in the failure of university-based activism in the 1960s and 1970s to touch base with industrial labour, even though much of the academic polit-ical rhetoric concerned 'class oppression'. With the 20/20 vision afforded by hindsight, we may say that the more ecological and libertarian features of campus radicalism held little appeal to organized labour, with its generally solidarist strategy for retaining factory jobs. Of course, the jury is out on whether the anti-globalization movement really serves the interests of those they claim to represent. Nevertheless, the movement already displays some distinctive contexts of interaction. The representatives and the represented – the protestors and the oppressed – are usually limited to 'photo-ops' in the broadest sense, ranging from the protestors briefly visiting oppressed habitats in the presence of the cable television news channels to the protestors themselves filming the oppressed to raise consciousness at home.

It is easy to see how such self-appointed representation of others suits a reduction of the politics of humanity to a 'politics of nature' (Latour, 2004). For example, animal rights activists do not organize animals to revolt against their human oppressors, nor do they necessarily spend much time around animals – though they visit sites of animal captivity, mainly to document the cruelty they suffer for the humans who might make a difference to their fate. While this political strategy is perfectly understandable vis-à-vis animals, it should cause the heart of any socialist to sink when applied to humans: *where are the attempts to persuade the locals that they should organize themselves to revolt against their oppressors?* Of course, in the current political climate, the few such attempts that do occur are regarded as 'treason' and 'terrorism' – indeed, as they were when socialists acted similarly in the 19th century. Yet, the original socialists were not deterred by the threat of state sanction because they believed that the locals could be persuaded of their point-of-view and, crucially, that fact would contribute evidence to the view's correctness. This result, in turn, would embolden the enlarged comradeship to continue spreading the word worldwide.

Here we see one of the many senses in which socialism tried to realize the spirit of Christianity in a secular guise (MacIntyre, 1994). Presupposed in the socialist project – at least in this organizational phase before it became the dominant state party of any country – was a sense that one's own faith in the project had to be tested against the unconverted. This gave socialism much of its heroic quality, but it also meant that the doctrine was responsive to the resistance it met from those on whose behalf socialists aspired to speak. In contrast, the anti-globalizationists are essentially a self-appointed emancipatory movement that does not require its subjects to confirm its perspective. Read uncharitably, the anti-globalizationists would appear to be risk-averse or dogmatic in their own sociological horizons. In effect, they have assimilated the plight of oppressed humans to that of the natural environment, whose consent they would also never dream of seeking. In this respect, they engage in a 'dehumanization' of politics – albeit a benevolently inspired one.

Other attempts to provide a post-welfarist grounding for sociology have foundered on the shoals of 'body politics'. In his keynote address to the annual meeting of the British Sociological Association in 2002, Bryan Turner, a founder of the popular speciality, 'sociology of the body', called for a division of labour within social science to recapture the distinction between a universal human nature and differences among particular societies. Perhaps unsurprisingly, the proposed division was a phenomenologically inspired one – between the universal experience of *pain* and the culturally relative manifestations of *suffering*. For Turner a supposed advantage of this redefinition is that it draws the boundary of the social's domain right at the interface with the natural world. Thus, Turner would extend sociology's remit to cover areas previously ceded to psychology and the biomedical sciences.

Unfortunately, this extension comes at the price of attenuating the definition of the 'social' in ways that, once again, give comfort to both ecologists and neo-liberals at the expense of the old left: In Turner's Brave New Sociology, 'the social' is reducible to a collection of traits possessed by individuals (the neo-liberal turn) and, moreover, these traits are defined such that their possessors need not be humans (the ecological turn). It marks a return to an ontology that sees the difference between 'species', 'race' and 'culture' as matters of degrees, not kinds, and a normative ideal that is fixated on the ideal member of one such group rather than the exemplary collective product that 'humanity' was meant to be.

FIVE

Towards a Renewal of Welfare and the Rediscovery of British Sociology

No one denies the unprecedented nature of what we know about the genetic constitution of humans and other animals, as well as our capacity for genetic intervention both *in vivo* and *in vitro*. What remains – and will always remain – in doubt is our control over the consequences. Genetics is an irreducibly statistical science. Indeterminacy occurs on at least three levels: interaction effects among genes in a genome, from genotype to phenotype, and the interaction effects between genetic makeup and the environment. In this respect, the very term 'biotechnology' masks a socially significant gap between knowledge and control. To be sure, at the dawn of the 20th century, when eugenicists learnt from the Hardy-Weinberg theorem that most disabilities would remain unexpressed in the individuals carrying the relevant genes, they did not admit defeat for their programme of selective breeding. Rather, they intensified their research, as if the indeterminacy were ignorance that could be eliminated through more precise genetic knowledge and invasive genetic technology (Paul 1998: Chapter 7). However, as one might expect of any complex phenomenon, this research has only succeeded in posing new problems as it solved old ones.

The statistical nature of genetic science provides the best chance for reviving the fortunes of both social science and socialism in the 21st century. But the realization of this future requires a genuine Hegelian 'sublation' of genetics. In other words, the status of genetics as a body of knowledge needs to be reduced before it can be properly incorporated into a renovated conception of 'society'. Specifically, it must come to be seen not as an autonomous, let alone foundational, science but as a 'mere' social technology that can be explained, justified, and applied by a wide variety of theories, ideologies, and policies. Ideally, this involves divesting genetics of its status as a paradigmatic science with a canonical history and fixed location on the intellectual landscape. Indeed, we should aim for the phrase 'genetic engineering' to become a pleonasm. Genetics must become like the economy, which is no longer the preserve of *laissez-faire* liberals but a generally recognized and multiply interpretable societal function. However, given the prevalence of what Richard Dawkins (1976) notoriously popularized as the 'gene's eye-view of the world', the public understanding of genetics continues to conjure up the spectre of totalitarian regimes, comparable to the public understanding of political economy, *circa* 1810, which evoked images of dehumanized exchange relations.

The analogy runs deeper, since Dawkins draws – perhaps unwittingly – on the reversal of means and ends that Marx used so effectively in *Capital* to illustrate capitalism's perversion of value. Just as money drives the exchange of commodities, 'selfish genes' use willing organisms to reproduce themselves. In contrast, with renewed sociological vision, genes should not be seen as the prime movers of life but organic by-products of procreation, a means by which people perpetuate several legally sanctioned social formations – most traditionally the family – as they bring the next generation into existence. To be sure, these organic by-products are themselves socially significant as regulators of individuals' bodily functions. Nevertheless, describing the genetic basis of humanity in such ontologically diminished terms draws attention to the subservient role of the gene, which through changes in the constitution of society and extensions in our biomedical capabilities (not least 'cyborganization') may itself come to be transformed, obviated, supplemented, or even replaced.

Moreover, in keeping with a welfarist sensibility, this sociological reval-uation of genetics places it squarely in the realm of human endeavour, specifically a product of collective labour that draws indeterminately on a common pool of resources in order to increase society's overall value. Moreover, the value of this product – the offspring – is measured by all the factors that go into its actual production rather than some inherent value of its raw material (as in the extreme bioliberalism of the 'right not to be born' rulings). The relative weighting of these factors and the identity of their bearers are the natural stuff of politics. Indeed, a society's genetic potential is the nearest that nature comes to providing a *res publica*, a focus for public deliberation and collective action.

At the moment, an important tendency in the history of the law – one normally associated with Enlightenment sensibilities – cuts against the idea of treating society's genetic potential as a *res publica*. It is the idea that greater knowledge entails greater responsibility for one's actions. The underlying principle is that if one recognizes the conditions under which one influences events, then one will have a clear sense of permissible and impermissible acts, and how one acts in a particular case – for good or ill – can be deemed deliberate. An important way that justice has remained 'blind' to special pleading and exceptional cases is to presume that people already know enough about themselves and others to anticipate (and hence prevent) situations where their actions might lead to disastrous consequences. In that respect, the more people are encouraged – or forced – to learn about themselves, the more the image of 'equality under the law' can be maintained in a regime that has effectively disciplined people to manage themselves in somewhat different ways. Thus, instead of a defendant in a drink-driving incident being presumed to know the alcohol blood level that counts as unlawful intoxication in all cases, a future with DNA-registered identity cards, an understanding of which is part of ordinary citizen education, will enable courts to hold defendants liable for different standards of intoxication under the guise of 'equal treatment' – because 'equality' will mean 'equal presumptive self-knowledge'.

All of this points to the centrality of a *politics of the gene* in an integrated welfare policy that encompasses the pre-natal situation, the conditions of birth and infancy, child-rearing and formal education, as well as preventive, diagnostic, and curative health care. As in debates over taxation, there are many possible points of intervention for influencing an individual's life chances. Each proposes to redistribute the costs and benefits across society rather differently, usually in accordance with some vision of justice. And as in debates over, say, the taxation of inherited wealth, we may look forward to the day when reasonable people disagree over specifically genetic interventions without demonizing those whose arguments test the extremes of political possibility. In the end, what matters is the democratic framework for taking these decisions, one that invites the regular examination and possible reversal of standing policies (Fuller, 2000a: Chapter 1).

It is clear that renewed attention to the concept and processes of redistribution should be central to sociology for the 21st century. In the first place, a property possessed by an individual may be normatively positive or negative, depending on the legal authorization for its transmission. There are even Biblical grounds for this notion. Biblical literalists concede that the only evil form of transmission is biological reproduction, which grants legitimacy to later generations simply by virtue of being a genetic descendant of Adam, the original sinner. A more sanctified form of transmission requires a formal renunciation of what was evil in this legacy, as in baptism or its secular equivalent, an examination that gives a candidate the opportunity to renounce one's former ignorance or prejudice. Moreover, even if we grant that people are 'by nature' selfish to the point of being prone to use violence to protect their individual inheritance, they may nonetheless improve their sociability simply by the legal transfer of these violent tendencies to the state as executor of their collective inheritance, which is tantamount to maintaining the conditions under which the people remain sociable. The 'arts of citizenship' from military training to regular elections encapsulate this species of political alchemy. Accordingly, potential combatants are compelled to focus on particular activities with clearly demarcated rules of engagement rather than 'taking the law into their hands'.

The reinvention of sociology will also benefit from the mutual recognition of the fundamental equality of individuals that accompanies a redistributionist ethic. 'Equality' here is meant in mainly negative terms, namely, the arbitrariness and potential reversibility of whatever conditions actually differentiate members of a society, be it to one's own advantage or disadvantage. This point may be seen as another way of sublimating the uncertainty that besets *Homo sapiens* in a Hobbesian state of nature (for example, the Rawlsian 'original position') or more positively – following Alasdair MacIntyre (1999) – as identifying humanity with a sense of reciprocity, that is, the capacity for giving and taking. Our achievements are largely due to the collaboration and license of others who neither question our motives nor themselves materially benefit from those achievements. They simply expect that we would act similarly toward them under similar circumstances. Included here are the background institutions that economists say 'minimize transaction costs'. (However, Alvin Gouldner (1973: 260–99) intriguingly suggested that it may be the *separate* development of the 'giving' and 'taking' phases of reciprocity – that is, beneficence and exploitation – that mark the human. This would certainly define the human in 'counter-evolutionary' terms.)

Regardless of aetiology, an egalitarian attitude counteracts both complacency about success and fatalism about failure: informed with a vivid sense that the future may well *not* copy the past, people will endeavour to make their collective efforts exceed whatever they might do individually or in a more socially restricted capacity. The outstanding question that remains is which individuals are eligible for this sort of equality: is the redistributionist regime limited to only and all those genetically marked as *Homo sapiens*? Whereas socialists traditionally answered yes without hesitation, today neo-liberals deny the 'all' and ecologists the 'only' premised in the question. In today's ideological debates over biotechnology, neither neo-liberals nor ecologists speak consistently on behalf of all of humanity, although it is clear that specific humans are likely to benefit from politically realizing one or the other side. Here a renewed socialist sensibility would make a point of *prioritizing* the maintenance and extension of specifically *human* traits, forms, and projects.

To compare genetic potential with labour power or inherited wealth is, in an important sense, to render the raw material of our lives banal. Moreover, from a sociological standpoint that regards humanity as a collective project initiated by *Homo sapiens*, that is exactly how it should be: our humanity lies *exclusively* in what we make of our genetic potential, not in the potential itself. In this respect, Aristotle was right to hold humanity to a higher standard of achievement than animals. But he had got the reason wrong: we are entitled to be held to a higher standard *only* because we have already achieved so much, not because our raw material is so much better. The task for sociology in the 21st century, then, is to reclaim the ground that *a posteriori* criteria like 'beneficial consequences' have unwittingly yielded to *a priori* criteria like 'virtuous capacities' in a time when major scientific advance has coincided with diminished expectations of the good that can be ultimately derived from it. I shall elaborate this point more fully in the Conclusion.

Perhaps surprisingly, the British intellectual tradition provides hidden resources for reorienting sociology's research and policy compass in the desired direction. Of the major Western nations, Britain is normally seen as having laid the weakest foundation in sociology. When the British contribution is discussed at all, a generic picture of utilitarianism is presented in which the likes of Mill and Spencer are lumped together, making too much of their common allegiance to the Liberal Party (for example, Levine, 1995: Chapter 7). But as we know today from membership in, say, the UK Labour Party or the US Democratic Party, this bare fact speaks more to common foes than common goals. Nevertheless, since Spencer frequently used the word 'sociology', he is treated as the figurehead of the British tradition. Yet, like Mill, he was a public intellectual rather than a proper academic. Consequently, 'sociology' was never institutionalized with a clear systematic vision. The academic discipline bearing that name emerged at the LSE in the first decade of the 20th century, fuelled by the institution's Fabian socialist founders but subject to internal disputes between those with philosophical and applied sensibilities, which across the country was eventually stabilized by creating departments of 'sociology and social policy' (Dahrendorf, 1995: Part I; Halsey, 2004: 10–13).

Attempts to promote a distinctive British tradition in sociology have not been helped by the post-Second World War tendency to emulate, at first,

American and then, largely under Giddens' influence, Continental European theoretical concerns. Indeed, a coherent history of British sociology has been written that regards theoretical concerns as externally imposed (Kent, 1981). Consequently, most British sociologists today probably regard their discipline as a foreign import. Without rekindling intellectual chauvinism – after all, I am an American of Continental European descent – it should be possible to recast sociology's historically distinctive national contexts as platforms for projecting alternative futures for the entire field. To appreciate the distinctive British context, we need to get behind the uneasy truce signalled by the expression, 'sociology and social policy'. In the LSE's history, the two figures who epitomize the two parts of the expression are, respectively, L.T. Hobhouse and William Beveridge. Together they represented two strategies by which the social sciences might institutionalize the Enlightenment: education and administration.

Hobhouse, an idealist philosopher and self-styled 'social liberal' and 'ethical socialist', was appointed to the UK's first sociology chair in 1907, which he held until 1929 (Collini, 1979). He stressed the role of education in self-actualization, what Humboldt had called *Bildung* at the dawn of the modern German university and which came to be most clearly marked in the British sociological tradition as a general emphasis on 'rights' and 'citizenship', notably in the work of Hobhouse's successors, Morris Ginsberg and T.H. Marshall (Halsey, 2004: 51–62). In contrast, Beveridge was an economist for whom the field was still 'political arithmetic', on the basis of which social policy could be made. He translated into an English idiom an equally German – this time Bismarckian – concern for administration. As the LSE's director from 1919 to 1937, Beveridge promoted the field of 'social biology' as the ultimate positivistic policy science before joining Churchill's wartime cabinet, where he became the architect of the British welfare state. Here he was finally given an opportunity to administer to the 'vital statistics' that constituted the subject matter of his beloved social biology (Dahrendorf, 1995: Part II).

On the surface, Hobhouse and Beveridge could not be more different. Consider their respective heroes: Thomas Hill Green and Thomas Henry Huxley. Green was the Oxford don responsible for infusing British philosophy with the spirit of Hegel. The names of Bradley, Bosanquet, McTaggart and Collingwood evoke a sensibility that was only gradually dispelled by the combined efforts of Bertrand Russell and G.E. Moore at Cambridge in the early 20th century. Huxley, of course, was the surgeon and naturalist who, when not defending and extending Darwinism in public debate, campaigned for the centrality of the natural sciences to liberal education.

Nevertheless, Green and Huxley both wanted to secularize organized inquiry without reducing its goal to the Epicurean imperative of maximizing pleasure and minimizing pain. The promise of social science for their followers, Hobhouse and Beveridge, lay in the prospect of a middle way between conceptualizing humanity in purely theistic and purely animalistic terms. The focus for this concern was the relationship between the 18th century concept of *progress*, which both continued to uphold, and the ascendant 19th century concept of *evolution*, which both did not wish to deny. Specifically, these British founders of modern social science promoted a sense of social progress that existed in dialectical tension with that of Darwinian evolution.

By 'dialectical tension', I simply mean that Hobhouse and Beveridge held that social progress requires not only the recognition but also the reversal and transcendence of evolutionary tendencies. This realization informed a *prima facie* puzzling, and certainly unfashionable, methodological position they shared: both defended a strong distinction between facts and values in research (Collini, 1979: 225–7; Dahrendorf, 1995: 250). Their motivation for sharpening the fact–value distinction largely complemented that of Max Weber, the person with whom the distinction is normally associated. As illustrated in his original reluctance to identify himself by the ideologically charged term 'sociologist', Weber drew the distinction to protect scientific integrity from political contamination in a nation-state inclined to subordinate social science to a nationalistic social policy. Thus, Weber maintained that science cannot determine the best course of action, except in relation to a goal and value structure specified by the client, which the scientist simply takes as given. In other words, the cost of scientists retaining control over the means of their knowledge production is that they would refrain from telling clients what to do with the knowledge so produced. Reflecting his training in economics, Weber believed that 'efficiency' was the only value about which science could speak authoritatively.

Hobhouse and Beveridge saw the matter from the other side of the coin: A strong fact-value distinction is equally needed to keep the sphere of political decision-making as open as possible in the face of science's tendency to prematurely naturalize its own theoretical horizons. To be sure, the two conceptualized matters somewhat differently: Hobhouse the Hegelian saw the future as potentially 'contradicting' the past, while Beveridge the positivist regarded the past as logically underdetermining the future. Weber, of course, also promoted this decisionistic aspect of the fact–value distinction, especially in pedagogical settings, where it served as an antidote to the dogmatism of lecturers attached to both Marxist determinism and German militarism – what Karl Popper (1957) would later demonize as 'historicism'. However, an even more insidious version of such premature naturalization is epitomized in the proposition, '*Laissez faire* is nature's way', whereby one is always as one ought to be. The default is thus taken as *ipso facto* divine. This objectionable tendency began with the formal separation of economics from political economy inaugurated by Jevons' professorship (discussed in Chapter 3) and canonized at the LSE in Beveridge's day by Lionel Robbins, who dis-cussed it under such misleading rubrics as 'value neutrality' and even 'positivism' (as if Comte and Mill had never existed), all of which have given protective colouration to economics over the past half century (Proctor, 1991: Chapter 13; Fuller, 2001a).

Such economic naturalism had been given wide public exposure by Spencer's version of Social Darwinism, which counted on people's 'natural benevolence' in a low tax regime to redistribute wealth at a sustainable level vis-à-vis the natural environment (Offer, 1999). Those who failed to benefit from this spontaneous display of sentiment probably did not deserve to live – or at least, were they to live, would impose a burden unfair to others and, indeed, a yoke on nature itself. Perhaps unsurprisingly, benevolence comes under severe censure in the history of distributive justice, as it would restrict our capacity for justice only to those with whom we can easily form affective bonds. For Rousseau, Kant and most other Enlightenment thinkers outside Britain, benevolence promoted a 'people as pets' mentality familiar from paternalistic forms of conservatism that demeaned human dignity by creating permanent dependencies, the sense of enforced indebtedness that Nietzsche would later find so abhorrent in conventional morality (cf. Fleischacker, 2004: 53–74). From this standpoint, the growth of the state has corresponded to greater social progress by educating people to care about those to whom they have *no* emotional attachments – indeed, may even be strangers – simply by virtue of a shared common identity as 'citizens', the Enlightenment prototype for 'humanity'. A range of successful state-organized activities from voluntary military service to anonymous blood donations empirically testify to the human capacity to be reoriented from mere benevolence (Titmuss, 1970). The philosophical residue of this issue is that whereas Spencer understood altruism as a natural extension of egoism, Mill drew a sharp distinction between self- and other-regarding attitudes that remains ensconced in contemporary moral theory. Nevertheless, as we shall see in Part Two, these neo-liberal times, especially under the influence of Peter Singer, have witnessed a revival in the bonds of benevolence – only this time crossing species boundaries, while leaving behind a significant chunk of *Homo sapiens*.

Our Brave New Semantic Universe

A good way to demonstrate the distance we need to travel to recover the sociological sensibility whose signs of life I have been seeking is to focus on a couple of words that have subtly but significantly shifted their meanings in the sociological corpus: – *mobility* and *innovation* – and the corresponding downgrading of *institution* and upgrading of *community* as supporting concepts. These shifts have been largely facilitated by the 'new production of knowledge' in which social science research is increasingly engulfed (Gibbons et al., 1994; Nowotny et al., 2000). It is basically contract-based, client-driven research, in which the university is only one of several sponsors, or 'partners' (Fuller, 2002a).

Historically the terms 'mobility' and 'innovation' have had a progressive ring. In classical sociology, 'upward social mobility' named an aspiration of the working classes, as well as the geographical mobility that enables people and artefacts to transform host cultures, typically by introducing innovations from which everyone ultimately benefits. In this context, 'order' and 'tradition' suggested at the very least conservatism and perhaps even stagnation and repression. However, in our brave new world, the key terms have shifted their meanings. In particular, their teleological connotations have disappeared. Thus, mobility and innovation are valorized *as such*, without regard to the consequences. Moreover, in keeping with the deconstructive sensibilities of these postmodern times, there is a tendency to argue that the very distinction between tradition and innovation is bogus, since there are traditions of innovation and all innovations recover earlier traditions. And in light of chaos and complexity theory, we can even say that different kinds of order are simply patterned mobilities (Urry, 2000: Chapter 5), thereby conferring new meaning on the maxim, 'The more things change, the more they stay the same'.

Lost in these semantic manoeuvres is the idea that there may be better or worse innovations and better or worse ways of diffusing them. Judgements of this sort presuppose a standard external to the process under investigation. Such a standard would be typically manifested in the investigator's adoption of a fixed standpoint – what used to be called a theoretical framework – in terms of which some of the phenomena under investigation would appear normal and others deviant. Whether the standpoint is treated as 'normative' or 'empirical' depended on whether its resistance to the phenomena is treated as grounds for disciplining the phenomena or altering the standpoint. In practice, science usually negotiated a settlement between the two extremes.

In Orwell's *1984*, this erasure of standpoint was accomplished by the continual rewriting of history to make the present appear as the realization of current state policy. The records department of the Ministry of Truth, where *1984*'s protagonist Winston Smith worked, was thus dedicated to a rather cynical implementation of the Hegelian motto, 'The real is rational and the rational is real'. Smith's society was one whose grounding norm was the reduction of cognitive dissonance, specifically through what social psychologists call *adaptive preference formation*. In short, one strives to achieve a state of mind in which one wants what one is likely to receive – to be sure, an ironic reading of socialism's aspirations to leave no human needs unmet. The political theorist Jon Elster (1983) has spoken of 'sour grapes' and 'sweet lemons' in this context, as ways by which people find the hidden good in *prima facie* bad outcomes.

The formation of adaptive preferences is facilitated by the elimination of reminders of previous goals, or at least the promotion of ambiguity through the compressed expression of those goals. In *1984*, copies of newspapers stating old government policies were placed in 'memory holes', pneumatic tubes that sent the documents to a fiery end. Of course, the systematic destruction of documents by itself could not erase the memories potentially triggered by the continued use of words appearing in those documents. Consequently, *1984*'s official language, Newspeak, tended toward neologisms that shortened words so as to minimize the time needed for thought before a response is elicited. These words, coined in the name of efficiency and convenience, provided a surface continuity that masked what were often radical shifts in policy import. However, it would be a mistake to regard Newspeak as the product of linguistic prescription in the sense of a standardized grammar and diction that in the name of national unity is legislated against the wills of many, if not most, native speakers. On the contrary, Newspeak's diabolical character lies in its ability to capitalize on the default tendency of linguistic forms to become condensed at the lexical, syntactic, and semantic levels through repeated use (Fuller, 1988: Part II). This tendency has been more effectively exploited in capitalist than socialist societies through the subliminal component of advertising, whereby a familiar phrase or slogan is given a new twist to stimulate consumer demand (Packard, 1957).

What's in a Name? 'Mobility'

The loss of a distinctly sociological standpoint is perhaps most straightforwardly illustrated in the case of 'mobility', a popular topic among sociologists of the post-classical generation, notably Pitirim Sorokin, the liberal exile from the Russian Revolution of 1917 who founded the Harvard Sociology Department. His work is conspicuous by its absence from more recent discussions (for example, Urry, 2000; Urry, 2002). Sorokin (1928: 747–52) would regard today's tendency to assimilate 'mobility' to the sheer statistical drift of individuals across regions or categories as 'pre-sociological', in that no judgement is made about the benefit or harm caused to either the mobile individuals or the host societies. Rather, the sheer persistence or increase in a tendency – 'survival' in its extended sense – is presumed to establish an emergent norm. This is very much how an evolutionary biologist or an epidemiologist sees matters. It has also gained increasing currency among social scientists who look to genetics for objective traces of large scale, long term socio-cultural mobility (for example, Cavalli-Sforza, 2000). Nevertheless, the sociologist's professional task would not be complete without considering what else needs to change to enable the emergence of certain patterns of mobility.

Whereas Sorokin himself pointed to the dissolution of traditional social bonds as a potential casualty of mobility, the US historian Christopher Lasch (1995: Chapter 3) has focused on the tradeoffs that have resulted from the elision of mobility and *opportunity*. For example, the drive to upward social mobility presupposes that membership in the working class – as either a mode of production or consumption – is not inherently respectable.

To achieve respect, and hence to realize their full potential as people, the working class have been urged to engage in substantial mobility of some sort. This implies that there is no *prima facie* value attached to who they already are, what they already do, or where they already do it. A more distant, but no less real, consequence of this elision of mobility and opportunity is a devaluation of politics in the conventional sense of party membership, voting, and public service: why go through the trouble of constructing an identity around a social position like 'working class' that other groups in your society largely regard as unfortunate and undesirable? More broadly, why struggle to redress injustices at home, when given the opportunity to emigrate to a more hospitable land? Thus, the decline of state-based citizenship has ushered an era of 'lifestyle politics' that is relatively indifferent to the location of its pursuit (Urry, 2000: Chapter 7). The dark side of this process is the tendency for such declining 'neo-liberalized' states to slip into a mode of governance by attrition, sometimes called 'post-facism', whereby those who cannot cope with the state's diminished circumstances are *expected* to leave or even die (Tamas, 2000).

Of course, the preceding remarks are not meant to belittle the plight of asylum seekers through the ages. But as the chequered but overall progressive history of democratic politics illustrates, long-lasting purposeful social change has typically required the mounting of organized resistance to dominant tendencies in the *domestic* environment. The result has been the construction of corporate persons – originally *universitates* in Roman Law – whose aims transcend those of its constituent members and whose perpetuation occurs by means other than hereditary succession. This category includes chartered cities, states, churches, universities, and – starting in the 19th century – business enterprises. The construction of these entities has involved the redistribution of powers and properties across a wide range of otherwise conflicting or indifferent groups of individuals by a procedure that Max Weber would have recognized as 'legal-rational' (Fuller, 2003b). In short, it has been the establishment of institutions – not the facilitation of immigration – that has enabled *homo sapiens* to overcome its animal origins, thereby making it a fit object for sociological inquiry. In this context, much more needs to be made sociologically of the role that returning exiles have played in revolutionizing their native societies (Fuller, 2005: 118–122).

Not surprisingly, the meltdown of institutions into mobilities has been accompanied by a renascent interest in the pre-institutionalized forms of social life epitomized in the word 'community', now understood more positively than in classical sociology. Here the German word, *Gemeinschaft*, stood for the residual structures of pre-modern world. These structures set biological and geographical parameters on the meaning of human existence, such that kinship ties provided the grounding ontology for face-to-face interactions, which were in turn regarded as the most authentic form of social life. In this context, Ferdinand Toennies originally spoke of *Gemeinschaft* as 'racial' rather than strictly 'political' in its social basis. Toennies wrote in the 1880s, when the unification of Germany was within living memory and the emerging German superstate clearly had imperial ambitions outside Europe that would entail the reorganization and integration of racially diverse peoples. In this context, *gemeinschaftlich* bonds placed obstacles in the way of what Norbert Elias has called, with respect to Europe itself, the 'civilizing process'. However, today's conceptually face-lifted version of 'community' does not require literal bio-geographical embeddedness. Its phenomenologically distinctive features may be preserved – or 'virtualized' – by the increasing immediacy afforded by the emergent information and communication technologies (Urry, 2002). Thus, the proliferation of mobile videophones puts paid to the alleged opposition between 'mobility' and 'community' – yet both terms remain resolutely anti-institutional in their focus.

The knock-on effects of this anti-institutionalism are subtle but pervasive. For example, the concept of *race*, whose exclusionary character always haunted classical sociological depictions of 'community', is beginning to receive a more acceptable face, one inflected with the idea of mobility. Fortified by the marriage of Mendelian genetics and Darwinian evolutionary theory, Cavalli-Sforza (2000) has revitalized the old ideal of 'racial purity' in the guise of 'genetic diversity' that needs to be maintained, especially against the various threats of homogenization and assimilation faced by so-called indigenous peoples. Evidence for human genetic diversity is tracked – just as the early 19th century German philologists had tracked racial purity – in terms of linguistic diffusion. (For a landmark critique of this first wave of 'scientific Aryanism', see Bernal, 1987.) To be sure, Cavalli-Sforza treats racism as an arbitrary form of discrimination, since any two individuals, while genetically identical in almost all respects, will display genetic differences at some level of resolution. Nevertheless, from this acknowledged arbitrariness, he concludes that one should target culturally salient genetic discriminations for preservation (a.k.a. segregation). Not surprisingly, this conclusion leads him to follow the movements of peoples across times and places, resulting in an endorsement of scientifically updated versions of theses prevalent in late 19th century anthropology. Thus, after asserting that political units such as the state are analogical extensions of the family, Cavalli-Sforza says, 'Cultural transmission is easier, faster, and more efficient when a powerful authoritarian chief forces the acceptance of an innovation' (182). His examples are the Pope and Mussolini. Sociology's hard won insight from the law – that institutional perpetuation can fruitfully cut across hereditary modes of succession – is alien to this line of thought.

If Cavalli-Sforza's co-valorization of authority and mobility appears strange to contemporary readers, then it is worth recalling that before Hannah Arendt firmly established the 'totalitarian' credentials of Nazi Germany in the minds of social scientists, close observers, both pro- and con-, of the regime regarded fascism as quite a flexible corporate actor. It was more Behemoth than Leviathan, to quote Franz Neumann's (1944) famous invocation of Hobbes' distinction in rule by weakly bounded coalitions versus a strongly bounded sovereign. Were it not for strictures of political correctness, we would now regard the regime as an especially supple 'actor-network' (Fuller, 2000b: Chapter 7). The secret of Nazi Germany's flexible fascism lay in its studied anti-institutionalism, which enabled local authorities to enforce the Führer's will however they saw fit, suspending rule of law in order to tackle more effectively the contextually specific ways in which the regime was subject to external threat (Scheuerman, 1994). Thus, doctors were not ordered but *empowered* to exterminate the disabled and the Jews – that is, if doctors voluntarily took such a decision, the state would back it (Browning, 2003). Not surprisingly, in these historically amnesic times, we find that the jurist who did the most in his day to confer intellectual respectability on this policy, Carl Schmitt, is now rehabilitated as a deconstructionist *avant la lettre* – of course, laundered of his painfully obvious Nazi associations (Latour, 2002; cf. Lilla, 2001: Chapter 2).

What's in a Name? 'Innovation'

Innovation is the first global policy craze of the 21st century. One could be forgiven for thinking that 'fostering', 'seeding', and 'nurturing' innovation are the most popular pastimes of public and private sector decision-makers *outside* the United States. The exclusion of the USA from this generalization suggests that one innovates mainly to catch up in the world political-economic arena. In this context, innovation is presented as the key to competitiveness. Of course, the USA realizes that it too must remain competitive to maintain its premier position in the global marketplace. However, the USA relies on such distinctly uninnovative activities as erecting foreign trade barriers, subsidizing domestic industries, and investing in controversial overseas political adventures. Without defending American policies, which have been criticized almost to the point of banality, I wish to question the contemporary fascination with innovation in the rest of the world. The most that can be said in favour of innovation as a normative economic strategy is that it is the prerogative of losers, as set out in the unjustly neglected thesis of the 'relative advantage of backwardness' (Gerschenkron, 1962; Fuller, 1997: Chapter 5).

In the UK and its overseas emulators, universities are increasingly urged to measure their worth in terms of the number of patents generated, perhaps the most facile indicator of corporate innovativeness, yet the indicator that is most easily met by academics trained to realize the fruits of their labour in a refereed piece of analytical writing (Fuller, 2002a: Chapter 1.4.2). To be sure, if policymakers were serious about converting universities into 'engines of economic growth', they would simply provide incentives to have academics seconded to industry in aid of implementing the ideas behind the patent papers (Granstrand, 1999: Chapter 6). Interestingly, despite a greater tolerance for academics volunteering their services to industry as consultants, there is no general policy encouraging the tendency. The reason has probably less to do with the objections of academic purists than the policymakers' own exposure to risk. After all, bringing an innovation to market, like any other trial-and-error process, typically requires significant prior investment before any payoff is delivered. The formal secondment of academics to industry, while increasing the likelihood that an innovation will pay off, would at the same time draw attention to any failure that might result. In contrast, the perpetually promissory character of innovation for its own sake – as measured by the endless generation of patents – would seem to square the policy circle, while incidentally pacifying academics who typically find writing a new kind of text (a patent) more palatable than interacting with a new kind of person (an industrialist).

Thorstein Veblen (1904) would have recognized what is going on here. In his terms, the imperative to innovate characterizes the dominance of 'business' over 'industry'. Veblen was one of the last political economists who tried to uphold Adam Smith's normative ideals in a time that had already left them far behind. Before the so-called 'Industrial Revolution' (a neologism in Veblen's day), Smith held, people bound to the land by birth were restricted from applying themselves freely to satisfy the needs of their fellows. Writing over a hundred years after Smith, Veblen saw society suffering from the opposite problem of *hyper-mobility*, as in the idea that markets should be regularly 'creatively destroyed' by self-styled innovators seeking to replace producers who might be already adequately satisfying consumer needs (Fuller, 2002a: 51–2). Whereas in the 18th century, the landed aristocracy were the parasitic class inhibiting industry, in the 20th century the corporate market-ing division – the business class – turned out to be new parasites, or more pre-cisely cancers that metastasize industrial effort.

In short, the business class manufactured new wants in the course of claiming that the new products satisfy old wants (cf. Jacques, 1996: Chapter 7). In this way, adaptive preference formation became institutionalized in the economy without explicit government intervention – except to allow business to grow to unprecedented proportions. Thus, once everyone had a car, adver-tisers insisted that one's entire automotive experience would be compromised without the possession of an air-conditioned, four-wheel drive car. (Compare the marketing techniques nowadays for upgraded software packages.) These observations received their most influential elaboration from John Kenneth Galbraith (1967), whose concept of the 'new industrial state' epitomized advanced capitalist nations in the middle third of the 20th century, when mar-keting came to overtake manufacturing as the focus of corporate enterprise.

Whence comes this endless drive to innovation? One may be initially tempted to draw on contemporary evolutionary psychology, which updates much perennial philosophical speculation about 'human nature': to be human is to be capable of genuine novelty. Unfortunately, this criterion suf-fers from obvious anthropomorphism. Might not the detectability of 'genuine novelty' be related to the perceiver's ability to find meaningful differences? (Of course, a Chomskyan who regards the 'generative' capacity of language as unique to *homo sapiens* would see nothing problematic here, since a native listener's ability to make sense of a novel utterance is precisely the criterion used to establish genuine novelty.) If, instead, one were to apply to humans the criterion normally imposed on animals – that is, to check whether apparent novelties significantly alter behavioural patterns outside the immediate context of utterance – then many of our own innovations would appear as so many contextually explicable local deviations that leave the basic patterns undisturbed. Here one would need to resist the lazy rhetoric of 'building on the past', which assumes that every innovation – especially if published and stored – remains indefinitely part of the living memory of at least some humans. One wonders how this 'building' might occur (except by some subliminal or genetic means), given two tendencies: the diminishing half-life of the average article cited in the scientific litera-ture and the strengthening of the boundary between historical and contem-porary scholarship in each scientific discipline (Fuller, 2000a: Chapter 5). It is more likely that our sense of recurrent novelty is somehow tied to a sys-tematic forgetting, and hence modified reinvention, of the past. I shall have more to say about this Orwellian point below.

Moving from species-general to more historically specific explanations of the drive to innovate, while Joseph Schumpeter (1934) may well be right that the creative destruction of markets constitutes the lifeblood of capitalism, the tightness of fit between innovation and capitalism comes from the tendency of innovation to involve 'capitalization' – that is, the conversion of non-capital into capital. This was certainly the spirit of Werner Sombart's coinage of 'capitalism' in 1902, to capture how traditionally non-commercial aspects of social status come to be spontaneously generated in market transactions (Grundmann and Stehr, 2001). At the most general level, 'capitalism' in this sense carried into the human realm the translation of physical substances into mathematical functions that had characterized the Scientific Revolution (Cassirer, 1923). The relevant 'function' in this case is the law of supply and demand. This shift in ontological sensibility is also captured in the memorable definition of the logician Quine, 'To be is to be the value of a bound variable'. At the level of our psychic economy, this principle implies that objects are valuable solely in relation to the desires they satisfy – or, in the language of political economy, a particular good has no value other than the cost of its replacement in supplying a particular demand, where demand is presumed to be elastic (Smith, 1994: Chapters 8–10).

According to this logic, the innovator thinks about existing goods as placeholders for demands that may be met by several competing goods, especially new ones that meet the demands more efficiently. Goods are what John Dewey called 'instrumentalities' – that is, ends whose value rests on being means toward still other ends. Thus, Carl Menger, Eugen von Böhm-Bawerk, and the Austrian school of economics from which Schumpeter descended famously countered Marx's labour-based theory of value by arguing that labour, like all other forms of capital, constitutes a market for second-order goods, whose values are determined in a competitive field, which may include *inter alia* automated technology (März, 1991: Part Two). In this respect, factory owners are consumers of labour power only because that is the most efficient means to produce the goods they need to sell. But this is a contingent fact of history that may be overturned by innovation in the future, not a necessary fact about the composition of the goods or the social relations governing them. One can also shift the focus from the factory owner to the customer and apply a similar strategy. Thus, when American institutionalist economists like Veblen and Galbraith wrote derisively of 'business', they meant those who innovate by manufacturing demand. Specifically, market researchers determine the various demands served by a good currently on the market and then develop goods that can meet each of these demands more efficiently, thereby multiplying the level of demand and hence the potential for sales.

To be sure, innovation works somewhat differently in the Austrian and American cases, though both share the Schumpeterian awareness of innovation as creative destruction. In the Austrian case, the consumer comes to accept a new product as worth the cost of replacing the old product. Thus, what might be lost in the details of craftsmanship is more than made up in the product's timely completion and delivery to market: at least this would be one reason for preferring automated technology to human labour. In making this judgement, the consumer – in this case, a factory owner – is trading off against competing desires that are satisfied to varying degrees in the human and the machine. In the American case, by contrast, the consumer comes to regard an old product as simultaneously satisfying several desires, each of which would be better satisfied with new products. Thus, rather than forcing trade-offs where previously there were none, the consumer – in this case, regarded as someone not directly involved in production – is led by the power of advertising to regard a heretofore satisfactory product as suboptimal along several dimensions, each of which needs to be addressed separately.

In both the Austrian and American accounts of innovation, 'creative destruction' does not cancel itself out, as its oxymoronic name might suggest. Rather, it exacts an additional cost of its own. That cost was adumbrated in our discussion of Lasch in the previous section: *innovation is correlated with a devaluation of what things have been in favour of what they might become.* Thus, people, products, and research are not valued in themselves but as means to still greater ends. At first glance, this places innovation in defiance of the 'discounting principle' in welfare economics, which, for example, justifies taxation on the grounds that, without coercion, people tend to prefer the gratification of baser desires in the present to nobler desires in the future (Price, 1993). However, the welfare economists had not anticipated that people might discount the past *in order to* discount the future. After all, the discounting principle stipulates that the future needs to be regarded in a certain way to avoid being 'discounted'. Not only must the future be seen as consequences of earlier people, things, and events, but these consequences must also be seen as enjoying their own autonomy, and not simply reflecting whatever we would now wish them to be. Unfortunately, the innovative mentality makes forsaking the past attractive by discounting the future's autonomy from the present in just this sense. In short, the past may be set in stone but the innovator believes that the future may be made in her own image. Thus, the innovator reduces the future to a mode of experiencing the present and hence a potential source of immediate gratification, as exemplified by the much advertised joys of risk-taking, in which 'speculation' on a future prospect takes precedence over the actual consequences of having so speculated.

The innovative mentality's discounting of the future generates a mystique surrounding innovation, especially the alleged genius of entrepreneurship. This mystique is tied to the ease with which precursors are forgotten as imperfect versions of what it would take to satisfy the ends defined by the current generation. Indeed, the shortened half-life of current achievements behind the compression of collective memory may both motivate people to innovate and allow them to recognize achievements as innovative. In this respect, the innovating impulse appears as the positive side of adaptive preference formation.

There is also a reflexive dimension to this situation, as empirical social inquiry into innovation tends to presume that everyone – including the very inventors – are taken by surprise by its consequences. This undoubtedly reflects the anchoring of recent social studies of innovation in the context of *failures* in the diffusion of new technologies, which casts aspersions on the very idea of a master planner, while celebrating the improvisational constructions of agents 'on the ground' (Latour, 1996). In effect, treating the object of inquiry as an 'innovation' de-sociologizes it by presuming that it does *not* follow from socio-historically embedded knowledge. One wonders what licenses such researchers to suppose that the increasingly well-informed people who commission and produce new forms of, say, biotechnology lack any anticipatory sense of the consequences of actions that might compel them, from a legal standpoint, to bear some responsibility for those consequences – unless, of course, they constitute profits! Yet, such a presumptive state of blissful ignorance is implied by the 'counterintuitive' results that social researchers repeatedly uncover about the diffusion of innovations.

The curious socio-epistemic status of innovation may also help resolve a conundrum that Karl Popper (1957) famously raised about the prospect of planning scientific progress – namely, if scientific progress consists of genuinely new discoveries, then if these discoveries can be predicted, then they must be already known and hence not genuinely new. This paradoxical conclusion stands as long as we assume that the 'new discoveries' are indeed truly new and not simply modified reinventions of a half-forgotten past. I say '*half*-forgotten' because we need to explain, despite famous examples to the contrary, how allegedly genuine novelties so often manage to diffuse *so quickly*. Why are they not more often the source of more general cataclysms in thought and taste, if not regarded with indifference or incomprehension? Rather than investing entrepreneurship with preternatural powers of genius, it might make more sense to credit innovators with repackaging – by design or accident – a past with which consumers are already dimly (a.k.a. 'subliminally') familiar. All that is required is that, as a matter of fact, a society's collective memory is never as finalized as the sales figures on corporate spreadsheets or the logical outcomes of truth tables would suggest: What fails to sell may still affect consumer behaviour, and what fails to be valid may still affect scientific inquiry. In other words, there is always room for a 'return of the repressed', as long as the past has not been completely segmented from the present in a self-contained market called 'history' (Fuller, 2003a: Chapter 9).

In light of the preceding discussion, two complementary conclusions may be reached about the nature of innovation. First, what is normally called 'the past' is the repository of lost futures. Put less paradoxically, the achievements consigned to history are normally ones that, had they remained in living memory, would have taken us to a different present. Their counterfactual character is signified by labels like 'false', 'remaindered' and 'ignored'. However, as long as the boundary between the past and the present is porous, these lost futures may be reactivated as 'innovations'. The ultimate model for this conceptualization of innovation is Plato's *Meno*, in which all learning is portrayed as a form of reminiscence (Polanyi, 1957). But whereas Plato himself seems to have thought that education worked by tapping into a genetic or racial memory, it is possible to update his theory of 'anamnesis' in a less metaphysically forbidding way by supposing that innovation – as a society-wide learning process – occurs through non-standard contact with such external memory stores as libraries and databanks. Some innovators may even see themselves as agencies of justice, championing ideas that had been previously discarded because they were 'before their time'.

The second complementary conclusion is that a highly innovative society wastes its potential by making poor use of its past. A charge of this sort is most familiar as a characterization of natural selection, regarded from a strictly economic viewpoint. Perhaps the strongest Neo-Darwinian argument against the existence of a divine creator is the amount of genetic wastage at various stages in the life cycle. For this reason, the kind of 'selection' that nature metaphorically performs is regarded as 'blind' (Hardin, 1959). That the market is not also normally seen as completely sightless has to do with capitalism's historic coupling of the alleviation of human misery and the manufacture of surplus wants. While the latter may involve an unnecessary expenditure of human effort, the former has been necessary for promoting and maintaining our general sense of humanity. However, as Schumpeter (1942) perhaps first saw clearly, capitalism's blind eye can interfere with its sighted one. The intensified expectations and disappointments generated by the boom and bust phases in the business cycles of the modern period – he was especially thinking about the 1920s – were due to an uncritical belief in the value of innovation.

In that case, socialism may be understood as an attempt to rationalize this situation by ensuring that more of the past is made more available to more of society. The sheer impulse to innovate would thus not interfere with the effective diffusion of innovations. Admittedly, this level of planning would destroy the mystique surrounding entrepreneurship, reducing it to a kind of social experimentation. But very much like the other great economic sociologist, Max Weber, Schumpeter regarded such 'disenchantment' as a fair price to pay for a more stable and just social order. Socialism would extend the mandate of social science from the empirical to the normative realm: whereas positivistic social science had demystified theological ideas of Grace and Providence, socialism would purge the last vestige of theology in secular social thought – capitalism's invisible hand (Milbank, 1990). Of course, the second half of the 20th century has itself witnessed a demystification of the promise of socialism, which has landed us in a situation not so different from the one for which Schumpeter thought socialism would provide a solution. However, as befits an Orwellian turn in the historical cycle, the term 'Neo-Schumpeterian' today is normally invoked by science policy theorists who stress the creative rather than the destructive side of Schumpeter's definition of innovation in terms of the market's creative destruction.

Steps toward the Re-instatement of Sociology

Is there a way back to sociology from the emerging post-sociological order? I believe that our very sense of humanity depends on an affirmative answer to this question. However, notwithstanding the argument of Part I of this book, it would be a mistake to attribute the decline of the sociological imagination exclusively to successful external replacements from the humanities and the natural sciences (*à la* Wallerstein 1996) or, as I have been arguing in the interlude, the perverse redeployment of the sociological lexicon. In addition, the seeds of sociology's self-destruction were sown at the discipline's outset. This general nature of this problem is unavoidable in a discipline that aspires to universality, yet has no choice but to be formulated in particular times and places: it is the Achilles heel of any science. Nevertheless, the diagnosis of specific failures should prove instructive to the re-institutionalization of sociology. A useful frame of reference is the *Gemeinschaft–Gesellschaft* distinction on which Tönnies founded sociology as an academic discipline.

The basic mistake made by sociology's founders was to include all market relations – from medieval trade fairs to transnational business firms – in the category of *Gesellschaft*. In retrospect, it is easy to see how this was done: the corporate character of modern business was assimilated to that of the state and other traditional corporations. However, business is a late arrival to the legal form of the corporation. Until the 19th century, most business activity could be understood within the two recognized categories in Roman Law prior to the 12th century innovation of the *universitas*: on the one hand, the firm was an extension of the household, with both ownership and control transmitted along hereditary lines (namely *via gens*). On the other, trade that cut across hereditary lines was conducted on perhaps a regular but temporary basis in centrally located market towns or overseas joint-stock ventures, in which the traders were presumed to act on behalf of their own or other households, to which they would return once the goods have cleared the market or the venture has achieved its promised goals (namely *via socius*). It was only when the state, the dominant form of *universitas* in the modern era, saw its own nation-building ambitions enhanced by scaled-up business enterprise that firms received the legal protection that enabled them to expand their markets overseas with relative impunity and distribute their ownership and control in ways that subverted hereditary succession. Academic sociology's founders flourished as this transformation was taking place, and they understandably projected it backward as the hidden potential of market relations. Thus, the market is made to look like the harbinger of all distinctly modern social relations.

The conceptual cost of this instance of syncretism is considerable. Sociologists have been blindsided by evolutionary psychologists who invoke concepts like 'kin selection', 'reciprocal altruism', and 'indirect reciprocity' to capture what they allege to be the biological bases of all social behaviour (Barkow et al., 1992). This invariably involves a reduction of sociology to a genetically programmed version of rational choice economics. To be sure, there have been several worthy attempts to undermine this strategy (Archer and Tritter, 2000; Rose and Rose, 2000). Nevertheless, sociology is itself largely to blame for keeping the door open to sophisticated forms of biological reductionism by blurring the pre-modern and modern forms of market relations. Even within economics, a pre-modern sensibility of the market remains in the Austrian school (though, to his credit, not Schumpeter). Thus, one finds evolutionary psychologists today postulating 'modules' for 'social accounting' in the brain that suspiciously look like the competence that Friedrich von Hayek (1948) attributed to traders in the sort of market that Adam Smith could still envisage in the late 18th century. Not surprisingly, a nebulous pseudo-*gemeinschaftlich* concept like 'trust' is then made to bear the burden of providing the ontological glue that links interpersonal transactions at the trade fair to the impersonal dealings that are most emblematic of modern social life. From this standpoint, the prospect that people's default behavioural tendencies might be constructively channelled through normative strictures – changes in the selection environment, if you will – is ridiculed as the *Standard Social Science Model* (or *SSSM*), from which even sociologists have begun to distance themselves.

But suppose, in contrast, we took seriously that the socially significant behaviours we call 'innovations' did not emerge spontaneously from the most biologically salient forms of social life but have required planned collective effort aimed at producing benefits for humanity that may not be fully realized by those engaged in them. Here we would have a sociological sensibility that breaks decisively with biology, which I believe was what sociology's founders intended. In that case, the value of innovation would lie primarily in the destructive side of Schumpeter's creative destruction, that is, the lifting of barriers on human potential. The state would then have an obligation to seed innovation – in the form of publicly financed education – as an extension of its trans-generational stewardship over part of that potential. That only a relative few so supported turn out to be genuine innovators, yet others manage to benefit quickly through the diffusion process, would no longer be regarded as a paradox but rather evidence for the relative equality of humans, rendering issues of priority a matter of luck, and hence grounds for regarding society in a very modern *gesellschaftlich* fashion as a whole much greater than the sum of its parts (Fuller, 2003b).

PART TWO

THE BIOLOGICAL CHALLENGE TO SOCIAL SCIENCE

SEVEN

The Hidden Biological Past
of Classical Social Theory

Professional sociologists typically regard the field called 'social theory' as made for export. It is a convenient means for non-sociologists to appreciate the distinctiveness of social scientific inquiry. Social theory may not exactly capture the cutting edge of empirical research, but at least it draws from roughly the same ancestry. Thus, the sociologists most capable of puncturing the pretensions of current social theory by revealing its empirical limitations and vagaries prefer to leave it in a state of benign neglect, as one might a reprobate uncle who only seems to come into his own at weddings and funerals. However, such neglect has now produced at least one generation of 'social theorists' who acquired off the shelf their history from Foucault, their economics from Marx, and their psychology from Freud. To those with the intestinal fortitude to suspend belief in these 'masters', the narrowness of the horizons so defined is astonishing – especially when mobilized in the name of 'progressive' politics. At the same time, it is only to be expected in a discipline whose mainstream practitioners claim to address contemporary societies, while continuing to define its domain in terms laid down by three late 19th century thinkers: Karl Marx, Émile Durkheim and Max Weber.

Thus, a pair of questions arises. Is social theory intimately tied to the letter of the classics, as much of the scholastic turn in the field would suggest? Or, is there some way of reactivating in contemporary terms the spirit that made the classical sociologists appear so seminal? In either case, we social scientists need to conjure up our own version of the 17th–18th century debate between the 'Ancients' and the 'Moderns', which turned on whether modern authors could improve on the ancient classics (Fuller, 1997: 93–4). This debate was updated by Matthew Arnold in the 19th century as what we now call the 'two cultures' problem between the 'Arts' and the 'Sciences' (Lepenies, 1988). On these matters, I side squarely with the Moderns and the Scientists (Fuller, 1998a,b). In particular, we should revisit the aspects of biological research from which the classical sociological theorists originally drew intellectual sustenance.

The histories of sociology and biology have been always intertwined. However, you would never guess this from how sociologists – and social scientists more generally – write their histories, either for legitimatory or even more allegedly scholarly purposes. The point is made whenever sociologists do a hasty shuffle through the contributions of Comte and Spencer, followed by pharisaic claims about the 'anti-racism' of Max Weber and other founders of the German Sociological Association. (They were anti-racist for the same reason they were anti-feminist and anti-Marxist: they wanted to protect their discipline from political check; cf. Proctor, 1991: Chapter 8.) Yet, the traffic between biology and sociology was remarkably fluid – at least until the disasters associated with Nazi and Soviet eugenics. To be sure, both sides trafficked in reified social relations (Fuller, 1993: 123–4). Still the clearest case of this cross-disciplinary traffic is Darwin's idea of natural selection, whose basis in Thomas Malthus' 1798 *Essay on Population* was well known and contributed to the largely positive public reception of *Origin of the Species* in pre-socialist Liberal Britain (Young, 1985). Thus, an early polemic against welfare policies for the poor was naturalized as the 'struggle for survival' in life more generally. All told, the most extreme social policy initiatives of the past 100 years have had strong biological backing by appealing to either the fundamental plasticity or immutability of some or all of *Homo sapiens*.

The terms 'sociology' and 'biology' were coined in the early 19th century by two French thinkers – Comte and Lamarck – who from today's standpoint mixed findings and metaphors on both sides of the disciplinary divide. Throughout the 19th and early 20th centuries, both disciplines attached significant explanatory roles to evolution, instincts, inheritance, adaptation, and functional differentiation. In these contexts, a biologically inflected sociology was thought to have substantial policy import, ranging from the control of individual behaviour to the governance of entire nations. Sometimes it licensed substantial intervention into the management of the most intimate relations; at other times it provided arguments for the futility of any such intervention. Biological research was at first supported for reasons that eventually became sociology's own, including an interest in comprehending and often containing life's diversity (hence the establishment of zoos and museums), improving the quality of life at home (hence the applications to medicine), and approximating the standards of the physical sciences (hence the development of statistical methods and mathematical modelling). The best history of these developments is Merz (1904), because it was written four decades *after* the publication of *Origin of the Species* yet four decades *before* all of biology was subsumed by the Neo-Darwinian synthesis.

With his usual uncanny candour, Bruno Latour (2000) has suggested that, once we forsake theoretical sloganeering for the hard graft of empirical research, what the anthropologist Paul Rabinow (1997) calls 'biosociality' and the entomologist E.O. Wilson (1975) calls 'sociobiology' may be separated by no more than the niceties of political correctness. Both blur the difference between biology and sociology that recalls the period just *before* the two fields of knowledge were distinguished in French. Nevertheless, political correctness counts for a lot in disciplinary boundary maintenance. As Runciman (1998) has observed, the otherwise encyclopaedic Anthony Giddens is conspicuously silent on the biological character of social life in his popular introductory textbook (Giddens, 1991) and downright hostile to it in his more strictly theoretical works, where it is relegated to the 'pre-given' vis-à-vis the 'new rules for the sociological method' (Giddens, 1976: 160). Yet, the elision of biological and sociological concerns can be found in the classics, that is to say, Marx, Durkheim, Weber, Simmel and Parsons. I shall now review these instances, including a detour through that proto-postmodernist, Edward Westermarck.

Marx and especially Engels followed debates in embryology, which threw up some suggestive concepts for their dialectical materialist account of history. These included the idea that organisms develop according to a plan, each stage of which is prepared by earlier stages and elicited by specific environmental conditions – the doctrine of *epigenesis*. The interest that Marx and Engels increasingly showed in biological evolution tracked embryologists' interest in demonstrating that individual development imitates species development or, as Ernst Haeckel famously put it, 'ontogeny recapitulates phylogeny' (Gould, 1977). This original embryological interest haunted Marxism throughout the 20th century as the 'socialism in one country' thesis, according to which Marx and Engels were read as claiming that the global march toward socialism was mirrored in the developmental sequence undergone by each country, with the UK having set the pace. (Influential capitalist versions of this approach include Rostow (1960) and arguably even Fukuyama (1992).) This microcosmic Marxism justified

Lenin's and Stalin's accelerated industrialization of the previously feudal Russian economy. It presented the prospect that even if capitalism retained its overall grip on the globe, there could still be autonomous socialist republics, whose numbers may grow over the years.

However, as Mendelian genetics came to be fully integrated into evolutionary theory in the 20th century, especially in the work of Conrad Waddington and E.O. Wilson, epigenesis lost its specifically stage-like character and was set against a broader ecological canvas that tolerated considerable variation in terms of what the environment might elicit (Dickens, 2000: Chapter 6). The developmental analogy for nation-based socialism had thus been undermined. It would seem that the followers of Leon Trotsky and their academically domesticated comrades like Immanuel Wallerstein and Andre Gunder Frank in world-systems theory, who envisage the conflict between capitalism and socialism exclusively in global terms, have had a more Darwinian sense of evolution than either Marx and Engels or even Lenin and Stalin. The last outpost of classical epigenesis, courtesy of Jean Piaget, is probably developmental psychology (Kitchener, 1986). As we turn to the more 'bourgeois' sociologies of Durkheim and Weber, this point acquires renewed significance. After all, if we do not expect all humans – let alone all human societies – to undergo the same mode of development, how do we tell the human from the non-human, the social from the asocial, let alone the progressive from the reactionary?

In terms of the history of biology, Durkheim and Weber came of age in the first generation to experience the impact of Darwin's *Origin of the Species*. Although the French were much more resistant than the Germans to Darwin's charms, both were caught in the intellectual transition between an essentialist conception of species, membership in which is established by an organism's inherent properties, and the more 'constructivist' Darwinian conception, whereby species membership is produced and reproduced through (notably but not exclusively sexual) transactions among organisms in an environment. Semantically the transition is felt in the shift in taxonomic interest in the phrase *human nature* from the former to the latter term. Thus, nowadays it is less significant that we stand out from nature than fit into it.

Of Durkheim and Weber, the former was the less Darwinian. He was famously influenced by Claude Bernard's definition of the organism as a self-sustaining 'internal milieu' in the face of external environmental resistance. Thus, Bernard placed experimental medicine on a scientific footing, a strategy Durkheim extended to capture how societies establish a strong systemic sense of inside/outside, normal/deviant, and so on distinctions that sociology may then explain and justify (Hirst, 1975). In effect, Bernard provided a positivistic elaboration of Aristotle's original definition of the organism as an entity that perseveres with its goals in the face of adversity. Like Aristotle, he presupposed a world infused with values, whereby, say, microbes and other potential challenges to an organism's health are considered in exclusively negative terms as 'disease', not entities in their own right. Death is the ultimate defeat. To be sure, this has become the default self-understanding of medical scientists and practitioners. But seen from the standpoint of modern evolutionary theory, it prejudges the question of who or what deserves to live, a question that will increasingly haunt us in the later pages of this book. Of course, this was not a problem for Bernard or Durkheim – not to mention the positivists or their Christian ancestors – all of whom privileged the maximization of human welfare. *They all interpreted 'human nature' as what allows us to remake nature to human benefit.* Durkheim's contribution to this tradition was to highlight the role of collectivization – that is, 'Society' with a capital 'S'.

As for Weber, he airbrushed the residual biologism lurking in Wilhelm Dilthey's 'sympathetic understanding' when advancing his own methodology of *Verstehen*. Like Dilthey, Weber assumed the species unity of *Homo sapiens* ensured that people would respond in similar ways to similar situations. If people in other times and places appear to behave strangely, that simply means we have yet to fathom the relevant features of their world that establish a proper connection to us. This is a job for the comparative historian, whose task was subsequently distilled and enshrined in analytic philosophy – with the historian replaced by an anthropologist – as the 'principle of charity', a phrase coined by the US auditor at the logical positivists' Vienna Circle, Willard Quine (Fuller, 1988: Chapters 5–6). As it turns out, the resident psychologist in the positivists' circle, Egon Brunswik, soon thereafter fled the Nazis for the USA, where alongside former Viennese colleague Paul Lazarsfeld spearheaded the golden age of quantitative social science methodology (Hammond and Stewart, 2001).

I mention Brunswik because he scientifically upgraded an idea that recurs throughout the German biological tradition from Goethe's and Schelling's *Naturphilosophie* to the *Lebensphilosophie* of Nietzsche and Dilthey: namely, that each animal species has a distinct 'sign-world' (*Merkwelt*) that characterizes the sensory interface through which it encounters the environment (Schnaedelbach, 1984: Chapter 5). When Brunswik was a student, this view was associated with the largely qualitative 'theoretical biology' of Jakob von Uexküll. Brunswik took it in the direction of statistical representation and experimental design, an indirect descendant has been the 'ecological psychology' of James J. Gibson, whose American followers have tried to capture, often by computer simulation, the geometry of the visual horizons of various species that (very) arguably operationalizes animal subjectivity. Back in the German countries, Uexküll's ideas continued to be developed under the Nazis as a qualitative science with strong ties to ecology and evolutionary theory called 'ethology' by Konrad Lorenz (Richards, 1987: 528–36). Today these ideas find a home in an evolutionary anthropology of the 'built environment' focused on human 'niche differentiation' (Rapoport, 1994).

Weber, Dilthey and the other early German social scientists were keen to synthesize the best of idealist philosophy and the ascendant science of evolutionary biology, as insurance against the unaffordable epistemological cost of scepticism – indeed solipsism – in the form of what philosophers call the 'problem of other minds', which places the burden of proof on those who believe that we can make sense of those with whom we do not have direct contact. (A selection of recent pieces still alive to this concern is Koegler and Stueber, 2000.) Nevertheless, the 20th century increasingly questioned the species unity of *Homo sapiens* underlying *Verstehen*, as it has become possible to discriminate human life at both a genetic and an environmental level. Two rather opposite conclusions may be drawn from this situation, both of which cause problems for the idea that the social sciences are closed under *Homo sapiens*. On the one hand, it may mean that any individual's capacity to understand another is more limited than was thought a century ago because people are now known to differ more substantially. On the other hand, it may equally mean that making sense of humans is, in principle, no different from making sense of any other sentient creature. In current political terms, the former conjures up the neo-liberal spectre that we can only understand those with whom we have contact or otherwise provide us with a tangible benefit, and the latter the ecological spectre that the social sciences can now be absorbed into an ecumenical natural science of 'sociobiology' – or 'biosociology'.

One of the pioneer questioners of our species unity deserves special mention: Edward Westermarck, the Swedish Finn who was the first anthropologist among the original sociologists at the LSE. The title of one of his last books, *Ethical Relativity* (1932), enjoys the dubious honour of having planted the stereotype of the social scientist as 'relativist' that remains a mental obstacle to many philosophers and enables latter-day sociobiologists to score untold points with the 'Standard Social Science Model'. In terms of actual research, Westermarck is generally known for two things that have been normally kept apart but are increasingly brought together. The first is his theoretical arguments for moral relativism, which spurred greater open-mindedness toward the customs of non-Western cultures, as well as anticipated logical positivist analyses of ethics as the expression of emotion toward people and objects. Secondly, he contributed empirical arguments against the uniqueness of the incest taboo to human beings, which are now cited as evidence for the continuity of social norms with the hidden logic of evolutionary fitness. Indeed, Westermarck is one of the very few classical social scientists cited appreciatively in the major recent attempt to synthesize all knowledge under sociobiology (Wilson, 1998: 189–96).

At first glance, Westermarck's two contributions seem to pull in opposite directions: the former is particularistic, the latter universalistic. However, this is to mistake the import of the Neo-Darwinian synthesis, whereby experimental genetics and natural history were finally integrated under one theoretical rubric. Starting with Theodosius Dobzhansky, *Genetics and the Origin of Species* (1937), evolution – or more precisely, natural selection – has *not* been regarded as a force like Newton's gravitational constant, which operates uniformly across physical environments. Rather, it has been seen as an emergent product of specific populations in specific ecologies. Thus, natural selection is now treated more as a single global process than a universally applicable principle. An anti-Christian in the style of David Hume (about whom more in Chapter 9), Westermarck understood this point intuitively before it became part of biology's official dogma. He was determined to remove the last vestige of God's 'top down' governance by revealing the self-sufficiency of its 'bottom up' organization. Westermarck was notoriously scathing about Christianity's claim to the civilizing mission of humanity, interpreting the very search for an 'essence of humanity' tied to its normative strictures as an ideological smokescreen for centuries of cross-cultural abuse.

The dynamic element of Newtonian mechanics had relied on the presence of a universal force that attracts all moving bodies, each otherwise subject to its own inertial impulse. A natural way of imagining such dynamics was as the Holy Spirit drawing all things out of their brute local natures into some cosmic harmony. Kant also envisaged his own secular variant on Christianity's Golden Rule, the categorical imperative, as modelled on this image, only now applied to the microcosm of the human condition. Similarly, though by different means, Durkheim conceptualized the relationship between collective and individual consciousness. However, evolution by natural selection lessened the intuitive hold of such a uniform force acting on a group to constitute them as a normative social order. As I suggested above, this had its most direct impact on social science through

Trotsky's interpretation of Marxism, whereby the completion of Communism as a global process may require the pursuit of disparate paths rather than a series of fixed and repeatable stages.

It is easy to forget that Westermarck and the first generation of normative relativists denied universalism not merely because they wanted to uphold local knowledge from the onslaught of hegemonic Westerners. Relativism was more fundamentally motivated by the desire to erase any ontological distinction between humans and animals, the final stage in the demystification of humanity's theologically inspired species pretensions. This motivation became more salient as the 20th century wore on, especially as the overwhelming genetic overlap among animal species reinforced the purely conventional nature of species distinctions themselves. In his day, Westermarck had recourse to what George Santayana then called 'animal faith', a kind of cross-species commonsense that made the avoidance of incest quite reasonable 'even' for ordinary animals. For him 'universalism' was no more than a scientifically neutral way of making reference to Christianity – that ultimate bastion of what I call in Chapter 11 the 'anthropic vision' – which Darwinism had conquered by relativizing the cosmos to the earth. Today's science and technology studies gurus, Bruno Latour and Donna Haraway, should thus recognize their indebtedness to Westermarck as the missing link required to render Darwinism postmodern *avant la lettre*.

In the history of social science, the status of the incest taboo turned out to be the litmus test of Westermarck's species indifferent sense of relativism (Degler, 1991: Chapter 10). Those who argued for the autonomy of the social fixated on the incest taboo as the primal moment when human beings took systematic efforts to resist and transcend their animal nature, seen in largely negative terms, as a 'genetic burden'. The wide range of theorists who held this position – including Edward Tylor, Émile Durkheim, and Sigmund Freud – averred to a secular version of Christianity as the self-conscious expression of humanity's uniquely 'civilized' status, which in turn demanded active maintenance, since it was under constant threat of recidivism. In contrast, Westermarck explained incest avoidance in terms of the de-sexualization of domestic life brought on by prolonged physical proximity, a phenomenon he observed across a wide range of primate species without any special need for sanctions – a variation on the theme of 'familiarity breeds contempt', to which we shall return in Chapter 10.

Finally, much has been made of the striking contrast in styles that Simmel and Parsons brought to sociological theorizing (Hall, 1999). Simmel never wrote a systematic treatise, which was all that Parsons ever seemed to write. Simmel proceeded by juxtaposing examples of a social form that had little more in common than his word that they exemplify the form in question. In contrast, Parsons comfortably cited rather different social practices as instantiating the same social function in different societies, typically by redescribing the practices in a theoretical language that abstracted from their concrete differences. There is a standard explanation of this difference in style: Simmel, whose Jewish background excluded him from a university chair in Germany for most of his life, was forced to court a public audience, whereas the White Anglo-Saxon Protestant Parsons enjoyed the captive student audience that Harvard had to offer. The one audience valued novelty, the other ritual. Of course, one could go further into their respective psychologies and contrast Simmel's mercurial nature with Parsons' plodding disposition. However, the most instructive difference may lie in examining their implicit biologistic turns of thought, which turn on alternative conceptions of *morphology*.

'Morphology' was coined by Goethe in the early 19th century but at that time was most closely associated with Lamarck's Parisian nemesis, Georges Cuvier, now known mainly for his 'catastrophist' explanation for the great geological periods (namely each layer of fossils marked a great Biblical flood). Morphology was meant to be the general science of life, which aimed to uncover correlations between the physical 'structures' and 'functions' of organisms across species, perhaps – but not necessarily – eventuating in a theory of the evolution of organic forms (Merz, 1904: 200–75). Originally, this task was interpreted in terms of examining the anatomies and physiologies of whole organisms, but by mid-century the discipline's terms of reference had begun to shift to the cellular level. Today morphology is typically concerned with the micro-task comparing the structural and functional features of particular genes.

The Holy Grail of morphology has been a cross-species demonstration that certain biological functions can be performed only by organisms possessing certain physical structures. If not exactly proof that such organisms possess these structures by 'design', it might at least provide a basis for assessing the relative 'fitness' of organisms to their environments. There have been even some attempts to regard structure and function as, respectively, a 'perfective' (i.e. developed) and 'imperfective' (i.e. developing) standpoint toward the organism in question. (Ernst Haeckel was closely associated with this approach, with which I have some sympathy when applied to human history; cf. Merz, 1904: 214; Fuller, 2000b: 207). However, those who entered morphology by searching for similarities of structure, or *homologues*, across species have tended to be more sceptical about teleological interpretations of evolution than those who have sought similarities of function, or *analogues*. Thus, whereas Lamarck sought analogues in nature, the great anti-evolutionist Cuvier approached morphology through a search for homologues. The latter strategy has also characterized today's scepticial 'cladist' school of systematic zoology (Gee, 2000).

The difference between homology and analogy applies no less to social as well as biological evolution (Runciman, 1998: 28ff.). In that case, Simmel represents the homologue strategy, and Parsons the analogue. Simmel focused on how the size and shape of groups constrained the possibilities for social interaction, independently of the group's recognized social function or even the intentions of group members. These 'social forms', as Simmel tended to call them, had lives of their own, which together did not add up to the stable 'social system' that would be the hallmark of Parsonian sociology. On the contrary, social forms could have dysfunctional consequences if they changed their size and shape, even slightly, over time. To be sure, Parsons had already taken on board from Durkheim (and classical political economy) the role of population size and distribution on the division of labour in society as a whole. But Simmel's formal sociology implied that changes in the dimensions of social sub-systems, including the micro-level of face-to-face interaction (for example, a shift from a dyadic to a triadic relationship), could destabilize the entire social system. In short, Parsons realized that Simmel's focus on social homologues excluded the idea of a stable social system that leaned heavily on analogues. Indeed, Simmel's rising stock in the postmodern era is no doubt traceable to his lack of any clear sense of 'society' as such, while still retaining a sensibility about the social nature of things, an idea that first branded Simmel as incoherent in the first comprehensive English treatment of his work (Sorokin, 1928: 497–507).

The ultimate circle that Parsons had to square was how to render these biologically based considerations compatible with physics, the gold standard of scientific theorizing. A good trace to follow here is the shifts in the meaning of 'function' across the sciences (cf. Cassirer, 1923). For example, the biological functions most directly relevant to Parsons' structural-functionalist sociology are recurrent features of an integrated system, the organism. However, in classical mechanics, functions appear as mathematical equations that depict the resolution of countervailing forces in what physicists call a 'dynamic system' (Comte is blamed for using 'dynamic' to refer to the theory of social evolution in Popper, 1957: 112–16). In other words, the Newtonian image of a physical system is one of permanently contained conflict between moving bodies. This point would have been familiar to Parsons as the animating spirit of Vilfredo Pareto's cynical vision of circulating elites as a long-term stabilizing force in a free society, the preferred Harvard antidote to the creeping Marxism of the 1930s. Indeed, Pareto occupies in Parsons (1937) the place we would nowadays accord to Marx (cf. Fuller, 2000b: Chapter 3; Fuller, 2003a: Chapter 7, where Pareto's Harvard significance is traced to the Harvard biochemist L.J. Henderson, an early theorist of homeostasis who read Pareto's work as a sociological analogue of his own).

While the Paretian vision may underwrite the separation of powers and checks and balances that characterize the US Constitution, it was still a far cry from Durkheim's 'organic solidarity', whose welfarist implications were closer to Parsons' political heart in the New Deal (Fuller, 1998a). Matters only get more complicated once we add chemistry's sense of 'functional' as 'substitutable', which had historic affinities with political economy. If there are potentially many physical structures that can serve the same socially salient function, then why not try to synthesize structures that do so with the least effort to the system? Thus, Wilhelm Ostwald introduced 'energeticism' – the bane of Max Weber's existence – as a pretender to scientific sociology (Schluchter, 2000). To be sure, it bore fruit as Taylorist time–motion studies of the workplace and lurks behind much of today's research into human–computer interaction (Rabinbach, 1990). But while the late Herbert Simon (1977) may have included sociology among the 'sciences of the artificial', it is unlikely that Parsons' organicist sensibility would have found this route to a scientific sociology palatable. Nevertheless, the unholy alliance of biology and chemistry turned structural-functionalism into a mixed metaphor and a promise unfulfilled. I shall try to redeem this promise, 21st century style, in the Conclusion.

EIGHT

Making the Difference between Sociology and Biology Matter Today

If we take Aristotle's view of the human species as *zoon politikon* at face value, biology and sociology were born joined at the hip. We are the only animals with a *public* life, which means that our interactions produce things that extend significantly beyond what is, even in principle, within the power of any individual. In a word, they possess *meaning*. These things – the aspects and artefacts of the human condition that require elaborate social structures – help to constitute the environment inhabited by later humans. I stress the word 'public' because so much of the philosophically inspired discussion about the mark of the human for the past century has rested on humans possessing a distinctive *private* life, or *consciousness*. However, from the perspective pursued here, which stresses the common ancestry of biology and sociology, 'consciousness' is little more than a dress rehearsal for public display and the so-called science of psychology nothing but the application of a society's ideology to matters relating to the individual.

Unsurprisingly, Comte could not find an object for 'psychology' in his scheme of sciences other than a secularized version of the Christian soul, something that in a positivist polity would be treated mainly in terms of its indoctrination and subsequent ministrations – that is, pedagogy and psychiatry. Individuals are thus exemplars or deviants. Once the Third Republic began to comprehensively secularize France in 1870, Comte's vision came to be belatedly realized by the likes of Durkheim. This explains France's conspicuous absence from histories of experimental psychology. Its main psychologists have been associated with either education (for example,

Theodore Binet, of IQ fame) or medicine (for example, Jean-Martin Charcot, arguably Freud's biggest influence). Indeed, the most important French psychologist of the 20th century, Pierre Janet, is known primarily for his work on the 'dissociated' personality, which psychologists gloss as 'schizophrenia' but sociologists could equally gloss as the individual's failure to integrate a variety of social perspectives into a coherent basis for social action. The latter possibility has been pursued by a wide range of philosophically underrated social thinkers from George Herbert Mead and Lev Vygotsky to Rom Harré (1984).

The legacy of this anti-psychologism is that sociology's key concepts refer to properties that people possess by virtue of their position in a system of relations, rather than intrinsically as individuals. Thus, the expression 'working class bodies' refers primarily to how class relations are manifested on the individual human body, which is treated as a physical site where the social analyst can witness the logic of capital being played out (Skeggs, 1997: 100). The key implication here, pursued nowadays most thoroughly in empirically oriented feminist sociology, is that while anyone's comportment – what Pierre Bourdieu calls 'habitus' – offers a window into capitalist social relations, each person's body provides a different point of view according to his or her place in the system. To be sure, class relations may continue to be expressed in the abstract terms of political economy, but there remain quite specific physical expectations about how to comport oneself as, say, 'aristocratic', 'bourgeois' or 'proletarian' that can turn out to be stultifying, both to those aspiring to 'class mobility' and comfortable with their current class identity (Lawler, 2005).

The concern with the corporeal dimension of social life is no more than a quarter century old, largely a reflection of Foucault's assimilation into the sociological canon (Turner, 1984). However, Foucault, himself trained in philosophy and psychiatry, contributed much more to sociology than he ever drew from it. His misleadingly named concept of 'bio-power' was based on highly individualized and physicalistic models of governance that owed more to Thomas Hobbes and Ignatius Loyola than to Émile Durkheim, let alone any biologist. This is unsurprising, since from the standpoint of the history of science, the body has been just as alien to biology as to sociology. The two disciplines share a historic preoccupation with 'structure' and 'function', properties of systems that do not require physical specification. The concept of the body was imported into both disciplines from physics, where in mechanics it refers to matter on which form is externally imposed. (This imposition is called a 'force', which is what 'idea' means to a materialist. Ask Ludwig Büchner.) Thus, in 19th century German debates over where to draw the line between the sciences of 'nature' and 'spirit', biology was treated as a hard case. There appeared to be strong *prima facie* grounds – going back to Aristotle, of course – for thinking that animals possess an internally driven 'life force', what Henri Bergson later called *élan vital*, the primordial impulse out of which Bergson believed intentionality evolved in humans. Therefore, social theorists who take their marching orders from Paris should learn that the fixation on the body nowadays associated with Foucault belongs to the tradition of reductionism that vitalism was designed to *oppose*, not support.

In the social sciences, anthropology has been the discipline most explicitly dedicated to narrowing the traditional Western philosophical gap between physical reality and the meanings attached to it. (Unsurprisingly, Bourdieu's concept of habitus originated in his early Algerian fieldwork.) Anthropologists have tended to see meanings as *inscribed*, rather than *projected*, on the body. This subtle difference in emphasis carries important – though not entirely explored – implications for the ascription of personal responsibility. In particular, if meanings are granted the obdurate sense of reality implied by inscription, then individuals can be held responsible for things they do based on qualities they possess without having consciously participated in their creation. Biology came to accept this implication once its most physicalistic branch – genetics – moved to the centre of the discipline, and (as we shall see below) intellectual property lawyers have begun to pursue its applications in 'bioprospecting'. However, social scientists primarily concerned with humans as 'meaning-makers' are generally much less comfortable with this disjunction of accountability and consciousness, which wreaks havoc on concepts like agency and identity – at least as long as autonomy is taken to be constitutive of them.

In short, there remain good reasons for sociologists paying closer attention to biology. One of them is to appreciate that biology is *not* our scientific superior, at least in terms of approximating the ideal of a unified science promoted by physics-envying philosophers in the 20th century. Instead biology is rather like sociology, a set of overlapping fields that in some cases even contradict each other in their fundamental orientation to research and the world more generally. Moreover, this feature of the social structure of biology has long been an open secret among those positivist philosophers who have done the most to keep alive the physics-based model of inquiry (Rosenberg, 1994). When sociologists express fear and loathing of biology as an aspiring physics of life, they are probably relying too much on the popularizations of trained biologists like E.O. Wilson and Richard Dawkins, as well as the policy implications drawn from biological research by such social scientific works as

Herrnstein and Murray (1994). That sociologists still base their opinions of biology more on such science popularizations than an understanding of biology's institutionalization as a form of knowledge speaks volumes to the need to integrate the sociology of knowledge into the ordinary sociology curriculum.

For example, popularizers often misrepresent Darwinism as implying that well adapted organisms 'reproduce' – in the sense of mechanically copy – their genetic information in their offspring. Here social scientists should attend to the biological controversies surrounding the exact features of one's genetic inheritance that are 'selectively retained' (cf. Brandon and Burian, 1984; Fuller, 1993: Chapter 3). Otherwise, sociologists might fall for the charms of Blackmore (1998), where a psychologist shortchanges *both* the sociological and biological literatures by advancing an 'imitationist' account of idea propagation – nowadays dubbed 'epidemiological' or 'memetic' – that fails to advance much beyond run-of-the-mill 19th century accounts of social cohesion (Fuller, 2004).

As I have suggested, there is one important respect in which the social structure of biological knowledge resembles that of sociological knowledge. Sociologists have made methodologically robust claims about virtually every aspect of social life, yet these claims have failed to amount to a coherent disciplinary presence. This is largely because the theories and methods pre-supposed by those claims have varied so widely. Similarly, the so-called Neo-Darwinian synthesis, which has enabled experimental geneticists and natural historians to rally around a common theory of evolution only since the 1930s, has involved methods as diverse as in sociology, including research that is field-based, fossil-based, laboratory-based and, increasingly, computer-based (Dupré, 1993). It may turn out that in the 21st century the last method comes to unify the field – at least such is the current promise of 'systems biology'. Indeed, this virtualization may signal the 'end of science' more generally (Horgan, 1996). But that would be for reasons to do more with the mounting economic and political (namely the objections of animal rights activists and religious fundamentalists) costs of *in vivo* and *in vitro* research than any specifically epistemic role that the computer will have played.

As it stands, biologists have not come up with any universally accepted, theoretically interesting means of integrating their various ways of gathering, arranging, and interpreting data. Instead, the Neo-Darwinian synthesis has marked the point at which the different biological camps agree to trust each other as being on the same epistemic team, which then licenses them to take accredited members of each camp as competent witnesses to the phenomena they report. If Neo-Darwinism imposes a regime on contemporary biology, it is not one of Thomas Kuhn's (1970) totalitarian paradigms but a minimal state, or even an *entente cordiale*. Thus, the validity of the different methodologies is simply taken as given, even though no one had justified all of them to anyone's satisfaction (Ceccarelli, 2001: Chapters 2–3). The only area of disagreement that surfaces among the Neo-Darwinian signatories concerns whether specific proposals for integrating the different biological phenomena enable the various sub-fields to pursue interesting research as defined by their respective methodological orientations.

Here it is worth recalling that Kuhn did not include something called the 'Darwinian Revolution' amongst his exemplars of scientific revolutions. That such a revolution occurred was the invention of the philosopher Michael Ruse (1979), an early foe of US Creationists who wanted to reduce the pedagogical status of Darwinian evolution to a 'mere theory'. Although Kuhn never explained why he did not count Darwinism among his revolutions, one can only guess it was because biologists had acted much more expediently than the strictures of a paradigm would permit. Researchers under the spell of a Kuhnian paradigm do not simply aim at a common picture of reality but also agree to certain ways of gaining access to that picture. Sociologically speaking, this may involve a totalitarian attitude towards knowledge production ('you are not an X-ologist unless you work according to this method'); at the very least, it implies that the discipline has a clear division of labour ('you are an X-ologist only if you believe that the kind of research you do contributes to the paradigm in this specific way').

Biologists have circumvented these Kuhnian options by not requiring a discipline-wide standard of methodological validity: the peaceful coexistence of multiple methods has been accepted in exchange for allegiance to the Neo-Darwinian world-view that the propagation of life results from differences in reproductive advantage that the environment accords to genetically variable individuals. This has been accomplished by sticking to Darwin's original unification of historical and contemporary biological change under the methodological assumption of *uniformitarianism*: the view that the kinds of changes that have made the most difference in the past (namely based on field work) are ones that we can still see in operation today (namely based on lab work). Readers can judge for themselves whether sociology's failure to reach such a diplomatic solution to its own internal conflicts constitutes a mark for or against its epistemic standing. In any case, the point bears on whether sociologists should take biological knowledge claims at face value.

Perhaps little surprise, then, that biologists hailing from diverse fields have discouraged social scientists from engaging with their discipline. The population geneticist Richard Lewontin, the neuroscientist Steven Rose and the palaeontologist Stephen Jay Gould come to mind. A common thread running through their arguments is that evolutionary change occurs over timeframes that transcend virtually all the interesting contexts that call for sociological explanation. Specifically, genetic change occurs either over too large a temporal expanse to interest professional sociologists or at a level too far below the humanly perceptible to interest the social agents that sociologists usually study. (Of course, this conclusion can equally provide comfort to the biosocial thinkers dubbed 'karmic' in Part Three, who believe that sociologists have mistaken the scale and scope of their field of inquiry.) Moreover, when discouraging sociologists from appropriating the fruits of their fields, biologists like Lewontin, Rose, and Gould may be motivated less by disciplinary modesty than a sense of paternalism that borders on condescension (cf. Segerstrale, 2000: Part II).

There is certainly a curious asymmetry in how biologists and sociologists tend to use each other's work, when they do. For example, sociobiologists confidently strip social scientific research of its theoretical overlay in order to reveal phenomena that can then be slotted into evolutionary explanatory frameworks (for example, Wilson, 1998). Boldness of this sort is typically accompanied by a certain methodological crudeness, since it is not clear that the phenomena can survive such a radical translation of theoretical contexts. This is the sort of problem that immediately strikes the trained sociologist but frequently eludes lay commentators impressed with the pronouncements of sociobiologists. Yet, social scientists themselves are methodologically much less adventurous toward biological research, either accepting or rejecting it *as a whole* – Lewontin, Rose and Gould advising the latter. But can't social scientists exercise some critical judgement in distinguishing the hype from the substance in biology to produce a more nuanced evaluation?

At the moment, sociologists tend to engage with biology, when they do, through the popular science literature, which is conveyed in an anthropomorphic rhetoric that often subtly and unintentionally influences the conduct of science itself (Howe and Lyne, 1992). Recall the succession of dominant images of humanity's biological core over the last quarter century. At the height of the Cold War, Konrad Lorenz's (1977) 'aggression instinct' defined human nature. Back then 'mutually assured destruction' was a genetically inscribed version of Freud's 'death wish'. However, the neo-liberal aftermath of the Cold War favoured that micro-entrepreneur, the 'selfish gene' popularized by Richard Dawkins (1976), which now may be yielding to the more communitarian and kinship based conception of Paul Rabinow's 'biosocial' primates. Getting a grip on this situation requires going beyond an uncritical acceptance of popular science and their pale reproductions increasingly found in sociology journals. But it does not mean that sociologists need to obtain degrees in biology. An elementary understanding of the sociology of knowledge should suffice to instil the requisite critical awareness.

Symptomatic of the problem is Sean Watson's (1998) attempt to provide a 'neurobiological' basis for the views of Gilles Deleuze, the late French philosopher of 'difference', to whom Foucault famously declared the 20th century belonged but who has only come into vogue in the anglophone world in the last ten years. (An early thorough assessment of Deleuze – that is, before the onslaught of his English fans – may be found in Descombes 1980.) Watson is singularly strident about sociology's current irrelevance to issues concerning our corporeal nature. His proposed cure is an intellectually lethal cocktail that valorizes biology at the expense of sociology without actually showing how any particular biological findings undermine, or somehow compel a reorientation of, sociological research. Instead of a constructive engagement, we are presented with yet another, albeit now postmodern, instance of sociology's prostration to biology.

Watson argues that if sociologists are to properly understand affective phenomena, they must incorporate recent research in neuroscience and some areas of cognitive science. This research models the mind as the pattern of neural connections distributed across the entire body – not just the brain – of an individual, which carry the traces of the person's unique experiential history. The model is to be regarded as the material infrastructure of various affective phenomena – especially one's sense of the 'idiosyncratic' and the 'uncanny' – which Henri Bergson and Theodor Adorno used to ground personal identity formation in their insightful but impressionistic way. Deleuze and his long-time collaborator, the psychiatrist Felix Guattari, bear on this proposal because the network of metaphors and conceptual associations in which they theorized came close to articulating the infrastructural account that Watson prefers. If it sounds as if Watson advocates physicalistic reductionism, then that is because he almost does. The content and perhaps some elements of the underlying ontology of the theories has changed, but otherwise the pecking order of the explanatory hierarchy remains unchallenged. Natural science theory provides the *explanans*, social science phenomena the *explananda*. While Watson does not present his case in quite these slavish terms, he is much keener to attack opponents than supporters of reductionism.

For example, like a good reductionist, Watson targets what cognitive scientists call the 'functionalist' theory of the mind, according to which the same thought process can be materially realized in a variety of ways. This variety, in turn, depends on the environment in which an agent operates and the media through which it conveys thought (for example our central nervous system versus a computer's central processing unit). Functionalism informs the efforts of artificial intelligence researchers who design computer programs to think human-like thoughts. It licenses their belief that questions concerning *how* a thought is embodied are to be kept separate from *which* thought is embodied. While there is some justice in thinking that functionalism is the scientifically respectable face of contemporary Cartesianism, it also provides the clearest argument for an autonomous science of psychology (Fodor, 1981).

This last point should interest sociologists, since an analogous argument – again travelling under the name of 'functionalism' – has been made for the autonomy of our own field by followers of Durkheim and Parsons (Fuller, 1993: Chapter 3). Thus, the same social function can be performed by a variety of institutions and practices, the exact one of which is determined by the history of the society in question. In this disciplinary context, functionalism enables cross-societal comparisons and generalizations that underwrite sociology as an empirical science. The renunciation of functionalism in psychology and sociology has also had analogous consequences – namely, a deflation of, respectively, mental and social ontologies. This deflation, in turn, eases the absorption of mind and society into the Neo-Darwinian sciences of life and the physical environment, especially sociobiology. So, while functionalism may be ultimately a flawed position, it should be rejected in full awareness of the intellectual consequences.

Watson objects to functionalism in psychology because (allegedly) one cannot think like a human unless one has the body of a human (Watson, 1998: 37–8). Thus, Watson wants sociologists to defend our biological integrity against would-be eugenicists and brainwashers by becoming shareholders in the intellectual stock of neurobiology in order to participate authoritatively in its development and application (24–5). Hopefully this means going beyond Watson's own practice of importing metaphors from neurobiology. In particular, what does it mean to have 'the body of a human', especially if each of our bodies is literally, namely at the level of neurobiological composition, unique? Here Watson follows Deleuze in trying to update the classical idea of human beings as biologically and sociologically closed under the concept of *species*, even though the integrity of this concept has been now challenged by *both* biology and sociology. On the one hand, the idea that a 'species' might refer to a natural kind or something essentially shared by a class of individuals is undermined by the fact that humans share 95+% of their genes with other mammals. On the other hand, an increasingly popular movement within the social sciences called 'cyborg anthropology' (after Haraway, 1990) has argued for the technologically mediated nature of the distinction between human and non-human bodies.

Deleuze's resurrection of the human body draws on the work of Gilbert Simondon, who was Professor of Psychology at the Sorbonne in the 1960s when he wrote the landmark *Difference and Repetition* (Deleuze, 1994). Simondon was fascinated by the metaphysics implied by the doctrine of 'epigenesis' in modern biology, whereby the environment is said to elicit and perhaps even shape an organism's development. Of course, the possible trajectories of this development are limited. Yet, even within those limits, two organisms that are 'virtually' identical – that is, begin with the same material capacities – may develop in quite opposing ways, based on the cumulative conditioning of their respective environments. Thus, one may preserve the idea that the organism possesses an essence corresponding to its shared material origins without thereby committing to a deterministic view of its individual development. Legal theorists are beginning to associate this metaphysics with the practice of 'profiling', whereby individuals (usually actual or potential criminals) are cast as 'correlatable data subjects' (Hildebrandt, 2004). The wider the range of data that can be collected about an individual, the easier it becomes to identify his or her propensities to commit certain acts in the future. However, this is *not* because more comes to be known about the individual *per se* but because the individual's acts participate with those of others in the construction of socially relevant statistical categories. In that respect, profiling may grant renewed scientific legitimacy to the legally discredited idea of 'guilt by association'. In other words, you might be deemed guilty (namely susceptible to criminality) simply because your behaviour is statistically associated with the behaviour of others whose pasts may nevertheless be significantly different from yours.

What is most striking about the importation of Deleuze – and more generally French post-structuralist thought – into sociology is its normatively suspended metaphysical fascination. Deleuze (following in the footsteps of Leibniz and Tarde) certainly challenges the classical opposition of the individual's uniqueness and society's commonality that is indeed captured by the rise of statistical profiling, which co-produces the unique and the common from the collection and combination of many acts from many sources. However, instead of worrying that such co-production might undermine the idea of autonomy – the source of freedom of thought and action that presupposes the capacity of individuals to resist social norms – Deleuzians seem more taken by their rediscovery of a principle long known to capitalist economists, namely, the tendency of revealed preferences to 'self-organize' so as to result in stable orders that do not require external coercion for their maintenance. Whether some such orders might be preferred to others seems to lie beyond the scope of their considerations.

Behind my concerns about the use of Deleuze is the failure to attend to matters of method. Deleuze was not Pierre Bourdieu, a social theorist whose conclusions are reasonably read as distillations of independent empirical research on specific human subjects. Rather, his insights are the product of imaginative interpretations of earlier philosophers and the current popular science literature. Given that the theoretical tastes of the sociologists attracted to Deleuze veer in the same direction, it is easy to adapt Wittgenstein's quip, that to invoke Deleuze's authority carries no more evidential weight than buying two copies of the same newspaper to check whether a story is true. Of course, one could read 'against the grain' of Deleuze, a self-proclaimed 'Neo-Bergsonian', by making more of the relationship between the intellectual development of Henri Bergson and that of his classmate at the École Normale Superieure, Émile Durkheim. For example, Bergson and Durkheim stood in quite different relationships to the emerging discipline of biology. Bergson wrote as a philosopher who tried to control the interpretive spin given to aspects of human experience closely associated with biological evolution, whereas Durkheim wrote as a sociologist eager to avoid his fledgling field's absorption into a variety of biological and psychological explanatory frameworks. Nevertheless, both drew on similar vitalist metaphysical resources, including an array of metaphors and arguments that continue to be invoked in contemporary neurobiology. Indeed, were we to go back the century that now divides us from Bergson and Durkheim – to when biology and sociology had yet to be sharply differentiated – models could be easily found for expressing the biosocial character of humanity that do not presume a trade off between biological and sociological perspectives.

More generally, history provides a valuable resource for constructing 'hybrid' and 'genre-blurring' discourses. Before a knowledge domain is divided into disciplines, the scientific imagination exhibits many of the desirable features associated with postdisciplinary forms of inquiry that aim to remove the boundaries separating fields of knowledge (Fuller, 1999). Nowadays it is common to epitomize the conflicts between biology and sociology as 'nature' versus 'nurture', but in the period from 1750 to 1900 there was no generally accepted account of genetics to underwrite a strictly biological concept of human nature. Consequently, more often than not 'nature' referred to the full range of possible psychosocial realizations of the human condition. Instead, 'human nature' referred to a *virtual* entity in the ontology of the social world that need not correspond to a specific physical substratum. Thus, such purveyors of Enlightenment in 18th century France and Scotland as Voltaire and Hume would be just as likely to turn to anthropomorphic accounts of animal life – latter-day versions of Aesop's fables – as to the actual history of *Homo sapiens* to illustrate so-called 'human nature'. Were sociobiology not so singularly beholden to genetics, it would be considered a natural heir to this tradition. Instead the mantle has fallen to science and technology studies, whose leading gurus, Bruno Latour and Donna Haraway, promiscuously mix fable, fiction (especially science fiction), speculation and facts about various animal species.

But beyond any substantive connections between the histories of biology and sociology, a 'shadow biologism' has also run through the history of social thought. What used to be called 'methodological holism' in the philosophy of the social sciences captures much of this tendency, reflecting its roots in 19th century 'organicist' philosophies that regarded societies as subject to the same developmental patterns as individual organisms (Mandelbaum, 1987). A keystone text was Tönnies' *Gemeinschaft und Gesellschaft* (1887), which linked Hobbes' original discussions of the 'body politic' to the social organicism of post-Hegelian thought. Common to this tradition is that the individual acquires its identity as a part of a larger social whole, especially through citizenship in a nation-state. Depending on the depth of one's ontological commitment, this whole came to be divided by 20th century social theorists into 'functions' or 'roles', each of which to be filled by one or more individuals.

More generally, behind any belief in naturally occurring human kinds, there usually lurks a commitment to some branch of biology as the metatheory of social inquiry. That branch may be *genetics*, which explains social life as emergent on the interaction of individuals possessing fixed properties; or *ecology*, in which case individual identities are specified by the set of roles they play in a self-sustaining social system. Thus, in the differences between genetics and ecology, we find the basis for the choice in theoretical frameworks that sociologists have felt they had to make: in a previous generation between behaviourism and functionalism, and nowadays between rational choice theory and structuralism. All of these options presuppose that purposeful action requires a clearly bounded unit that operates in an environment that offers varying degrees of resistance.

However, modern biological research poses a special challenge to sociologists who would assimilate its findings: no ordinary social meaning is associated with the sorts of collectives that count as bounded units in both genetics and ecology. To their credit, both sociobiologists and ecologists have realized this problem and offered one logical response, namely, a radical revision of the terms in which social life is conducted and interpreted. For example, according to what Richard Dawkins has called the 'gene's eye-view of the world', contemporaneous individuals interrelate so as to enhance the likelihood that their genes will be propagated. Thus, relationships that sociologists regard as constitutive of society appear, from the gene's point of view, as merely instrumental to genetic reproduction, since, biologically speaking, an individual's sights are ultimately set not on his or her contemporaries, but rather on future generations that carry his or her genes. At the other end of the biological spectrum, 'ecosystems' typically refer to units that array humans and non-humans in ways that cut across existing social formations. A typical result is that creatures with a wide capacity for action, such as humans, are urged to exercise self-restraint, so as to ensure the survival of creatures whose capacities range much less widely. In practice, this may mean discouraging people from activities that consume considerable natural resources, even if those activities would be rated highly in a purely anthropocentric value system, such as consumer capitalism.

In sum, the general biological challenge to sociology amounts to a query about the scope of the 'we' that is presupposed by an assertion of 'I'. Is my primary reference group the humans to whom I am legally and culturally bound, or is it restricted to my descendants, or rather bounded by some combination of humans and non-humans who inhabit a common stretch of space-time? Interestingly, these three options have been shadowed by the cosmologies of the world-religions. The great monotheistic religions, starting with Judaism, anticipated the sociological sense of 'we' that is restricted to human ancestors and descendants (by virtue of their special relationship to God). In contrast, the Hindu doctrine of the transmigration of souls constitutes a spiritualized version of the gene's eye-view of the world, with the Buddhist path of enlightenment presaging the ecological standpoint in its prescribed movement from a luxurious upbringing to an ascetic lifestyle. (For an explicit recognition of contrast, see Singer, 1994.) In Chapter 11, I shall discuss this matter explicitly in terms of the *anthropic* versus the *karmic* world-views.

The specific challenge posed here is that sociology's spatio-temporal perspective may turn out to be ephemeral. While the directions taken by social policy may make a recognizably big difference over one or two generations, humanly significant changes in the gene pool or the ecology are unlikely to be felt for several generations, by which time the then-current crop of humans may have reoriented their value system to mitigate the significance of the changes that have occurred in the interim. Of course, one possible conclusion is that biology's frame of reference is irrelevant to sociological inquiry. But equally it could mean that a society's self-understanding is inevitably an ideology designed to foster a sense of control over an uncontrollable situation. The doctrine of unintended consequences, periodically invoked as an explanation for enduring tendencies in social life since the 18th century, only begins to scratch the surface of this potentially troubling interface between biology and sociology.

But if a thoroughgoing biological approach to social reality undermines modernist policy pretensions, it equally challenges the nostrums associated with postmodernist conceptions of identity. This is not because contemporary biology retains modernist metaphysical assumptions; on the contrary, it rejects them at least to the same extent as postmodernism does. The ascendancy of Darwinism has meant that each species is not a well-bounded set of organisms whose collective history is clearly set off from the histories of other species. Instead, species turns out to be a rather conventionally defined group whose members consist of genetic material that may also be present in the constitution of other species existing at other times and places.

Postmodernists should have no problem with this 'de-essentializing' of species identity. However, Darwinism also treats spontaneous genetic diversity and mutation as problematic, that is, more offspring are produced than ecologically sustainable. Herbert Spencer canonized the result as 'the struggle for survival', fuelling an ongoing debate over who is 'fit to live'. Postmodernists have so far evaded the issue, as they presume that the proliferation of individuals with open-ended identities occurs in an environment that exhibits a similar degree of open-endedness. To be sure, in our new biological age, the environment is restricted neither by brute nature nor an authoritarian eugenics policy. Rather, the restrictions appear in the characteristically diffuse neo-liberal projects like *offspring design*, which we briefly considered in Chapter 4, and *bioprospecting*, to which we now turn (Croskery, 1989).

Even more than offspring design, bioprospecting exemplifies the role of capitalism in mediating the production and social relations of biological knowledge. It has the potential for subverting taken-for-granted notions of who is 'rich' and 'poor' (for example, genetically rich peoples may be economically poor) and who 'owns' one's genetic identity (for example, oneself, one's tribe, all of humanity, the holder of the biotechnology patent)? At stake is no less than what it takes to constitute a normative social order and who counts as a member of such an order. Behind this issue is a very general concern about the future of the social bond itself, especially when Darwin-inspired criteria are used to select desirable traits in offspring. Eugenicists usually argue that only a restricted subset of humanity's naturally occurring traits deserve to be transmitted to future generations. Not surprisingly, the accompanying exclusionist rhetoric has cast a dark shadow over the motives of even the most Fabian of genetic engineers. However, in our own time, a more inclusionist rhetoric has come to the fore, one associated with the 'Human Genome Diversity Project' (HGDP). It aims to sample and register the full range of human genetic differences. When examining the Newspeak surrounding 'mobility' in Chapter 6, we considered Luigi Cavalli-Sforza, perhaps the world's leading theorist of genetic diversity, who has supported HGDP with arguments that bear an uncanny resemblance to those historically used for racial purity. Nevertheless, the minute differences in the constitution of the overall human genome on which HGDP focuses may also provide the key to understanding what makes a group susceptible or immune to certain widespread human ailments. On that basis, new biochemical medical treatments may be developed.

When HGDP had yet to be endowed at the levels enjoyed by the more famous Human Genome Project (HGP), which aims to map the genetic features shared by all humans, biotechnology companies made lucrative offers to cultures with relatively self-contained gene pools – in Papua New Guinea, Maori New Zealand, and Iceland – to allow the conversion of their genetic information to intellectual property (Schwartz 1999). This conversion, the legal basis for bioprospecting, was highlighted in the 1999 United Nations Human Development Report as meriting the highest priority from social scientists as a topic of investigation and critique. In bioprospecting, knowledge that a eugenicist can use to control the means by which others reproduce themselves coincides with the knowledge a capitalist can use to control the means by which others increase their wealth. We have thus reached the lowest common denominator between the most extreme forms of planned and unplanned social regimes. (For an early and still pertinent critique of this tendency, see Glover, 1984.)

However, in April 2005, IBM teamed up with *National Geographic* magazine to endow a re-branded HGDP as the 'Genographic Project', trading on the name of a commercial software package for amateur genealogists. Thus, the Genographic Project encourages the donation of rare genetic material and information relating to the migration patterns of their human bearers in what is euphemistically called an 'open source' environment, which in practice means 'pay-for-play'. In other words, you must first make a contribution to draw on the contributions of others. At first glance, this looks like a version of the Marxist principle 'From each according to their ability to each according to their need'. To be sure, the increase in the number of poorer players in an open source environment helps to sustain this impression – not to mention the Project's own public relations, which suggests that each contributor will help the others complete their family trees. But the concept of open source also arrives with a prior history in information technology, where contributors to a common software pool are not prohibited from *also* developing their own more exclusive software. Thus, the democratic rhetoric of 'open source' *de facto* provides protective coloration for the extra-curricular activities of the wealthier contributors, demonstrating once again that public goods cannot be reliably produced without a corresponding policy to regulate the production of private goods (Lessig, 2001: 67). In the case of the Genographic Project, it would be easy to imagine wealthier genetic donors exploiting their access to contributions of less wealthy donors to cultivate a lucrative sideline in designer drugs that end up widening the gap between the genetic 'haves' and 'have nots'.

The Genographic Project points toward a self-administered version of bioprospecting, perhaps relieving the role traditionally played by a sector of the social science community: medical anthropologists. Their involvement reveals a clear trajectory that leads from the treatment of people as objects of scientific inquiry, through the treatment of the fruits of that inquiry as intellectual property, to the treatment of intellectual property as a source of power in society at large (Fuller, 2002a: especially Chapter 2.7). However, the arguments against social scientists participating in this process are not as clear as they might first seem. To be sure, there are general utilitarian considerations of distributing something held by a few so that many can benefit – especially if the few are not demonstrably harmed in the process. Indeed, even the few may benefit by negotiating royalties from the profits reaped from commercial exploitation of their genetic resources. A moral space for this possibility is opened once one believes that in arenas where nation-states fail to act, the market provides the most efficient means of distributing goods and services.

As for Marxist-inspired concerns that bioprospecting compromises a culture's biological integrity by subjecting it to exchange relations, these often presuppose a genetic essentialism that both evolutionists and postmodernists would oppose, albeit on rather independent intellectual grounds. The difficulties inherent in appeals to biological integrity periodically surface in the rhetoric of the target cultures, which veers between talk of racial identity and market monopoly. This is especially true of cultures that enjoy significant economic autonomy: objections that begin by decrying the commodification of life *per se* may end by claiming injustice in the way the fruits of commodification are distributed. Indigenous peoples alive to their unique genetic makeup sometimes seem to resent that they were not the first to exploit it (Griffiths, 1997; Brown, 2003). There are two interesting features of the value confusion bred by bioprospecting, to which we now turn.

First, bioprospecting appears to be shifting the burden of proof in disputes over the value placed on indigenousness. Given the success of biochemical treatments based on rare genetic material, barriers to the sharing of this information are increasingly seen as akin to property owners who do not want their grounds despoiled by ramblers and developers – unless tres-passers are willing to pay a price. Needless to say, this analogy does not project an especially sympathetic image of indigenous peoples. One way around this emerging public relations problem is for indigenous people to play the political economy game and argue that the value contained in their genetic material should be interpreted as *labour not property*. In other words, the genetic uniqueness of people is less like inherited wealth to which the current generation contributed nothing than the ongoing work it takes to keep the population relatively inbred. In the current geopolitical scene, this requires upholding the value of cultural purity and continuity, in the face of capitalism's global tendency to dilute the differences between people. This shift in value orientation highlights the active and risky character of culti-vating a distinctive genetic profile. After all, inbreeding is just as likely to result in harm to the inbred individuals – be it from racial prejudice or con-genital defects – as good to members of other populations who receive treatments synthesized from the products of such inbreeding.

The second interesting feature of bioprospecting is its reversal of the economic orthodoxy when it comes to locating the source of value in new knowledge. Economists tend to see the value of new knowledge as a product of the scarcity associated with its origins, typically in self-selected commu-nities or the minds of exceptional individuals, neither of which are trans-parent to publicly accessible forums. Thus, tacit knowledge is valued more highly than explicit knowledge, often figuring as the 'something extra' that explains the difference between innovative and routinized economic systems once the usual factors of production are taken into account – that is before codification eliminates the competitive knowledge afforded by such knowledge. In short, economists tend to analyse new knowledge as if it were a magical ingredient in the manufacture of goods, which inclines them toward scepticism about the possibilities for managing, cultivating or expe-diting the growth of new knowledge (for example, Dasgupta and David, 1994). In this respect, economists treat new knowledge as occurring just as 'naturally' or 'spontaneously' as climatological changes, which also affect a society's productive capacity in significant yet largely unforeseeable ways. In contrast, bioprospecting dismisses this brute conception of nature, be it human or physical. Instead, new knowledge is treated as akin to the primary sector of the economy: a natural resource that can be farmed, fished or mined – in any case, 'captured', to use a favourite metaphor. Of course, like natural resources, the full extent of their exploitability may not be known. But by the same token, considerable effort may be devoted to developing replacements for resources that may run out in the long term; hence, the emergence of computerized expert systems and biomedical syntheses of genetic materials as growth areas in knowledge-based industries. At this point, we enter the field of 'knowledge management', the hottest research topic in business schools today (Fuller, 2002a).

A helpful way of thinking about the challenge posed by the application of biological knowledge in a capitalist world to social conceptions of value is to regard bioprospecting as undermining the privileged status of human beings shared by all the major modern economic paradigms – Marxist and institutionalist, Austrian and neoclassical. To be sure, these paradigms differ substantially in their depiction of the human: for example, Marxists regard humans as unique contributors to the means of production ('labour') whereas the Austrians subsume human activity under the general category of property: namely if everyone owns their body, then each person can dispose of it as he or she sees fit (if at all). But bioprospecting opens up the additional possibility that the bodies of all organisms, including humans, are mere means, if not outright obstacles, to expediting the rate of wealth production, a process that like some undifferentiated life force is taken to be an end in itself, regardless of its beneficiaries. From this point of view, *Homo sapiens* is a rather volatile carbon-based technology whose basic principles must be mastered for purposes of replacement by cheaper and more secure means. Bioprospecting would thus complete the incorporation of humanity 'as such' into the logic of the history of technology, which up to this point has been limited to various – but largely unconnected – aspects of our mental and physical condition (Fuller, 2002a: Chapter 3). In this brave new regime, claims to the uniqueness or inviolability of human beings, which historically informed the descriptive and normative sides of the social sciences, no longer carry merit.

NINE

Beware of Darwinists Bearing Leftist Gifts

The Struggle for Marx's Successor

The threat posed by bioprospecting to the integrity of humanity comes from the dynamic side of capitalism that always attracted Marxists for its promise of ever more efficient modes of production that, under the right political regime, might eliminate human misery altogether. Bioprospecting – and biotechnology more generally – continues to extend that promise. In contrast, a far greater threat to our humanity comes from the static side of capitalism, which I epitomized in Chapter 5 as '*Laissez faire* is nature's way', only now repackaged as a successor to Marxism! I refer here to the *Darwinian Left*, a nascent movement that will increasingly figure in the rest of this book. The Darwinian Left officially aims to revive the fortunes of progressive politics in today's post-Marxist world, but in practice it would reinforce current prejudices by justifying the policy path of least resistance to those who already happen to exist. The Darwinian Left is the brainchild of Peter Singer (1999a), the Australian philosopher of animal rights who now holds a privately funded chair in 'Values and Society' at Princeton University. Singer is often portrayed in the mass media as the world's most influential and dangerous living philosopher. I believe his influence has only begun to be felt.

Quoting Richard Dawkins, Singer portrays Darwin, not Marx, as Hegel's true heir:

> Although 'We are built as gene machines,' [Dawkins] tells us, 'we have the power to turn against our creators.' There is an important truth here. We are the first generation to understand not only that we

have evolved, but also the mechanisms by which we have evolved and how this evolutionary heritage influences our behaviour. In his philosophical epic, *The Phenomenology of Mind*, Hegel portrayed the culmination of history as a state of Absolute Knowledge, in which Mind knows itself for what it is, and hence achieves its own freedom. We don't have to buy Hegel's metaphysics to see something similar really has happened in the last fifty years. For the first time since life emerged from the primeval soup, there are beings who understand how they have come to be what they are. (Singer, 1999a: 63)

An important assumption that Singer makes – which I share – is that the Left requires a 'scientific' foundation because progressive politics needs to legitimize any substantial deviation from past policies. After all, the people who, in the first instance, would have to endure any proposed policy changes are precisely the ones who have endured the policies that would now be changed. In the modern world, science seems to provide the only consistently persuasive basis for believing that systematic change is better than stasis. Nevertheless, Singer's vision of a 'Darwinian Left' does little to exploit science's role as an *alternative* source of authority to tradition. If anything, his use of Darwin reinforces traditionally conservative, what starting in Chapter 11 I call 'karmic', views that would place *a priori* limits on the scope for social change. Simply consider the ease with which Singer quotes Dawkins (in the sentence before the one quoted above) who asserts that altruism 'has no place in nature, [is] something that has never existed in the whole history of the world.'

This missing aspect is epitomized by Hegel's phrase, 'the quest for recognition', the most eloquent recent expression of which has been Francis Fukuyama's (1992) *The End of History and the Last Man*. Without completely endorsing Fukuyama's sanguine democratic liberalism, nevertheless I believe he has tapped into a deep current in Western thought that remains unrepresented in modern biological science, including Singer's appropriation. However, rather than propose a heroic synthesis of the Darwinian and Hegelian strands in evolution, I shall discuss how greater attention to the Hegelian strand would overturn an intuition Singer shares with many interpreters of the human condition, namely, that greater familiarity should breed charity – rather than contempt – of those interpreted. Let me begin by contrasting Singer's and Fukuyama's coroner's reports on the demise of Marxism. The overall shape of my argument is presented in Table 9.1.

Both Singer and Fukuyama agree that, on a global level, Marxist socialism has been decisively defeated by liberal capitalism. Yet, Singer shows no

Table 9.1   *Fukuyama v. Singer: the struggle over struggles*

Theorist	Francis Fukuyama	Peter Singer
The point of it all	The uniquely human struggle for recognition	The pan-species struggle for survival
Political tradition	Plato to Hegel	Hobbes to Darwin
Why Marxism failed	Suppressed struggle for recognition in the name of egalitarianism	Ignored human adaptiveness to inegalitarian regimes
Equal or unequal?	All humans equal and superior to all animals	All species equal and some of each superior to others of their own
Moment of reproduction	Combat emblazoned in memory	Sex inscribed in genes
State of nature	Relative abundance	Subsistence
Relevant scarcity	Forgetfulness and distraction	Food and shelter
Image of humans	Risk-seekers trying to extend their claims over others	Risk-avoiders trying to defend what little they have
Explanation for altruism	Unlimited competition for superiority (who can give the most)	Limited protection of own interests ('tit-for-tat')

regret about what might have been lost in the process, whereas Fukuyama keeps the normative question open – of course, not so much that he would have preferred a Marxist future to a liberal one. He clearly agrees with Singer that Marxism is a bankrupt political tradition, taken on its own terms. However, Fukuyama also sees Marxism as the main vehicle by which a certain ennobling image of humanity was projected on the world stage, one that appears to have escaped Singer's notice.

In contrast to Singer's perspective, Fukuyama (1992) is striking in that its sense of the species-wide struggle derives no intellectual sustenance from contemporary biological accounts of human genetic survival. Rather, it is steeped in classical Greek sources. Fukuyama's proximate philosophical debt is Hegel's attempt to define humanity in terms of its endless *struggle for recognition*, even at risk to one's own life. To be sure, this quest has undergone considerable metamorphosis in the history of Western culture. It first entered Plato's thinking as an aristocratic warrior ethic, and at the peak of Marxism's popularity it had become a rallying cry for uniting the dispossessed peoples of the world. But regardless of its manifestation, the quest for recognition has not fitted comfortably with the selfish image of *Homo sapiens* – and animal life more generally – common to Darwinism and its English roots.

Specifically, it does not reflect a first-order desire for goods that are enjoyed privately, or 'excludably', as economists would put it. Rather, it is a second-order 'desire to be desired' that cannot be achieved without the participation of others. Indeed, the personal goods that normally mark the achievement of recognition – such as titles and honours – are in themselves fairly trivial. What matters is the swirl of public activity licensed by these symbols.

Ultimately the quest for recognition cannot be reduced to selfish behaviour because those engaged in the quest are not afraid to risk their lives – or at least a substantial portion of their material well-being – to do things that typically benefit others much more than themselves. Not surprisingly, rational choice theory finds recognition-seekers *prima facie* irrational. To square the struggle for recognition with the utilitarian calculus, it is sometimes said that they are sacrificing themselves for the greater good of some favoured group, but this end is more often assumed than proven. Moreover, one can never be recognized too much, whereas the law of diminishing marginal utility teaches that desires can be rendered pointless once they have been sufficiently indulged. Fukuyama observes that the selfish human that has anchored the English political imagination from Hobbes to Darwin presupposes a world of scarce material resources, in which staying alive is the order of the day (Fukuyama, 1992: 143–61). This leads to an identification of rationality with risk-averse strategies. Thus, one always obtains food for oneself and for others only if the level of personal risk is low or the likely benefit outweighs the risk.

To be sure, Fukuyama's preferred alternative – the political tradition that runs from Plato through Hegel – is equally aware that in the long run we are all dead. Nevertheless, in that tradition's state of nature, a hospitable physical environment renders the maintenance of life unproblematic. After all, the Athenians could turn to philosophy by virtue of the leisure they enjoyed in a political economy that did not valorize endless material growth. In this context, the relevant sense of 'scarcity' was that of *cognitive* limitations – that is, the finitude of consciousness and memory, which over time threatens to erode any achievements in recognition. Nevertheless, the posthumous memory of ancestors and the survival of their artefacts show that some have managed to acquire this scarce resource, which amounts to having their spirit borne by later bodies. Consequently, rationality comes to be aligned with continuous risk-seeking, or what Fukuyama calls the 'thymic' political imagination, after Plato's word for courage. Resting on one's laurels is not an option in a world governed by distraction and forgetfulness, especially where the material resources are available to do more than one already has to attract attention.

Marx is aligned with the thymic tradition because his faith in the success of the proletarian revolution presupposed that capitalism's productivity is sufficiently high to absorb any short-term costs that might be incurred by the workers' violent overthrow of the existing relations of production in their struggle for recognition. The world of *Capital* is much better endowed than that of *Leviathan*, even though the struggle for survival features in both. To be sure, as a diligent student of both classical philosophy and classical political economy, Marx integrates the struggles subsequently divided up between Singer and Fukuyama. The 'struggle for recognition' pursued by Marx's proletariat combined a desire for both material security and political status: that is, epistemologically speaking, to be sheltered from the mistakes others make and to be permitted to make their own mistakes.

However, alloys of Hegel and Hobbes need not always have such salutary results. A good case in point is the perpetually acquisitive nature of capitalism, even once the system has produced considerable wealth. Marx saw this as capitalism's tragic flaw, which would be played out in the falling rate of profit as capitalists try to outdo each other by producing the most goods by the cheapest means. Max Weber traced it to the inscrutability of divine justice behind the Protestant Ethic, while Thorstein Veblen and later Fred Hirsch (1976) pointed to the competitive consumption practices in contemporary capitalism. It would seem that Hegel gets his revenge on Hobbes, since capitalists always crave new 'states of nature' in which they can prove their superiority. Fukuyama himself sees this development in more hopeful terms, as it spurs entrepreneurs to seek out new markets, which (he claims) ultimately spreads the wealth around the world. Yet even Fukuyama sometimes bemoans consumerism as a degraded version of the struggle for recognition, coming close to endorsing Nietzsche's suggestion that a 'good war' (even a 'cold' one) would revive the old quest in all its heroic glory.

If capitalism's compulsive acquisitiveness exemplifies Hegelized Hobbesianism, an instance of Hobbesified Hegelianism would be postmodern identity politics. On the surface, the call to 'respect' traditionally disadvantaged social groups appears to continue the struggle for recognition. However, postmodern practitioners of identity politics do not generally mean to risk transforming or losing their identity in the hope of representing the interests of humanity. That would be to envisage women or minority ethnic groups as Marx did the proletariat, namely, as the vanguard of a worldwide revolutionary movement. To be sure, liberal and socialist feminists have entertained just such a vision, but they are not typical of contemporary feminism. Rather, identity politics tends to pursue the narrower goal of securing social space for its group within an existing power structure whose defining features are seen as uncontrollable, if not exactly unchangeable.

An important benchmark here is the recent turn in identity politics toward 'performativity' popularized by Judith Butler (1990) but ultimately derived from Michel Foucault's unfinished work on the history of sexuality. The politics of performativity should be seen as the latest moment in the trajectory that includes Hume and Wittgenstein, whereby an epistemological radicalism belies political quiescence by 'naturalizing' (or 'empiricizing') the scope of normatively appropriate action. In Butler's championing of the ethic of 'drag', a renovated concept of identity provides *a posteriori* grounding for what had been previously seen as only *a priori* groundable. The two genders remain as the normatively appropriate forms of self-presentation, but which biologically sexed persons occupy which gender depend on the social consequences of one's particular self-presentation, a.k.a. 'passing' as male or female. Thus, in providing an epistemological basis for 'being queer', Butler has opened up social space – but only slightly – by altering what counts as legitimate practice but not the practice that is thereby legitimated.

As in Hume and Wittgenstein, here too significant change is said to occur mainly as the unintended consequence of reproducing institutionalized practices at a local level, not some global strategy that lays claim to meta-level knowledge of a wide range of locales. As a concrete political strategy, this means that women's impersonations of men and vice versa are the most likely vehicles for redressing gender-based discrimination in a world profoundly structured by gender differentiation but at the same time providing resources for both men and women to work the system to their advantage. From one standpoint, Butler's gender performativity appears to be the final frontier of egalitarian politics. From another, it looks like a sectarian strategy for those who already enjoy considerable social, economic, and political freedom – such as middle class gays and bisexuals who live in the San Francisco Bay area.

To put the politics of performativity in perspective, recall some alternative strategies for redressing gender discrimination. The more familiar ones have been largely state-mandated, such as affirmative action and equal pay legislation. They presume that most women have neither the opportunity nor the inclination to impersonate men to improve their standard of living. A more distant political possibility is the complete diffusion of gender identity, as organic reproduction is institutionally and technologically separated from sexual intercourse. It is one thing to advocate free sexual passage between the two genders, but quite another to call for a multiplication of gender identities that ends up emptying the concept of gender of all meaning.

Gender performativists start to worry at this point, and some have hinted at a backlash comparable to those who celebrate the free passage of individuals between racial or cultural identities but then baulk at the prospect that inter-marriage, hybridization, and sheer globalization might serve to render race and culture meaningless social categories. Yet, even here, Hegel may have the last laugh on Hobbes. As Marxists are still fond of observing, members of the bourgeoisie who demonized the unearned wealth of the nobility and clergy in the French and Russian Revolutions simply ended up having a version of that very argument turned against them – in the name of 'capitalist exploitation' – by the working class, thereby removing any temporary advantage the bourgeoisie had gained by it.

Singer blames Marxism for failing to realize that humans are biologically constituted to resist the sort of comprehensive societal transformation promised by a Marxist revolutionary order. But he is no libertarian. The problem is not that Marxism constrained people's 'natural liberty', but that it failed to take seriously the evolutionary adaptiveness of persistent social arrangements, especially ones that contradict the revolutionary's most cherished ideal, egalitarianism. In developing this argument, it soon becomes clear that Singer is targeting a particular form of socially engineered equality – namely, between the sexes. Here Darwinism's causal focus on sexual reproduction as the key to species survival in humans is alleged to contain some valuable political lessons for the Left:

> While Darwinian thought has no impact on the priority we give to equality as a moral or political ideal, it gives us grounds for believing that since men and women play different roles in reproduction, they may also differ in their inclinations and temperaments, in ways that best promote the reproductive prospects of each sex. (Singer, 1999a: 17–18)

Given Singer's long-standing interest in extending rights to animals (for example, Singer, 1975), also inspired by Darwin, the apparent ease with which he excuses gender discrimination may seem odd. However, it is characteristic of the English philosophical tradition, on which both Darwin and Singer draw, to argue on 'naturalistic' grounds for *both* breaking down any hard ontological distinction between humans and other animal species *and* reinforcing persistent social distinctions within humans. What has varied across thinkers and centuries in this tradition is exactly how one proceeds to bridge the gap between humans and non-humans and which persistent human social distinctions are legitimized.

Armed with the Neo-Darwinian synthesis, Singer can point to the vast majority of overlapping genes between animal species to warrant the extension of rights to animals. Sigmund Freud, a pre-Mendelian Darwinist who appreciated the English tradition, could treat human beings as distinctive physiological channels for generalized animal energies, while recoiling from John Stuart Mill's call for gender equality – even as he was translating *The Subjection of Women* into German (Appignanesi and Forrester, 2000: 421–3)! Darwin himself, by no means an activist for the rights of either women or animals, originally learnt to blur the human–animal distinction from David Hume's account of reason as an instinct common to all animals but expressed in varying degrees in different species and even different races, given Hume's views on the multiple origins of humans from apes (Richards, 1987: 106–9; Harris, 1968: 87–8). Since Hume both exemplifies the mentality that informs Singer's discussion and continues to enjoy totemic status in contemporary anglophone philosophy, a brief digression may be in order.

Historians of modern philosophy have observed, usually in perplexity, why Hume, now seen as the most reasonable and well reasoned of the British empiricists (Mill included), was consigned to minority status for the 100 years following his death – that is, until the rise of Darwinism in British intellectual culture. While Hume's staunch anti-clericalism is usually cited as the reason, that is only part of the story: he was an anti-clerical Scot who upheld the English monarchy because of its proven ability to keep the nation united in peace and prosperity. Before the widespread acceptance of naturalistic arguments for the maintenance of tradition – often under the rubrics of 'adaptationism' and 'functionalism' – there was no obvious ideological niche for a secular Tory thinker like Hume. Secularists tended to be republicans, monarchists theists.

This point is often lost because of Hume's much vaunted 'scepticism' and his association with such Enlightenment icons as Jean-Jacques Rousseau. However, Hume was sceptical only about *a priori*, not *a posteriori*, means of grounding authority. The intended targets included not only the divine right of kings and innatist forms of rationalism, but also attempts to overturn authority by appeals to 'the rights of man' and the sort of *a priori* normative principles that would motivate the French Revolution. Hume liked Rousseau for his views about the oppressive effects of corrupt institutions, not his more utopian urges to return humanity to some pristine state, be it noble savagery or ancient republicanism. More to Hume's liking was Montesquieu's refashioning of Aristotle's 'Man is born into society and there he [*sic*] remains'. In short, Hume was 'radical' in much the same sense Wittgenstein was, namely, someone who wanted to revise how we justify common practices without necessarily revising the practices themselves. While this strategy does little to change what happens on an everyday basis, it significantly alters what counts as legitimate grounds for change – diminishing *both* the presumption of the incumbent and the motivation of the pretender: neither *lex tyranni* nor *vox populi* is treated as absolute and universal. The plausibility of such a modulated view of things assumes that the greatest evil is to violate the 'if it ain't broke don't fix it' principle. It implies that one should oppose those who would exchange a stable social order for an untested ideal, while resisting the urge to redress persistent local injustices that can be ultimately explained as part of a global adaptive strategy. For the generation after Hume, and posterity more generally, this view would receive its most eloquent expression by the Whig politician, Edmund Burke.

Historically, this view has suited a landed gentry suspicious of tyrants who advanced their fortunes by speaking for society's lower orders in ways the poor themselves had not previously spoken. Perhaps the most robust descendants of this line of thought in the 20th century, the anglophile Austrian school of economists championed by Friedrich von Hayek, earned their liberal credentials with an early and vigorous opposition to all forms of totalitarianism, but then remained conspicuously silent on the long-standing forms of class, race, and gender discrimination that affirmative action legislation has been designed to counteract. It is just this combination of a high sensitivity to power emanating from a concentrated source (for example, a tyrant, the Politburo) and a low sensitivity to its emanation from a diffuse source (for example, locally enforced class-, race-, gender-based prejudice) that marks Singer's Darwinian Left as heir to this ultimately conservative tradition.

For these heirs of Hume, diffuse forms of power are recognized as natural, not coercive, especially when there are beneficiaries who deem their situation a 'stable environment'. Consequently, they have difficulty seeing how a countervailing form of concentrated power would improve matters. In times of domestic tranquillity and no foreign threats, a policy of benign neglect would seem to be licensed. The result is the following attitude toward women, taken from Hume's 1751 work, *Enquiry Concerning the Principles of Morals* (Section III, Part 1):

> In many nations, the female sex are reduced to like slavery, and rendered incapable of all property, in opposition to their lordly masters. But though the males, when united, have in all countries bodily force sufficient to maintain this severe tyranny, yet such are the insinuation,

address, and charms of their fair companions, that women are commonly able to break the confederacy, and share with the other sex in all the rights and privileges of society.

Here Hume defends the *de facto* oppression of women by men on the grounds that women manage to find ways of mitigating their disadvantage to lead fulfilling lives and influence society. In the sentences prior to these, Hume had denied the natural equality of all humans on the evidence of their vastly different levels of civility, while at the same time regretting that European colonists have slaughtered native Americans and impressed Blacks into slavery. Hume's concern here was with the actual misery caused, not any transcendental concerns about the violation of human dignity. Hume's policy message seemed to be that lesser peoples should be either subject to paternalistic governance or left alone in their sub-civilized state. The proven 'success' of male–female relations testified to the former strategy, whereas the pre-colonial existence of Blacks and native Americans testified to the latter.

Because ideological allegiances have shifted so much over the past two centuries, it is easy to forget that Hume's 'balanced' counsel was seen in his own day as strategic complacency. The reformists back then were Scottish clerics like James Beattie, who argued for universalism on the basis of the species essentialism that the Bible granted to humans, allied to the then-popular idea of an innate 'commonsense' faculty through which God communicated with us. In terms of cosmology, Beattie et al. were unable to see how Hume could so vigorously oppose the idea of divine creation on *a priori* grounds, while remaining confident in the 'uniformity of nature' on *a posteriori* grounds. For Beattie, as for Darwin's theistic opponents, laws of nature were *ipso facto* evidence for God's existence. Yet, for his part, Hume's opposition to divine creation mainly concerned the idea that God could intervene in the physical world as he pleased (namely breaking the laws of nature through miracles), which is analogous to how a tyrant would impose his will on the social world. Although Hume was not as explicit as, say, Voltaire on this point, his view was compatible with God as *deus absconditus:* someone powerful enough to create the best possible world and hence capable of remaining indifferent to its subsequent development. This attitude is comparable to the political conditions under which constitutional monarchies have been maintained.

Nevertheless, the view from the Scottish clergy was that Hume's defence of the English monarchy was designed to arrest any further extension of rights beyond what already had benefited the anglophile property-owning class and its aspirants. In that respect, Beattie's appeal to universalism was not unlike today's Scottish Nationalist Party's support for the European Union as a countervailing force to Her Majesty's Government. To be sure, with the hindsight of two centuries, Beattie's reform-minded universalism reads as condescending calls to uplift the 'natives'. However, his sentiment is better seen as anticipating affirmative action legislation. Without the welfare state formally redistributing income from rich to poor through taxation, the only available strategy for equalizing human differences was to deploy the resources of the leading non-governmental organizations, the independent churches, which funded their missionary work through the devout's subscriptions (Toulmin, 2003).

Peter Singer would have us return to Hume, now armed with Darwin, with the slight twist that incentive schemes are used to encourage the rich to transfer income to the poor by appealing to the likely consequences of their failure to do so, namely, that they might lose (through damage or theft) what they already possess – be it by achievement or inheritance (a distinction to which Singer is remarkably indifferent). This strategy seems to be targeted to societies where there are zones of wealth in ambient poverty, and both rich and poor are sufficiently knowledgeable of the contribution that each makes to the other's situation: namely large urban centres. Such incentive schemes are unlikely to move those either secure in their wealth or despondent in their poverty. Whatever else the 'Darwinian Left' may be, it is an ideology with diminished political ambitions.

TEN

Who (or What) Deserves Our Sympathy?

So, does the biological turn in social thought potentially threaten our humanity? You would have to be naïve or disingenuous to deny this possibility. Our sense of humanity is underwritten by the *sympathy* we can establish with the life circumstances of others. At the very least, this means that we can relate to them at a level they would recognize as relevant to their existence, typically because we share many of the same problems and concerns. However, there are tried-and-tested ways of severing that moral bond. For example, as Hannah Arendt observed with respect to the Holocaust, one can capitalize on the division of labour in bureaucratic societies to render evil a banality. Thus, the atrocity associated with populating concentration camps can be reduced to a set of discrete tasks, each of which appears routine and neutral to the person performing it because he or she lacks the opportunity to acquire a concrete sense of the consequences of the task's execution.

Similarly, in our own time, biotechnology permits a highly mediated sense of genocide in which potential parents are individually persuaded to take decisions that have the cumulative effect of propagating and eliminating certain traits from the human gene pool. Such is the *telos* of bioliberalism. No doubt many will deem this reference to genocide an exaggeration, if only because they envisage the process to be much less deliberate and centralized than what they imagine to have been Nazi efforts to promote Aryanism. However, the differences may not be so great. On the one hand, as we already noted in Chapter 6, the Nazis were never as systematic as their enemies made them out to be (Neumann, 1944). On the other hand, contrary to the fantasies of invisible hand theorists, our decisions are not nearly so independent, especially once we include the role that marketing campaigns and public service announcements are likely to play in influencing people's orientation to offspring design. Even if specific responsibility for the overall social outcome of genetic choice remains diffuse, the outcome itself will probably be strongly correlated with the messages that are widely broadcast.

Of course, the elimination of heritable diseases is generally regarded as a worthy goal. Nevertheless, licensing even this form of genetic adjustment entails accepting the appropriateness of such traditionally eugenicist metaphors as 'cultivating' and 'pruning' the harvest of humanity. And, lest we forget, those metaphors acquired widespread currency through Darwin's image of nature 'selecting' offspring much as farmers do, when selectively breeding livestock. Nevertheless, from a strictly scientific standpoint that does not presume our ability to second-guess the Great Cosmic Farmer, deviant species members – from mutants to those deemed 'disabled' – are just as likely to be harbingers of new forms of life as failed versions of old forms. It all depends on the selection environment, over which humans happen to have more control than all other species. On the principle that greater knowledge brings greater responsibility, the category of 'disabled' has thus gradually shifted from a natural to a moral category, in which we assume more responsibility for whether such individuals live or die.

Sympathy requires an important intellectual and emotional bond between people far apart in space and time. Our biological age has reopened questions about the nature of this bond. For example, had the relevant biotechnologies been available just a generation ago, there would probably have been a strong bias toward preventing the birth of blind and deaf people. The lack of a spontaneous sense of bonding between 'us' and 'them' would have been largely to blame, albeit papered over by utilitarian policy considerations. Yet, people born with these 'disabilities' have developed a strong sense of identity politics, distinctive literatures and other forms of expression, not to mention concessions by the rest of society to admit their 'normal' status in, say, the design of new buildings. Can we not then imagine that in the future someone may allow a blind or deaf offspring to come into existence, not merely because it is the natural product of human parents but because its altered sensory capacity contains the potential to *enhance* the society into which it is born? A positive answer requires the development of a *critical sympathy* with future generations that escapes the prejudices of current beliefs, desires and practices.

A critical sense of sympathy implies loosening our sense of what it takes to be sufficiently 'similar' to others for them to engage our sympathy.

If the last 150 years of social thought has taught anything, it is that our understanding of normality is more a product of historical provincialism than genuinely universal intuitions. Thus, a critical sense of sympathy serves as a reminder that the proper object of sympathy is a common *future* co-habitable by ourselves and others to whom we would extend sympathy, regardless of the differences that most immediately strike us – *qua* decision-makers – at the moment. It may require a sceptical attitude toward calls to eliminate certain heritable traits because the offspring themselves would supposedly not want to be brought into existence. This counterfactual judgement assumes that the unborn offspring don't place much hope in our capacities for accommodation and change.

Nevertheless, a temporary shortfall in the socio-technical imagination should never be equated with a permanent failure in the gene pool. In particular, a 19th century conception of an 'independent' existence still tends to pervade our assessment of the disabled, even though an increasing number of 'normal' people today go through much of their lives heavily medicated and/or under regular supervision. (Indeed, today someone who 'suffers' from Downs syndrome has a life expectancy somewhat longer than the norm for 1900, namely 60–65 years.) The suffering we so freely attribute to the disabled and the downtrodden without their consent masks that it is *we* who find their existence insufferable. In other words, any principled refusal to permit a certain kind of birth reflects the limitations we envisage in *our own* capacity to adapt to a different environment, one populated with a significantly different sort of person. Such refusals, however legitimate, say more about the judges than the judged. A recognition that in these matters we are always engaging in discretionary moral and political judgement – and not simply yielding to scientifically incontrovertible facts – is essential to retain our own sense of humanity in a time when it can be all too easily lost.

There are many ways to think of the relationship between 'selfishness' and 'altruism' in roughly Darwinian terms. If we stick to Richard Dawkins' original formulation of the 'selfish gene', then everyday instances of altruism are reduced to epiphenomena, namely, macro-behavioural consequences of one organism enabling another of its kin to reproduce their common genes (Dawkins, 1976). This is called 'Hamilton's Rule', after Dawkins' Oxford mentor, W.D. Hamilton (Segerstrale, 2000: Chapter 4). Since a gene's very purpose is self-reproduction, it needs to produce individual organisms as vehicles. On this view, the organisms themselves are neither selfish nor altruistic. They are simply used by the gene for *its* own purposes.

Sometimes Dawkins is criticized for overextending the metaphor of selfishness. But in reality the metaphor is an anthropomorphically fuelled equivocation. On the one hand, Dawkins means that genes subject everything else to their own ends. On the other, he wants to suggest that altruism exists only as a gene-driven illusion. However, obscured in this equivocation is that everyday instances of *selfishness* are just as illusory as those of altruism, since any increase in an individual organism's advantage is always a macro-effect of the advantage gained by the genes that the organism carries. An organism's selfish or altruistic interests may or may not coincide with the conditions that enable the organism's genes to reproduce themselves. In this respect, Dawkins has seriously misled Singer into thinking that Darwinism 'proves' that organisms are more 'naturally' selfish than altruistic. If there is no other reason for attending to levels of causation in policy-relevant arguments, it is to avoid such confusions.

This deconstruction of the selfish gene metaphor allows us to witness the ease with which attributions of selfishness are transferred between the individual organism and its genetic constituents. But can the transfer be made ontologically upstream, that is, between an individual and the society of which it is a member? It seems not. Consider the rhetorical viability of concept of the *selfish society*, understood *not* as a society of selfish individuals but a society that consumes its individual members just as Dawkins says a gene consumes its organic carriers. To be sure, it would be easy to tell the history of sociology in these terms, with Émile Durkheim, Talcott Parsons and Niklas Luhmann marking three successive moments in articulating the implications of regarding human beings as vehicles for reproducing the larger social system to which they belong. Indeed, by the time we get to Luhmann, the social system has become so self-organizing, or 'autopoietic', that in principle humans could be replaced by other animals or machines as bearers of the relevant social functions, including even personhood. (For the clearest – and perhaps scariest – presentation of this position, see Fuchs, 2000.) Yet, interestingly, the selfishness metaphor is rarely extended sociologically. On the contrary, the sociologists in question are normally seen as advancing a theory of the social system in which individuals are 'sacrificed' or 'subordinated' to a larger presence that exerts *power* over them.

Dawkins's selfish gene metaphor has tapped into an implicit convention whereby selfishness is a bottom-up and power a top-down relation. We are inclined to say that society, not selfishness, exerts power over the individual, whereas 'naturally' selfish individuals constitute society. However, matters are complicated once genes figure in the equation because genes can be understood either as specific parts of a whole organism or as vehicles for the expression of properties common to many organisms. Most logical paradoxes rest on confusing part–whole and one–many relations, and gene-talk continues this venerable tradition with a vengeance, as epitomized in the question: will greater knowledge of genetics enable us to design people as we please or force us to confront the terms of our natural enslavement? Singer, a follower of Dawkins, wants to answer yes to both questions. Moreover, it *is* possible to have it both ways, once we understand the interaction effects of different genes in an organism that expresses its unique genetic constitution under the distinct environmental regime that constitutes its history. But unfortunately, our imperfect knowledge of these effects encourages an expedient switching between these two metaphysical rhetorics.

On the one hand, a *part–whole* rhetoric is used to capture the libertarian impulse that is animated by the recent discovery of a 'gene for X', where 'X' is a socially salient trait. Here genetics is about physically localizable things in specific individuals. On the other hand, the more deterministic *one–many* rhetoric is used for a widespread trait that appears intractable to policy interventions. Here genetics is about elusive tendencies that are unpredictably manifested in a general population. Thus, Singer licenses the pre-natal manipulation or abortion of genetically disabled human foetuses, while (as we saw earlier) virtually excusing the long-standing discrimination against the advancement of women in the workplace. Of course, when it comes to legitimating a socially controversial trait like homosexuality, its antagonists will appeal to genetic rhetoric to nip it in the bud, whereas its supporters will mobilize the very same rhetoric to underscore the trait's inevitability (and hence normality) in the existing population. In both examples, the current state of our genetic knowledge provides the pretext for letting, respectively, the ease and the difficulty of strategic intervention carry more metaphysical weight than it might otherwise.

Yet, there is an important difference between the relative ease with which a *prima facie* undesirable situation can be altered and the utility that would be ultimately served by altering it. Temporal perspective typically makes the difference. For example, even if we can now easily prevent certain physical disabilities, those disabilities may have historically served to expand our collective capacity to experience and conceptualize reality. From the standpoint of philosophy, psychology and linguistics, deafness and blindness are the obvious cases in point (Rée, 1999). Too quick assent to Singer's call for eliminating 'genetic defects' overlooks the cultural value derived from having nurtured them in the past and having forced 'abled' people to extend their imagination and ingenuity to accommodate them (Lewontin, 1993). This is not to say that disabilities should be indefinitely perpetuated; rather, it is to argue, on Singer's own utilitarian grounds, for cultivating naturally occurring disabilities, at least until their distinct perspectives are absorbed into our common inheritance. To be sure, this strategy needs to be tempered by the findings of genetic science, since certain foetal abnormalities may result in individuals whose *genuine* suffering cannot be alleviated by *any* reasonable social adjustments.

To his credit, Singer realizes that little more than a metaphor connects Dawkins' appeal to selfishness and the phenomena with which selfishness is normally associated (Singer, 1999a: Chapter 4). Nevertheless, he allows Dawkins' 'gene's eye-view' to anchor his discussion of the policy prospects for altruism. The result is that Singer accords undue weight to selfishness at the level of human behaviour and, more importantly, presumes that there is usually a trade-off between self- and other-oriented action. Thus, while Singer grants that some selfish behaviour can be made to benefit others with the right incentives, his prescriptions tend toward veiled threats and explicit penalties, as in 'pay higher taxes now or else expect more crime in the future.' This suggests that he believes that promoting the cause of altruism is an uphill struggle against our selfish inclinations.

Instead, however, of simply importing a gene-based conception of the selfishness/altruism distinction to explain behaviour, we might observe the implications of the distinction at the behavioural level itself. A provocative frame of reference for this discussion is the *handicap principle*, which purports to explain altruism as a limited form of self-sacrifice that animals undergo to mark their status to members of their own species and sometimes of others (Zahavi and Zahavi, 1997). Without such altruism, it would be difficult for animals to orient themselves around their world, in both sociological and epistemological terms. The handicap principle is meant to be quite general, covering mate selection, the mutual identification of predator and prey, not to mention basic representational practices. The last sort of case is especially revealing, since the use of signs is normally explained in terms of economy of effort, as if the salient relation were between the word and the thing to which it refers. The point, then, would be that saying the word is usually more economical than providing the thing (Fuller, 1988: Chapter 2). However, according to the handicap principle, the evolutionarily salient relation transpires between the word and its utterer. Why would someone feel compelled to say anything in the first place? The answer to this question is not obviously economy of effort, since saying nothing at all would take less effort and the utterance often benefits the addressee more than the addresser. Similarly, one might ask: why do potential mates – or predator and prey, for that matter – announce their status (for example, by engaging in song or displaying plumage) before enacting it.

To focus on the difference that the handicap principle makes, consider a representational practice as basic as my telling you something you did not know. I am 'handicapped' by spending time talking to you that I could have spent doing something of more direct benefit to me. Moreover, by telling you what I know, I have eliminated any advantage I might have had over you by knowing it. Yet, these costs are offset by your recognition that I am a reliable source of information and hence someone to whom you should defer in the future. In short, you come to depend on me because I took the initial risk of reaching out to you and it turned out to have mutually beneficial consequences, even if not in the same sense. For, ultimately, altruists aim to display their superiority ('magnanimity') to those who benefit from their actions. This interpretation of altruism goes to the heart of the concept, as it was originally popularized in mid-19th century arguments for philanthropy. It presupposes a world that is sufficiently rich in resources that individuals will be inclined toward risk-seeking behaviour that aims to extend one's claims over others. Here we begin to see a possible evolutionary basis for the struggle for recognition. Yet, it is in marked contrast to the more Hobbesian world presumed in modern evolutionary accounts of behaviour. In that case, individuals are struggling to maintain what they already have, and hence are averse to taking risks unless a clear benefit can be foreseen. Under the circumstances, selfishness is understandable.

It might be useful here to sketch the contrasting genealogies of the selfishness- and altruism-based accounts of evolution by arguing that after Hobbes' secularization of Adam's fall, Darwin and his followers have sought non-theistic redemption in some chance combination of genetic dispositions and environmental expression. In contrast, like Fukuyama's account of the struggle for recognition, the handicap principle begins from a position more akin to the Greco-Roman than the Judeo-Christian tradition, namely, individuals regard themselves as gods in the making who demonstrate their admirability by their success at self-extension. Once the *Iliad* replaces *Genesis* as the creation myth, it becomes easy to see how the handicap principle may instill a spirit of 'competitive altruism' as you and I try to outdo each other in displays of superiority. The net effect is that we sacrifice more of ourselves, and in the process leave more traces of our accomplishments and failures, from which our successors may benefit.

The flamboyant gift-giving practices of the Kwakiutl of British Columbia that so fascinated Franz Boas and Marcel Mauss in the early 20th century – in which the natives would often risk their own welfare in the name of tribal recognition – obviously fall into this category (Boas, 1921; Mauss, 1954). But so too would the development of elaborate information and communicative exchanges, be they conducted in the polis, on the playing field, in the pages of a scientific journal, or over the internet. It would be difficult to reduce these instances of competitive altruism to latent self-interest because often the recipients benefit more in the long term than the benefactors. In the larger biosphere, this holds especially across species, as potential predators and prey demonstrate their respective status to each other. Yet, the true prevalence of competitive altruism may be obscured by a stigmatic label like 'obsessive-compulsive' behaviour, which presumes that one *should* do more for one's kith and kin than for a set of anonymous others whom one regularly encounters in rather specialized settings.

Moreover, competitive altruism cannot be assimilated to the 'reciprocal altruism' introduced by Robert Trivers (1971), which tries to turn altruism into a form of extended self-interest whereby one gives to another expecting to receive something of comparable value in return. In game-theoretic circles, this is known as the 'tit-for-tat' strategy. Singer himself has probably done the most to turn this strategy into an ethical principle, but it remains a very limited basis on which to ground altruism, since it is anchored in the interest one has in others of one's own kind (Singer, 1981). Singer then argues for extending the relevant sense of 'kind', mainly on the basis of biological and more broadly ecological considerations that cast doubt on the idea that human welfare can be addressed independently of animal welfare. His basic strategy for expanding what he calls 'the circle of ethics' – his surrogate for altruism – is to show that certain physiological and genetic similarities between humans and non-human animals compel us to include these non-humans in our calculations of welfare. This then entails a re-evaluation of human life, since the greater good of this expanded circle (and even its constituent individuals) may be served by, say, allowing a healthy pig to live, while consigning a disabled human infant to death. The need for such trade-offs clearly presupposes a policy regime with irremediably scarce resources. Here Singer proceeds tactfully, unlike his precursors in the racial hygiene movement, whom we shall encounter in Chapter 14.

Singer's defence of altruism relies heavily – perhaps too heavily – on a Scottish Enlightenment conception of concern for others modelled on Newton's inverse square law of gravitational attraction, according to which the Sun controls the motion of the planets by the inverse square of their distance from it. By analogy, concern diminishes as social distance from oneself increases (Singer, 1999b). This conception fails to acknowledge that as we acquire a scientifically nuanced understanding of our fellows, we start to question their moral worth, which sometimes reverses the salience of the social distance principle. For example, one reason many well-heeled, middle class people feel more immediate concern for caged laboratory animals than, say, homeless people or even the latest dispossessed African tribe is their belief that other *specific* humans, if not the parties themselves, are more directly responsible for their plight. The result, of course, is that relatively little is done to improve the condition of these humans, yet no one feels especially guilty: 'Not *my* problem!' In other words, greater knowledge of the causes of the oppression among humans than animals may lead us to lose a sense of the human condition as something for which we are all equally responsible. (A rare text that seems to grasp this point is Geras 1998, though it is focused more on indifference to violence that is *massed* like the Holocaust than *diffused* like poverty.) But courtesy of Singer, that sense of 'universal victimhood' is in the process of being transferred to animals.

We have here a secular version of the Genesis story of Adam and Eve eating of the Tree of Knowledge of Good and Evil. The more we learn about the diverse historical trajectories of the human condition, the psychologically harder it becomes to treat 'every man as my brother' – the traditional Christian expression for regarding each human as possessing divine ancestry. Jean-Paul Sartre was probably the last major thinker to argue with complete sincerity for a secular version of this perspective when he declared that all humans are complicit in such singular acts as Hiroshima or the Holocaust. A robust conception of *negative responsibility* – which would hold people accountable for failures to act when action would have probably issued in better consequences – can still make good on Sartre's intuition (Fuller, 2003a: Chapters 15–17; Fuller, 2005: 29–31). Nevertheless, nowadays our knowledge of animals is arguably closer to the knowledge of humans that originally made the universalist ethic of the monotheistic religions so compelling. In contrast, we may know *too much* about each other to engage in genuinely 'humane' relations with human strangers.

Robert Solomon (1999), the leading US interpreter of existentialism for the past 30 years, has criticized Singer's strategy for sacrificing compassion at the altar of reason. He argues that, according to Singer's logic, not only would the disabled infant be left to die, but so too the homeless person who refuses to find work. If one knows with moral certainty that a given human will be of more cost than benefit to the expanded circle, then that person should be removed from the circle. By analogy, consider Johannes Kepler, the 17th century astrologer whom we now credit with having discovered the elliptical orbit of the planets. He originally proposed the inverse square law to capture illumination as a function of distance from a light source. Perhaps then, by increasing the power of the light source to enable the illumination of more distant objects (cf. healthy pigs), one may unintentionally consume less distant ones (cf. homeless humans) in flames.

I agree with Solomon that all this seems to follow from Singer's argument. But I disagree that it points to Singer's uncompassionate hyper-rationalism, born of an uncompromising utilitarianism. On the contrary, without under-estimating his utilitarianism, Singer is better seen as a *compassionate hyper-empiricist* who lets his greater empirical knowledge of the differences in the behavioural patterns and motivational structures of human beings vis-à-vis those of non-human beings prejudice the value weightings he assigns in his utilitarian calculus. In other words, one can know (or think one knows) *too much* about individuals to make an appropriate moral appraisal. The bene-fit of the doubt is then accorded to those we know *less* about. On that basis, I would say that Singer is biased *against* humans.

The legal system regularly counteracts the perils of hyper-empiricism in the circumscribed procedure of courtroom trials: who can be a juror in a case, what counts as permissible testimony, and so on. John Rawls (1971) famously conferred philosophical respectability on this practice by arguing that decisions about the most fundamental principles of justice require a 'veil of ignorance' in which the decision-maker knows only the most general fea-tures of her society but not her particular status therein. Nowadays political theorists tend to treat Rawls' veil of ignorance as merely an intriguing artifice propping up a theory of justice that merits our endorsement on other grounds. However, the veil also reflects the deep need for a stopgap against any undue influence that the varying degrees of knowledge we have of our fellows may have on our normative judgements. Although Rawls himself jus-tified the veil of ignorance on transcendental grounds, it is better defended on 'reflexive naturalist' grounds (Fuller and Collier, 2004: 59–62; cf. Fuller, 1985, which first explored the epistemic import of the veil of ignorance). In other words, among the empirical components of our normative judgements should be the 'meta-fact' that the historical development of human know-ledge has been uneven, both in terms of what is known and who knows it. Contrary to Rawls' own construal of the veil of ignorance, failure to recog-nize this point is not limited to letting greater knowledge of our own situa-tion disadvantage others socially distant from us. At a more general level, it provides ironic vindication of La Rochefoucauld's maxim, 'Familiarity breeds contempt.' Specifically, our greater familiarity with humans vis-à-vis animals can breed contemptuous interpretations of fellow humans. (On the rationality of this and related psychological mechanisms, see Elster, 1999.)

That familiarity might breed contempt goes unnoticed because the socio-biological literature on which Singer relies often presumes that our knowledge of non-humans is in some normatively relevant way *better* than that of humans, since humans are presumed to engage in more complex behaviours than other animals, given the supposedly more complicated ways in which our genetic potential interacts with the environment. Of course, sociobiological accounts of non-humans are full of covert, unconscious, and otherwise unacknowledged borrowings from Marx, Durkheim, Weber, and Freud. The problem is getting sociobiologists to see Marx et al. as relevant to the *human beings* for which their theories were originally designed! A charitable understanding of this topsy-turvy situation is that social scientific theories typically identify only a few variables as salient for explaining human behaviour. Sociobiologists find this too simple, unless these variables can be located in morally 'simpler' organisms that then provide evolutionary precedents for human behaviour. Ants thus become the bearers of epistemic authority.

However, once we lay to rest the chimera that we might know more about non-humans than humans, is there any way of justifying the La Rochefoucauldian interpretive principle? Yes, but it requires that we transcend the perspectives of both humans and animals, and instead adopt the standpoint of *God* – but in the specific Enlightenment sense that made *deus absconditus* such an attractive image for Voltaire and his fellow deists. For them, 'the best of all possible worlds' implied that humanity was created in the image and likeness of God, including the freedom allowed to God. However, it was a deliberately imperfect reproduction designed to challenge humans to use their freedom to earn their salvation. In contrast, animals were created in a perfectly amoral state. Whereas animals are always all they can be, humans can always be more than they are. On this basis, familiarity with humanity's potential may breed contempt for what particular individuals make of it. This attitude is traceable to La Rochefoucauld's own origins as a mid-17th century French aristocrat very familiar with how members of his own class squandered their privilege, ultimately ceding it to the absolute monarchy of Louis XIV. Thus, he looked more charitably upon those who improved upon, rather than degraded, their inheritance. What distinguishes Singer's interpretive stance from La Rochefoucauld's is the former's failure to take seriously what can be added through will and effort to one's genetic endowment. In this sense, Singer remains deaf to the struggle for recognition, at least in the human species and probably others as well.

PART THREE

HUMANITY AS THE ENDANGERED SPECIES OF OUR TIMES

the species indifference of genetics and then ultimately dissolved in a probabilistic distribution of subatomic particles. I would not be surprised if soon some Neo-Darwinist disabused of the anthropic vision explicitly argues that all species are worth understanding in their own right, and that the continued fascination – say, by evolutionary psychologists – with looking to animals for clues to the human condition is tantamount to using modern astronomy as a source of astrological insight. In both cases, the non-human is subsumed to the human in a thoroughly superstitious fashion. After all, astrology, like evolutionary psychology, assumes that both humans and non-humans are effectively alternate arrangements of common matter, which in turn explains why studying things as remote as celestial motions happening far away or different species living long ago can illuminate everyday life today. The analogy is useful in reminding us that a superstition reveals a society's refusal to acknowledge the disproportional value weighting it gives to some facts over others.

Nevertheless, the social scientific understanding of religion has often obscured the depth of the anthropic–karmic distinction. To be sure, many of the distinctive methods (for example, 'interpretation') and objects ('meanings', 'consciousness') of the social sciences are secular descendants of Christian concepts that originally demarcated humanity's unique spiritual existence from the rest of the animal and material world. In this respect, the anthropic roots of social science are very clear. But at the same time, the conception of 'society' on which the founders of social science fixated was the nation-state, whose general *modus operandi* was to supplant the traditional seats of religion – the church and the family – as the primary locus of authority and allegiance. At best, 'religion' in this sense referred to a functionally differentiated ('private') part of society; at worst, it represented an atavistic form of social life altogether. Thus, common to the practices we continue to call 'religions' today – a motley array of monotheisms, polytheisms, pantheisms, and atheisms that range across the anthropic–karmic divide – is simply their capacity to organize social life into complex, long-lasting, and far-flung patterns of behaviour without requiring the agency of the nation-state. Of course, states and religions have often enjoyed symbiotic relationships, but typically the religions have predated and sometimes even helped to create the states with which they would then later come into conflict.

The idea that Science and Religion – in their capitalized forms – have been in perennial conflict is a Western myth invented in the last quarter of the 19th century, sparked by the rise of Darwinism, which was then projected backward by ideologically inspired historians to cover, say, Galileo's persecution, which in its day was understood as an in-house dispute among

Christians (Brooke, 1991). Moreover, the conflict's mythical status was recognized by Eastern intellectuals almost from its inception, which in turn eased the assimilation of Western science in countries like China and Japan that had previously restricted their access to Western ideas (Fuller, 1997: Chapter 6). The myth has two related sources. The first pertains to the use of 'religion' as a technical term in the emerging social sciences of the period, and the second to the specific struggle between theology and the natural sciences for control of national educational systems in the Europeanized world. These facts should give pause to today's 'cognitive anthropologists' who, impatient with the actual complexity of history and ordinary social science, try to localize religion in an evolutionarily adaptive 'mental module' – to use the politically correct expression for instinct (Atran, 2002). In cognitive anthropology's Newspeak, the phrase 'cognitive impenetrability', a defining feature of a mental module, is used to update and positively re-spin the unfashionable concept of irrationality (Fodor, 1983).

As noted above, anthropologists and sociologists originally used 'religion' to mean any form of social organization whose cohesion and perpetuation do not rely on the existence of a nation-state. It was thus largely a residual term designed to cover all so-called 'traditional' forms of social life, ranging from small non-literate tribes that were objects of both curiosity and contempt by 19th century 'ethnologists' to the complex Hindu caste system whose literary canon had attracted many Western admirers in the same period. Not surprisingly, the quest to find something epistemologically salient or common to all religions has turned out to be a red herring. They certainly don't share a belief in gods, let alone a common experience of the 'sacred'. If anything, what all forms of social life called 'religion' seemed to share is the presence of a stable normative order that is not traceable to a social contract spelling out a rational basis for collective agreement on the basis of which performance may be judged against promise.

Because of this shared negative quality, religious societies were often regarded as 'backward' in two distinct senses:

First, normative conformity was justified through simple induction, the sheer repetition of rituals previously performed. In this context, traditional societies mask the imperfect reproducibility of the past by propagating 'myths' that undermine the prerequisites for registering rational progress, namely, the recognition of historical change and individual responsibility (Brown, 1988). Thus, in many modern minds, religion came to be seen as synonymous with superstition.

Secondly, the social order was transmitted 'backward' instead of 'forward', that is, by inheritance not achievement. In traditional societies, sociology coincides with sociobiology. Thus, the site of biological reproduction, the family, is the ultimate unit of social selection. In contrast, from Auguste Comte onward, sociology has based its scientific autonomy on humanity's species uniqueness, which is only fully realized in modern societies. In such societies, humans systematically resist and even overcome their biological nature, most notably through the legitimation of corporate entities (*universitates*, in medieval law) like states, which reorganize human relationships in terms that break down traditional kinship ties and barriers.

In terms of these defining features of religious societies, the monotheistic 'religions of the book' (Judaism, but especially Christianity and Islam) occupy a distinctive albeit problematic place because their explicitly universalist aspirations and proselytizing tendencies have often put their members at odds with the dominant beliefs and practices of their societies. Rather than shoring up tradition, these religions have often been the vehicles by which societies have come to question and reform themselves, typically in the name of self-transcendence. For this reason, it is unsurprising that Christianity and Islam have provided the twin religious basis for modern science. Even the two original icons of the anti-religious defence of science, Galileo and Voltaire did not oppose the religious control of the universities. Galileo simply wanted theology to adjust its doctrine in light of scientific discoveries, whereas Voltaire was content to promote 'academies' that enjoyed royal immunity from the religiously dominated universities.

It is clear that Galileo and Voltaire distinguished the sociologically pre-judicial sense of religion sketched above from the intellectual project of theology, and indeed appealed to science to protect theology from succumbing to the religious imperatives associated with training the next generation of civil and ecclesiastical officials. This Enlightenment sensibility would provide the basis for establishing theology as a 'critical-historical' discipline in the renovated German university system of the early 19th century (Collins, 1998: Chapter 12). However, a half-century later, the tables were turned, as scientists – both natural and social – threatened to replace theologians as the intellectual guardians of societal reproduction. In Britain, this reversal of fate was epitomized by Thomas Henry Huxley who, buoyed by the largely positive reception of Darwin's *Origin of the Species*, aggressively campaigned to replace theology with the natural sciences as the centre of academic life. Yet, even that campaign only took systematic root at the senior levels of university administration after the First World War, a generation after Huxley's death.

Sociology's role in this process was most enthusiastically taken up by Émile Durkheim, who was pivotal in the design of secular moral education for France's Third Republic. He was best positioned to realize Comte's positivist dream of a 'religion of humanity' that would result from infusing the institutional form of the Roman Catholic Church with the content of modern science. Though descended from a rabbinical family and keen to avoid Comte's visionary excesses that had made him an academic pariah in his lifetime, Durkheim nevertheless agreed with Comte that Christianity's universalism has historically provided the most promising vehicle for human progress. Unfortunately, the Christian churches – especially Catholicism – fell afoul of their universalist promise by remaining aligned with reactionary political factions, such as the Bourbon restorationists, who claimed a hereditary basis for their legitimacy that, even at the end of the 19th century, was sometimes expressed as a 'divine right'.

Christianity's redeeming feature was a monotheism that concept-ualized the deity as the ideal extension of human qualities. In secular guise, such a God personified a worthy goal – namely, a state of collective being governed by principles that apply equally to all and to which all have equal access. From that standpoint, the great Eastern religions were dismissed wholesale for their failure to accord spiritual privilege to humanity, often in the name of 'pantheism'. This, in turn, explained (to Western satisfaction) the apparent indifference of Eastern religions to actual human lives, and hence their failure to develop adequate medical and legal support systems for the widespread promotion of human welfare. As for Christianity's rivals, Judaism was treated as atavistic for its residual insistence on a kinship basis for religious allegiance, while Islam was cast as a decadent Christianity that fetishized the Qur'an and devalued subsequent human achievements. Marx, Weber and Durkhem basically agreed on all these points – though they dif-fered over the extent to which social science should be explicitly identified with the project of secularized Christianity.

Now that more than a century has passed since the declaration of this mythical war between Science and Religion, we may begin to sift out its grain of truth. It goes without saying that the early social scientists were self-serving and ill-informed about the heterogeneous character of the religions on which they passed judgement. Nevertheless, they may have been right about the more general point that their imperfect array of data and opinion sug-gested: *Not all religions value human life to the same extent, and only the monotheistic religions of the book confer a metaphysical privilege on humanity.* This point is reflected in the very fact that the interface between the divine and the mundane is not some unmediated version of nature but an artefact – a book – to which humans have privileged access because, in the plenitude of Creation, we are the only ones who could have made something like it. Thus, the 17th century Scientific Revolution was launched by the metaphorical reduction of nature to a book written in the language of mathematics that would be decoded by the likes of Galileo and Newton. In the following century, the non-natural 'human sciences' were founded by the 18th century Neapolitan jurist Giambattista Vico, whose *La Scienza Nuova* converted this sacred bond with God into a secular epistemic principle: *Like the Creator, we know best what we make.* Ernest Gellner (1989) has updated the book metaphor to capture the idea that humanity truly comes in its own when it is emboldened to correct and perhaps even re-draft the original manuscript on which it is based.

Unfortunately, the historic connection between the privileging of humanity and the advancement of science in the modern era has been often made the basis for a clearly invalid inference – that the religious failure to privilege humanity implies other-worldly, anti-scientific attitudes. Nothing could be further from the truth. On the contrary, there is a unique world-historic tension between anthropocentric world-views – be they inspired by monotheism or secular humanism – and fully naturalized, non-dualistic conceptions of the universe – be they openly atheistic or laced with a diffuse sense of ecological spirituality. *Both* can lay equal claim to scientificity. Indeed, a common tactic used by self-styled vanguard thinkers in the West to resolve tensions between science and religion involves appropriating Eastern ideas and practices, typically as leverage against reactionary positions associated with Christianity (Clarke, 1997). Sometimes this strategic appropriation left a lasting impression on Western thought. For example, in the late 17th century, Leibniz cited Chinese ideograms as an inspiration for his project of a universal language of thought, which as 'symbolic logic' became one of the signature developments of modern Western philosophy.

Historically the tactic of playing off alternative theologies for scientific advantage has focused on physics. In the past century alone, a broad spectrum of scientists and humanists – including Niels Bohr, Joseph Needham, Carl Jung, and Fritjhof Capra – argued that such Chinese concepts as *ch'i*, *li*, and *tao* offered the holistic metaphysical background needed for a comprehensive appreciation of the more cosmic implications of the revolutions in relativity and quantum physics. These concepts clearly situated the observer in the world observed, thereby undermining the detached, perhaps even alienated, 'view from nowhere' that was presupposed by classical mechanics, itself modelled on Newton's understanding of the standpoint of the Christian deity toward his Creation. But how will the relationship between science and religion change, as biology replaces physics as the cutting edge scientific discipline in the 21st century?

From political interest and financial investment to philosophical debate and media attention, one paradigm shift is undeniable: The molecular biology laboratory has replaced the particle accelerator as the preferred place of scientific worship. Ours is a 'biotech century' (Rifkin, 1998). However, as the disciplinary focus shifts from physics to biology, so too will the source of Eastern metaphysical inspiration – specifically from China to India. If the 20th century was marked by a struggle between broadly 'mechanistic' and 'holistic' world-views, the 21st century will bring the conflict between anthropic and karmic perspectives into sharper relief. Metaphysically at stake is no less than the idea that reality is a single unified entity to which humans have privileged access – that is, literally a *universe* and not a *pluriverse* (Collins, 1998: Chapter 15).

Universalism presupposes a standpoint from which everyone can be treated equally – whether one thinks of this 'equal treatment' in terms of the physical or juridical versions of 'natural law'. The monotheistic God has been the historical personification of this perspective, since God stands in the same relation of absolute superiority vis-à-vis all Creation. In the case of humans, having been created 'in the image and likeness of God', the deity operates through two senses of 'natural law', not simply the physical version that Newton came to express as the principle of gravitational attraction, but also the juridical version that has been often invoked as a basis for solidarity and revolution in modern politics. In this respect, anthropocentrism is the ultimate example of what Marxists call a 'hegemony', whereby one perspective dominates and reduces all others. Anthropocentrism even displays this tendency in its own development, as Western wealthy white males have lorded over the rest of *Homo sapiens* in our allegedly collective quest to remake the world in our image and likeness. However, precisely because non-Western, non-wealthy, non-whites and/or non-males have been recognized as unequal by a *common* standard, the justice of those judgements could be always appealed – sometimes peacefully, often not.

However, once 'The One True God' is removed, the standpoint for making epistemic and ethical claims at once universal and anthropic is seriously threatened, if not completely undermined. The social sciences' historic strategy for reinstating this standpoint has been 'humanity', understood as a project that completes, if not outright replaces, The One True God. But if – or once – this project is deemed a failure, processes of *universalisation* yield to those of *globalization* (for example, Wallerstein, 1996). Whereas universalization implies an equality of individuals with respect to the same second-order entity, globalization implies a mutual accommodation of individuals as parts of the same self-contained system – that is, without need of an external

Creator to set a standard and possibly correct the system. In the latter case, system maintenance may demand unequal treatment and even elimination of parts that cannot figure as part of a stable equilibrium. The result is the political expedient of consensualism raised to the level of ontology, whereby only those who can get on without inconveniencing the rest too much are entitled to survival.

Nobody denies that in a world of infinite resources, all creatures should be allowed to live the fullest lives possible. But as a matter of fact, we do not live in such a world and are unlikely to do so in the foreseeable future. The open question, then, is whether those of us already here – regardless of species and capacities – should take the path of least mutual resistance or try for an external, arguably 'higher', standard that would force some hard decisions. The world religions differ significantly on what to make of this situation. The Western world religions (Judaism, Christianity and Islam) privilege human beings – regardless of their capacities – above all other creatures, while the Eastern ones generally hold a more egalitarian attitude toward the plenitude of nature. This difference helps explain the enormous significance that Western culture has traditionally attached to the birth and death of individual humans, refusing to reduce these events to transitional phases in larger cosmic processes that engulf all species. This sensibility has spawned a variety of Western contributions to world thought that might otherwise seem unrelated, ranging from modern medicine to existentialist philosophy. Of course, it equally means that the Western religions – especially Christianity and such secular successors as Positivism and Marxism – cannot completely escape responsibility for the environmental despoliation that has attended the global march of capitalism, as it too has been justified as a radical extension of humanity's God-like creative powers over nature.

So, then, how are we to learn from past errors? Do we simply junk the project of humanity as so much excess modernist baggage, or do we attend to the exact nature of the errors so as to see the project to completion? It should be clear that I wish to press forward. In any case, one implication of the Eastern alternative is already clear: *A society that supports both science and religion need not provide a safe haven for human beings.*

The 20th century was full of international conferences in which leaders from many religious faiths and scientific disciplines pasted over doctrinal differences in a diplomatic discourse of 'interfaith dialogue' full of vague abstractions and strategic omissions. This is neither surprising nor entirely blameworthy. An ecumenical attitude toward the relationship between science and religion emerged in the late stages of European Imperialism and peaked in the Cold War. Throughout this period, science and technology clearly contributed to exploitation and militarization, not least because they were so unevenly distributed across the globe. It was therefore easy to reach agreement that we all share the same ultimate ends but are divided by the means at our disposal. Ecumenism thus became a religious strategy to reorient science from its more destructive and divisive uses. Unfortunately, this admirable goal has been underwritten by an exclusive and unified association of, on the one hand, 'ends' with religion and, on the other, 'means' with science. This distinction is both historically and philosophically suspect. Moreover, as the balance of global economic and political power is slowly but surely being redressed, with the secular state only one among many players in the process, the course of scientific inquiry is re-opened to competing religious sensibilities backed by a range of corporate sponsors.

Just as it is nonsensical to speak of a perennial battle between Science and Religion, as if they were locked in some timeless Manichaean struggle of Good versus Evil, it is equally foolish – though undoubtedly more pleasant – to assert that all scientific and religious doctrines are mutually compatible or even complementary. Indeed, the latter error probably poses the greater threat to any genuine integration of scientific and religious interests. In the 21st century, a decision of world-historic proportions will need to be taken between coalitions of sciences-and-religions. As I have suggested, the choice turns on the difference between the monotheistic religions that place humanity at the centre of science and politics, and non-monotheistic religions (Hinduism, Buddhism, Jainism, Confucianism, Taoism), which regard humans as constituting only one among many forms of life that deserve equal scientific and political treatment. This is just another way of expressing the difference between *anthropic* and *karmic* versions of the science-and-religion duplex.

Contrary to the rhetoric of some of its most famous popularizers, the dominant tendency of biological research done under the Neo-Darwinian paradigm has been to discredit claims to a unique 'human nature' that have traditionally provided the empirical basis for the anthropic orientation. Instead, the overwhelming genetic overlap between us and other life forms point to a karma-friendly pan-naturalism that sees humanity as continuous with the rest of nature. I say 'karma' because that word captures a generic 'life force' in many of the great Eastern religions, especially Hinduism, Buddhism and Jainism. It is a broad-gauged term whose function is comparable to what August Weismann originally called 'germ plasm' and modern evolutionary theory calls 'genes'. Four claims are common to karmic and genetic discourse:

(a) that one's own actions are somehow constrained by past lives, be it as a potential or a necessary determinant;
(b) that actions can be taken in one's own lifetime (often related to lifestyle) to mitigate, but not completely eliminate, the worst aspects of one's legacy;
(c) that there is no inter-generational or inter-species sense of progress, unless the goal is defined as peaceful physical extinction;
(d) that the life force is common to all life forms, regardless of surface differences in appearance and emotional attachment.

The closest ancient Western tradition to the karmic sensibility is atomism and the associated ethical doctrine of Epicureanism, which espoused the minimization of suffering in the face of the irreducible contingency of things. A sign of karma's recent theological ascendancy is that the minimization of suffering has been proposed as the foundation for an 'ecumenical anthropology' (Charry, 1987). From an anthropic standpoint, this is to set the standard of religious observance much too low.

To help the reader follow my argument, I have summarized in Table 11.1 the main differences in position that characterize the anthropic and karmic world-views.

The contrast between the two world-views becomes most explicit in their answers to the following three questions:

1 *Religious*: does humanity have a privileged relationship to God?
2 *Scientific*: are the social sciences autonomous from the natural sciences?
3 *Political*: is humanity a collective project above the self-interest of individuals and their loved ones?

For each of these questions, the anthropic world-view answers *yes*, the karmic *no*. At this point, perhaps the contrast that requires most immediate explanation concerns 'Metaphysics', especially given the multifarious – and largely negative – uses to which the term 'positivism' has been put. After all, why have positivists stressed the procedural, typically sensory, basis for epistemic judgement? The general answer is that they have believed that reality transpires at a level that humans normally encounter or at least could encounter with minimal additional effort. Whatever else one wants to say about this view, it presupposes that reality is anthropocentric in a very profound sense, which is understandable given the movement's roots in Comte and its historical association with the extension of democratic governance. To be sure,

Table 11.1   *The two great scientific-religious world-views*

Worldview	Anthropic	Karmic
Metaphysics	Reality is co-human (Positivism)	Reality is infra-human (Atomism)
Theology	Monotheist	Poly/Pantheist
Humans	Agents	Vehicles
Evolution	Self-realization	Natural selection
Culture	Resists and transcends nature	Accepts and mirrors nature
Ethics	Maximize welfare	Minimize suffering
Justice	Corrects natural inequality (Distributive)	Restores natural order (Commutative)
Life	Humans privileged	Species egalitarian
Mortality	Medical problem	Biological fact
18th century icon	Condorcet	Malthus
19th century icon	J.S. Mill, T.H. Huxley	J. Bentham, H. Spencer
20th century icon	J. Rawls, F. Fukuyama	M. Foucault, P. Singer

positivism may be faulted for not living up to its egalitarian sentiments, as it would seem that scientifically trained sense organs are 'more equal' than untrained ones. Nevertheless, its karmic opposite, atomism, denies the very idea that reality should be epistemically accessible to most – if any – people. Thus, its epistemic politics have veered between the extremes of scepticism and expertism, in which the restricted access to particle accelerators may be seen as a modern-day equivalent to the restriction of literacy to members of the Brahmin caste.

My construction of the anthropic–karmic dichotomy is strongly influenced by the 1893 Romanes Lecture of Thomas Henry Huxley, to which I have alluded. Huxley, known in his day as 'Darwin's bulldog' was a Pauline convert to Darwinism – unlike, say, Herbert Spencer, who piggybacked his own long-standing evolutionary naturalism on the popular success of *Origin of the Species*. Thus, Huxley continued to struggle with issues that had been already resolved in Spencer's mind. Perhaps this explains how Spencer could develop a seamless system of thought, whereas Huxley most naturally expressed his thinking in debates and polemical essays. Huxley understood what was at risk in forsaking monotheism in a way Spencer did not. However, Huxley has fallen afoul of political correctness, both in his own day and ours. Addressing an audience already largely converted to Darwinism, Huxley sounded like an old man (aged 68, two years before his death) trying to hedge his bets in case God turns out to exist. Over a century later, we still find his message hard to take. After all, Huxley argued that the West was morally, though not epistemically, superior to the East. Such a judgement is easily dismissed as a typical piece of Victorian hubris, yet the terms of his evaluation bear further scrutiny.

Aside from his contributions to the biomedical sciences, Huxley was conversant in the Judaeo-Christian and pagan classics, as well as the history of philosophy more generally. He observed that the ancient Eastern doctrines of karma provide a metaphysical basis congenial to the development of Darwin's theory of evolution by natural selection. Yet, it took Victorian England to produce Darwin. Moreover, Huxley equally realized that the West had spawned karmic-style metaphysics early in its own history – namely, atomism and scepticism. Yet, neither encouraged substantial empirical inquiry until the 17th century, when the likes of Galileo and Newton tried to render these views compatible with Biblical aims. Ironically, Huxley concluded, for humanity to make the most of Darwin's theory, it may have been necessary for at least a couple of centuries of sustained empirical inquiry to have passed, informed by the sort of anthropocentric world-view encouraged by the Bible. For without a proven track record of human achievements in science and engineering, law and medicine, Darwin's very persuasive case that blind natural processes could have produced the appearance of cosmic design would have been dispiriting – as it probably was whenever such a case had been raised in the past. In this respect, monotheism appears to have endowed humanity with sufficient confidence, if not arrogance, in the meaningfulness of life to be immunized against the potentially disempowering implications of Darwinism. For Huxley, unlike, say, Spencer or Peter Singer today, this immunity is the source of our uniquely 'human' ethical sensibility.

Huxley's lessons are profound. The emergence and spread of Darwinism is itself just as historically contingent as Darwinism says life is. The normative question, then, concerns the frame of mind for regarding this fact: Should we position ourselves as agents or recipients of this dual contingency? Huxley's answer was clear: *agents*. Unfortunately, Huxley did not anticipate the strength of prejudice that favoured treating the two levels of contingency differently, itself a reflection of human reluctance to take collective responsibility for decisions that in the past would have been delegated to God. (Christians would see this cowardice as the residual taint of Original Sin, a view that would not have endeared Huxley to his secular audience.) To put the matter bluntly: if – as Darwin says – it is normal for species to produce more offspring than is ecologically sustainable, why should medicine be so fixated on keeping people alive as long as possible? Aren't we simply creating more problems for those already alive and crowding out the lives of those yet to come? Wouldn't it be more rational simply to think of medicine in terms of facilitating the transition between states of being – 'from welfare to farewell', as the political theorist Steven Lukes (1996) put it when satirizing the dystopian society of 'Utilitaria'? We live in times inclined to succumb to the doubts expressed in these questions, what I called at the start of this book, the *casualization of the human condition*. It marks a resurgence of the karmic sensibility that Huxley tried to counteract.

The most sociologically striking feature of the karmic sensibility's re-absorption of the human into the natural is the strengthening of the distinction between the normal and the deviant or pathological, at the same time it dissolves distinctions among forms of life. Most obviously, this implies a symmetrical treatment of health and illness across species. Richard Dawkins puts the point with characteristic vividness:

> People who cheerfully eat cows object violently to abortion. Not even the most vehement 'pro-lifer' would claim that a human foetus feels pain, or distress, or fear, more than an adult cow. The double standard, therefore, stems from an absolutist regard for the humanity of the foetus. Even if we don't eat chimpanzees (and they are eaten in Africa, as bushmeat) we do treat them in otherwise inhuman ways. We incarcerate them for life without trial (in zoos). If they become surplus to requirements, or grow old and miserable, we call the vet to put them down. I am not objecting to these practices, simply calling attention to the double standard. Much as I'd like the vet to put me down when I'm past it, he'd be tried for murder because I'm human. (Dawkins, 2001)

Examined a bit more closely, the normal–deviant binary is recast in markedly aristocratic terms as 'the best versus the rest'. In other words, an enforcement of equality *across* species requires greater discrimination *within* species. This, in turn, justifies a relatively permissive attitude toward the termination of human and proto-human lives, as well as the high value placed on non-humans who seem to excel in qualities normally associated with humans, such as intelligence, sentience or sheer 'loveability'. In this much at least, the Nazis and Singer are in agreement. What differs, of course, is the political means at their disposal for realizing their ideas.

A series of ontological conversions are at work in the karmic worldview by which nature's plenitude is encompassed as a closed ecological system. It is as if nature as a whole were itself treated as one species, with all former species respecified as nature's constituent organisms. What had been previously regarded as individual organisms would now appear as more or less functioning parts of this new superorganism called 'Nature', with some deviant individuals – say, a surplus population of humans living in economic or ecological squalor – acquiring the status of parasites or cancers. If this seems far-fetched, it is worth recalling that legal arguments for granting constitutional rights to animals typically presuppose that all humans already enjoy equal protection under the law unless they have been specifically excluded for legal or medical reasons (Wise, 1999). It is interesting to consider what 'all' might mean here, given the obvious fact that many humans beyond those formally excepted remain excluded from such protection. Not surprisingly, in opposing the formal recognition of animal rights, Germany's Christian Democratic Party has reasonably argued that the efforts to ensure such rights would deflect attention from the injustices that persist among classes of humans (Connolly, 2002). No doubt many animal rights activists believe that the persistent failure to enforce human rights might itself provide indirect evidence of the unsustainability of the current human population.

Postmodernists should recognize that I am also telling their story, since Michel Foucault's distinctive 'archaeological' method was acquired from Georges Canguilhem (1989), his teacher in the history and philosophy of science at the École Normale Superieure. Canguilhem spent his career deconstructing the *normative* basis of the normal–pathological binary in the biomedical sciences promoted by positivists like Comte and Bernard. What distressed Canguilhem most was the impulse – also found in Durkheim – to treat cases or individuals that strayed from statistically tolerable levels of deviance as *corrigible*. In other words, 'pathology' was always conceived as something that through scientifically informed legal or medical mediation could be rendered 'normal' in the sense of 'normatively acceptable' (Hirst, 1975).

Canguilhem rightly saw that this sensibility, which has licensed practices ranging from invasive surgery to radical therapy, was incapable of seeing statistics as anything other than a measure of our ignorance of the means required to realize our ends – where 'our' refers to those with the power to speak for 'us'. He responded by adopting a strong realist view toward stochastic processes. He read statistical uncertainty as representing real indeterminacy. Thus, he had an indiscriminate respect for spontaneously generated expressions of life without any special concern for the class of life normatively defined as 'human'. It is as if Canguilhem longed for Aristotle's original sense of 'distributive justice', which amounted to a recognition and respect for individual differences as a natural fact without further need for intervention, let alone *re*-distribution (Fleischacker, 2004: 19–20). Sometimes this turn in Canguilhem's thought is characterized as 'existentialist' or 'libertarian'. However, it would be more accurate to call it by its 19th century name, recently resurrected in the writings of Gilles Deleuze and other neo-Bergsonians, which divests the sensibility from any vestiges of humanism. That name is *vitalism*. One simply recognizes what one is simply because that is what it is. Here then lies the metaphysical basis for the ongoing battle for the soul of the left between the politics of identity and welfare (Fraser, 1997).

Redressing the balance in favour of the anthropic perspective means breathing new life into the idea of a distinctly *human* progress. But this will require taking the closeness of humans to God more seriously than vitalists have been prepared to do. Monotheists have been protective of the sanctity of human life, and hence have traditionally opposed suicide, euthanasia, and abortion, while their secular descendants in biomedicine have struggled to delay the moment of death as long as possible. Notice that both of these affirmative stances toward the human condition are primarily focused on the value of individual lives in their lifetimes. Yet, part of the privilege of being human is that we can take risks *voluntarily* on behalf of future generations. This may involve either heroic feats of self-sacrifice or rather more calculated investments in speculative financial ventures – neither of which always have salutary consequences. But in the wake of Nazism's coercive experimentation on humans, we have become reluctant to include participation as subjects in scientific research as part of this life-enhancing risk-taking. Instead, we prefer to rely as much as possible on animal-based experiments, as if either humans were the only species afraid to die or animals should be regarded as mere means to human ends. This is bad both ethically and epistemologically (La Follette and Shanks, 1997).

Of course, human health care has benefited from research that presupposes significant genetic overlap between humans and other animals. However, an overestimation of this point, combined with an excessively short term, risk averse sensibility, is equally responsible for the medical disasters associated with, on the one hand, the widespread use of chemotherapy and thalidomide and, on the other, the delay in recognizing the link between smoking and lung cancer (Greek and Greek, 2002). So far the case against animal-based research has been mostly presented from the side of the incarcerated animals rather than the humans who are treated on the basis of the animal results. My concrete suggestion along these lines is that we should come to regard participation in scientific research – as either investigators or subjects – with the sense of civic duty traditionally associated with jury service, voting, and military service. In all these cases, humans organize themselves for a fixed period, sometimes at personal risk, in order to affirm their joint commitment to a collective project.

My proposal may be regarded as an updated version of William James's 1906 speech, 'The Moral Equivalent of War', which called for a wide-ranging programme of national service for Americans, elements of which eventually made their way to FDR's New Deal and LBJ's Great Society programmes in the middle third of the 20th century. James believed that humanity's oldest means of collectively resisting threats to its social existence – warfare – may become obsolete in a 20th century overtaken by the peaceful pursuit of self-interest through free trade. In an obvious sense, James's recommendation turned out to be just as premature as Fukuyama's (1992) post-Cold War concerns about the fate of 'the last man' at 'the end of history'. Nevertheless, the spirit of such proposals is worth taking seriously. Typically the proposals are pitched at the level of the nation-state. However, I mean here to rekindle the positivist ideal of humanity as itself a collective project that cannot be realized by single individuals, or even single nation-states, but only together in opposition to a common foe, be it defined as ignorance or infirmity.

The failure of modern politics, epitomized by the Nazi jurisprudence of Carl Schmitt (1996), has been its continued stigmatization of fellow humans as 'the enemy' against which the republic is then constituted and legitimated. Consequently, the quest for universals in human knowledge and morals has been seen as orthogonal to – if not completely removed from – the particular divisions that seem necessary for political life. The ascendancy of the karmic sensibility in the new century threatens to exacerbate this tendency, only now with groups of humans and non-humans mobilized against other groups of humans and non-humans in the name of 'political ecology' (Whiteside, 2002; Latour, 2004). However, there is historic precedent for reversing this prospect, namely, the perpetuation of institutions whose self-defined and self-organized projects transcend biological patterns of reproduction (for example, the claims of family inheritance), resulting in a regular redistribution of wealth and power in society at large, with the aim of ever expanding and renewing the horizons of humanity. In Roman law, such institutions were called *universitates* (Fuller, 2003b).

TWELVE

Understanding the Fundamentalist Backlash against Secularism

Modern science imperils much less *the divine* than *the human*. Empirically speaking, nations traditionally dominated by karmic religious cultures are producing an increasing proportion of the world's scientific knowledge. This is a by-product of a growing middle class in places like India and China, who have aspirations to be players on the world's scientific stage. The significance of this fact should not be underestimated. Perhaps the most resilient vestige of Eurocentrism is the presumption that one must reproduce European cultural history – especially its modern science-religion conflicts – to become truly scientific. This is to commit the genetic fallacy, which consists of confusing what philosophers of science call the 'context of discovery' with the 'context of justification'. That Europe was the origin of the theory of evolution by natural selection does not imply that Europe (let alone, America) has provided the most hospitable environment for its reception. Indeed, the Far East much more quickly accepted evolution than socialism, as Herbert Spencer predated Karl Marx in Chinese and Japanese translation by several years. (See Fuller, 1997, Chapter 6, on Japan's 'defensive modernization'.)

However, Westerners sometimes mistakenly interpret the relatively easy acceptance of Darwinism in the Far East as evidence for the universal truth of evolution. This is to look at matters the wrong way round. It is far more likely that the monotheistic privileging of humans over other life forms has impeded the acceptance of Darwinism *at home*, since religions upholding the plurality of nature and the fundamental equality of life forms should find – and have found – Darwinism metaphysically quite congenial. There is a general lesson here: claims to epistemic universalism are often little more than a superstitious response to a tortuous tale of legitimation. Specifically, someone whose work is at first dishonoured at home (admittedly a gross exaggeration in Darwin's case) may end up being honoured somewhere else, which then enables the work to be reabsorbed at home, but now in the guise of having been independently vindicated. The superstition here lies in the mystified notion of 'independence', which masks the fact that the work is subject to each reception-culture's normal evaluative procedure, the overall import of which is to lend a transcendent air of 'universality' to the work, simply because the evaluative standards vary across cultures (Fuller, 1996).

Aside from the growth of science in parts of the world detached from European cultural history, the future existence of humanity is threatened by two other sources that will be the focus of this chapter. The first is that scientists from nations traditionally dominated by anthropic religious cultures are becoming sceptical of their own ability to improve the human condition. This largely Western tendency has crept into orthodox scientific thinking much more than the catch-all term 'postmodernism' would suggest. It is marked by subtle turns toward a more karmic sensibility, including an acceptance of 'fate' as an irreducible feature of reality and a belief that the sheer abundance of humans – a.k.a. 'overpopulation' – poses a serious threat to the global ecology. The second and insidiously overarching tendency is the increasing susceptibility of the direction and application of scientific research to market forces. This serves to dissolve any unified sense of human welfare into a set of discrete exchanges between knowledge 'producers' and 'consumers'. This tendency represents the negative side of what I have called the *secularization of science* (Fuller, 1997: Chapter 4; Fuller, 2000a: Chapter 5).

Any discussion of secularization should always recall the historical specificity of European Christianity. I say this not to 'relativize' Christianity in the sense of limiting its historic significance, but rather to flag barriers to extending the Christian message to those not sharing its previous history. Secularization consisted of the formal separation of church and state (Martin, 1978). Because the churches could no longer count on the state to bolster their authority (or finances, for that matter), they had to engage in recruitment campaigns. This period is usually said to have begun with the Treaty of Westphalia in 1648, which ended the Thirty Years War between German Catholics and Protestants. It led to a form of proselytism known as 'evangelism', in which the representatives of many Christian denominations realized that they were competing against each other. This newly created market environment influenced the evangelists' arguments, which led them to stress the direct relevance of universal doctrines to their potential converts' lives in a way that had been unnecessary when religions enjoyed state monopolies. Later in this section, I shall delve into this much misunderstood re-specification of universalism.

The post-Cold War devolution of state support for science worldwide, most of all in the West, should be understood as an intensification of just this process of secularization. The idea of science as the state church of the modern world has received much rhetorical, philosophical, and institutional support, ever since the emergence of German Idealism and French Positivism in the early 19th century. Both aspired to replace the popular narrative of Christian salvation with that of scientific progress, be it redeemed by philosophy or physics. For the rest of the century, the European nation-states assumed and consolidated the educational responsibilities previously in the hands of the Christian clergy and delivered them to those secular surrogates for the old monks and priests: that is, researchers and experts, respectively. However, as these secular surrogates have become entangled in the forces of social and economic reproduction in the 20th century, their own authority has been met with charges of both compromised judgement and doctrinal error. Martin Luther would knowingly smile – were it not that this latest round of secularization has opened science to a decision-making environment in which choice of epistemic authority is significantly constrained by market forces, the metaphorical equivalent of jumping out of the frying pan and into the fire. The next two paragraphs provide a religious and an economic elaboration of this point.

The sequence of consolidating, corrupting, and reforming epistemic authority – first in the clergy and now in the scientific community – may be unique to Christianity among the great world religious traditions: a pagan Greek fixation on seasonal cycles married to an internalized persecution complex, in a word: *heresy* (Evans, 2003). Science has secularized this process as an endless generation of hypotheses and tests. The heresiological roots even extend to the excommunication of unrepentant deviants, who may nevertheless go on to found their own churches (a.k.a. 'disciplines'), all the while claiming allegiance to a conception of truth that covers themselves and their persecutors. While it is common for religions to condemn desecration and blasphemy, and some like Islam are deeply divided over the prospect of living a sacred life in a secular polity, Christianity stands out for its schizoid tendency to *both* encourage the profession of personal witness to God and persecute those whose witness significantly deviates from the community norm, regardless of the sincerity of the witness. Karl Popper's much vaunted 'method of conjectures and refutations', which is meant to epitomize all that is rational about modern science, updates this tendency by attenuating the epistemic status of the scientist's 'profession of faith'. Thus, a conjecture or a hypothesis is no longer to be seen as an unshakeable commitment but an entertaining thought, whose refutation would allow its entertainer a second chance (Fuller, 2003a: Chapters 10–11). All told, Christianity's preoccupation with heresy may help explain the West's unique ability to excel in *both* high levels of intellectual innovation and resistance to innovation, while the East displays simultaneously low levels of both.

From an economic standpoint, the increasing exposure of science to market forces has occurred at a time when all nations with relatively large GDPs – including highly populous ones that still have relatively low GDPs per capita – have developed scientific elites. Much of this is attributable to the capitalist mode of production expanding more rapidly than compensatory regimes of social welfare provision. This situation has made the global future of science more volatile than ever. And as the idea of a unitary path for the development of science loses its material basis in the state, so too does the idea's intuitive grip on the minds of intellectuals. The concept of postmodernism, which Jean-François Lyotard (1983) invented in a 1979 'report on the state of knowledge', was designed to highlight the diverse origins of the 20th century's key scientific innovations, which include such decidedly non-academic settings as war and commerce. Lyotard himself wanted to undermine the university's claim as the premier site of knowledge production, a goal that indirectly demystified the state's power to direct the overall course of knowledge – especially given Europe's traditionally nationalized university systems. Cynics with the benefit of hindsight might conclude that Lyotard provided financially overburdened states with just the excuse they needed to offload academic research activity to those willing and able to pay for it (Fuller, 1999).

In any case, Lyotard's report unintentionally issued a licence for the *customization* of knowledge to particular constituencies. In this context, it is important to draw a sharp distinction between two types of customization. On the one hand, everyone might be invited to convert to one's own religion in order to enjoy the benefits of science. This strategy updates the old evangelical model of competing universalisms. Most recently, it has spawned movements often called 'Creation Science' and 'Islamic Science'. On the other hand, the benefits of science may be restricted to those who meet some financial threshold, regardless of how the money was made and why the science is wanted. This new and profoundly relativistic reduction of knowledge to exchange relations appears in the emerging intellectual property regimes. Both versions of customized knowledge retain elements of universalism, but only the former remains faithful to the classic Enlightenment idea that knowledge is not truly universal until it is within everyone's reach, and hence functions as an instrument for diffusing, rather than concentrating, power. Given the religious basis for Creation Science and Islamic Science, their latter-day alignment with Enlightenment goals is ironic – to say the least – but not unfounded.

The frequently heard charge that Creation Science or Islamic Science is 'relativistic' should be dismissed as resting on a confusion of medium and message. The message remains as universalistic as ever, but the medium requires a personalized appeal. When religion is protected by the state, there is no need to appeal to personal justifications for belief. Religious instruction is simply mandated by the state educational authority. However, once state backing is removed, then 'the product cannot sell itself', as the marketing people say. This does not necessarily make the product any less worth buying (namely it does not diminish the universal status of a religion's knowledge claims), but it does increase the need to make explicit the reasons why particular people should make a purchase (namely how the religion's universal knowledge claims are to be realized in one's life). Western defenders of the scientific orthodoxy have become so accustomed to state monopolies on knowledge production that they often turn hostile to the audiences whose sympathies they now explicitly need to cultivate. The repeated rhetorical failures of evolutionary biologists in US public school forums provide a striking case in point (Fuller, 2002b).

Nevertheless, to those used to science policies based on state monopolies, there is something vaguely suspect about the evangelism associated with the promotion of Creation Science or Islamic Science. However, for purposes of comparison, it is worth noting the form that science evangelism has taken in the West since the end of the Cold War, as the locus of funding has shifted from physics to biology. Physics had reigned supreme as the state church of science by purporting to benefit everyone at once, say, in terms of military defence or renewable energy, both of which economists reasonably dub 'public goods' (Fuller, 2002a: Chapter 1.4). The benefits flowed from laws of nature so fundamental that it would cost more to exclude 'free riders' than to include everyone. However, with the era of the nuclear holocaust (hopefully) behind us, continued public support for secularized science must be increasingly justified in more instrumentally specific terms. Thus, the latest (2003–8) five-year plan of the UK's Biotechnology and Biological Sciences Research Council is entitled, 'Towards a More Predictive Biology'. The theme of this report is that basic research in biology has reached a critical mass, and now it is time to focus the field in delivering products that will assist in policy-making, healthcare, and environmental protection. To be sure, these products will benefit some more than others, but then that is suited to a science whose knowledge claims are statistically grounded and hence cannot guarantee returns on investment.

Moreover, by loosening their state science monopolies, Westerners have intensified secularization to a point that threatens to undermine any robust sense of the universality of scientific knowledge. This turn is epitomized in new regimes of intellectual property. As the race to map the human genome first brought to light, knowledge producers are being forced to compete against not only other public-spirited producers but also profit-oriented ones who promise consumer-friendly knowledge products in return for private ownership of the means of knowledge production. This disturbing situation was most clearly driven home in the recent settlement by transnational pharmaceutical companies to supply South Africa with drugs for the treatment of AIDS at discount prices, in exchange for South Africa not developing its own biomedical industries (Fuller, 2002a: Chapter 2.1). Widely reported as a victory for South Africa (home to 15% of the world's AIDS sufferers), nevertheless the settlement marked a blow to the idea of knowledge that is both applicable *and* available to everyone. The transnational companies have effectively driven a wedge between the ability to produce and consume knowledge, thereby converting universalism from a doctrine of emancipation to subordination.

This conversion pattern is all too familiar from economic history. The world-systems theorist Samir Amin (1991) has distinguished ancient from modern forms of imperialism in terms of the dominant power's impact on the local political economy. In the ancient empires of Rome and China, the dominant power taxed its subject-nations but left their local modes of production and social relations largely intact. In contrast, the modern empires emanating from Western Europe radically restructured, or 'rationalized', local economies to make them efficient producers of surplus value for continually shifting and expanding markets, resulting in what both the British liberal John Hobson and the socialist Lenin recognized as the emerging global division of labour. The analogous movement in the global knowledge economy is from a situation in which Western science, technology, and medicine coexisted – in harmony or tension – with local knowledges to one in which the Western forms either pre-empt or absorb local knowledges by the imposition of intellectual property regimes. The South African case exemplifies pre-emption, the epistemic equivalent of mercantilism. As we saw in Chapter 8, perhaps the most serious form of absorption, the epistemic equivalent of capitalism, is *bioprospecting*, or the alienation of genetic information for commercial purposes. Knowledge that a eugenicist can use to control the means of biological reproduction coincides with the knowledge a capitalist can use to control the means of economic production. Thus, bio-prospecting forges an unholy alliance of the most exploitative tendencies of planned and unplanned economies.

In the wake of the destruction of New York's World Trade Center on 11 September 2001, intellectual and political leaders are perhaps more scep-tical than ever that religious fundamentalism could be a reasoned response to anything. Nevertheless, a strand of *monotheistic* fundamentalist thought constitutes a worthy counterbalance to the specific deformation of secular-ized science previously described (cf. Armstrong, 2000). Given that specifi-cally Islamic fundamentalists have taken responsibility for the acts of terror against the secular world since '9/11', the focus on monotheistic religions adds relevance to my argument. (In contrast, so-called Hindu fundamental-ism is a specific political project that forges karmic religion and postmodern science in the crucible of Indian national identity: cf. Nanda, 2003.) My main point here is that the distinction between what might be called 'fun-damentalist' and 'liberal' responses to the contemporary scientific world order roughly tracks what in the previous chapter I called 'anthropic' and 'karmic' orientations to the science-and-religion duplex.

Without further elaboration of the analogy, the reader may be surprised that I associate fundamentalism with the anthropic perspective and liberal-ism with the karmic one. After all, do not fundamentalists resort to suicide bombing, while liberals have been, all things considered, exceptionally cau-tious about risking human life in retaliation? More generally, have not fun-damentalists opposed the extension of civil rights to women, persecuted people for pursuing deviant lifestyles, and arrested the development of science and technology – all of which have been championed in liberal soci-eties? The answer to these questions is, for the most part, yes. Nevertheless, I urge that the resurgence of fundamentalism be interpreted as a reminder to liberals of the long-term dangers of doing the right things for the wrong rea-sons, or perhaps simply forgetting the right reasons for doing the right things (cf. Fuller, 2001b, 2002c, which initiated the British sociological response to '9/11'). In this context, we need to explore the significance of two com-plementary terms currently in vogue: *Orientalism* and *Occidentalism*.

In post-colonial studies, 'Orientalism' signifies the West's pejorative construction of Islam (and sometimes the East more generally) in the modern period. The term is due to the late Edward Said (1978), a Palestinian Christian schooled in the UK and USA, whose academic speciality was that great novelist of the colonial imagination, Joseph Conrad. Like the field of the post-colonialism he spawned, Said's intellectual centre of gravity lay somewhere between the early Lukács and the early Foucault. His use of 'Orientalism' alludes to the field of 'Oriental Studies', which emerged in the late 18th century from European interest in Sanskrit as possibly the source of all European languages and gradually became the intellectual infrastructure of imperial administration in Asia. (The textual focus of Oriental Studies, reproduced in the work of Said and most of his followers, may be contrasted with the ethnographic basis of African Studies, from which anthropology emerged as a distinct social science in the early 20th century. The difference is a residue of the old 'civilizationist' perspective whereby one must 'resort' to fieldwork only when a society is incapable of providing its own official record. The last stronghold of this mentality was Western science, whose first ethnographies appeared only in the late 1970s.)

Said's original usage of 'Orientalism' was rather ambivalent, since the targets of Orientalism often unwittingly lived up to the Western stereotype. In this respect, Orientalism alerted a variety of European scholars and writers over the last 200 years of the decadence into which their own societies could easily fall if they did not follow the righteous path – in this case, of secular progress. After all, Islam and Christianity share the same roots, and indeed Muslims were largely responsible for preserving and consolidating the Greco-Roman intellectual heritage that enabled the Christian revival of learning in the High Middle Ages. However, whereas the Christian world carried forward this heritage into modernity, the Islamic world remained locked in a medieval dogmatism, squandering their initial material advantage over the West. To Europeans unsure about the changes undergone by their own societies through industrialization and secularization, the contemporaneous state of the Islamic world stood as a living reminder of what might have been their own fate, had they rejected modernity. Thus, the spectre of Orientalism bolstered Western resolve to push ahead with modernization.

This sense of the threat posed by Islam in the Orientalist imagination should be strongly distinguished from the popular 'clash of civilizations' thesis advanced in Huntington (1996), which in the post-Cold War era, positions Islam as the chief 'anti-democratic' civilization, whose growing numbers allegedly pose the biggest long-term threat to global stability. Huntington's big mistake is his failure to see the so-called Islamic threat as a projection of Euro-American fears about its own future. The more profound clash of civilizations likely to matter in the coming decades is, as I have argued, anthropic *versus* karmic – with Islam, like Christianity and its secular successors, firmly on the side of the anthropic. From this perspective, the struggles surrounding the caricatures of both Orientalism and Occidentalism are alternative anthropic demonizations of the karmic world-view. The more comprehensive clash between anthropic and karmic visions will occur less on battlefields than in trading zones, as states yield increasing control over their citizens to private agencies and individuals whose interests are unlikely to be aligned with the totality of humanity. This is the crucible in which bioliberalism is currently being forged, to which Occidentalism directly responds.

The term 'Occidentalism' was designed as the mirror image of Said's 'Orientalism' (Buruma and Margalit, 2004). Both terms capture a demonized stereotype of 'the other' by a party anxious to justify and extend its own sense of virtue. A sense of Occidentalism begins with the common ancestry of Islam and Christianity, but now focused on their shared conception of the unique relationship between the human and the divine. From that standpoint, the secularization of Christianity has been marked by an increasing indifference to the material differences between people. The West has thus lost sight of the anthropic vision Christianity originally shared with Islam. For example, the very idea of progress presupposes the existence of more advanced humans who show the way so that the rest of humanity might catch up. However, the progressive promise has often turned out to be empty because the maintenance of differences between people itself became the standard against which some people were judged to have succeeded, or are better than others.

Behind this relativization of standards is the idea that the advancement of humanity can be judged on *comparative* rather than *collective* terms: that is, the relative status of humans with respect to each other rather than the overall state of humanity with respect to common matters that threaten their survival. The doctrine of progress destroys the sense of a universal human community. Consequently, Western societies – as epitomized in the isolationist foreign policy normally pursued by the United States – are characterized by a profoundly asymmetrical perspective to humanity at the extremes: on the one hand, they are acutely sensitive to risking the lives of their own citizens in principled conflict; but on the other, they blithely ignore the regular non-violent termination of life that poverty produces elsewhere in the world. They would much rather minimize the suffering than maximize the welfare of humanity. As the Occidentalist sees it, this is empiricism and Epicureanism run amok: 'out of sight (or touch), out of mind'.

Occidentalism may be understood as a moralized version of classical scepticism's singular lesson to philosophy, namely, that the relentless pursuit of the means of reason can easily undermine the ends of reason, if the ends are not themselves regularly recalled as a second-order check on the means. Put more bluntly, mindless attempts at improving the efficiency of a practice can destroy the point of engaging in the practice. Thus, one must periodically return to 'fundamentals'. A very interesting analysis of this situation has been recently provided by the US psychiatrist George Ainslie, who argues that classic Western religious conceptions of *sin* amount to self-defeating behaviour that arises from either an ignorance or an unwillingness to engage in what economists call 'inter-temporal comparisons' – that is, the impact of short-term on long-term satisfaction. According to Ainslie (2001), it was in the hope of remedying this deficiency that the concept of *will* was invented. Contemporary fundamentalists may thus be seen as chastising liberals for a failure of will.

From a more scholarly standpoint, an Occidentalist could cite two features of Europe in the 17th and 18th centuries that are relevant to this point, which Marx had already recognized as a perverse application of Hegel's 'cunning of reason' in history (Adorno and Horkheimer, 1972). The first is the severing of feudal ties between lords and serfs, which produced a putatively free labour market. The second is the creation of academies whose independence of church control enabled free scientific inquiry. Both measures officially aimed to realize the full potential of humanity, but their unchecked pursuit turned out to be dehumanizing, indeed perhaps raising the West's tolerance for inhumanity. Thus, capitalism dissolved the concept of humanity into an ethic of individual responsibility, while scientism dissipated it into a species-indifferent respect for life. At the level of political economy, human value has been reduced to sheer labour-power, a material factor replaceable by technology. At the level of philosophy, humanity's unique species being has been reduced to marginal differences in genetic composition that encourage tradeoffs between the maintenance of particular humans and non-humans, depending on their capacity to live full lives of their own kind. Little surprise, then, as we first saw in Chapter 9, our own latter-day Herbert Spencer, Peter Singer (1999a), has recently synthesized both strands of this Enlightenment heritage in an explicitly post-Marxist call for a 'Darwinian Left'.

The preceding discussion of Occidentalism may be summarized in the following paradox: *Fundamentalists are intolerant of the indefinitely tolerant, while liberals are tolerant of the intolerable.* From that standpoint, the terrorists intellectually aligned with fundamentalism are best understood as having taken advantage of the liberal's 'value neutral' attitude toward education in science and technology to promote a specific normative agenda. After all, if one passes the relevant examinations and can pay the relevant fees, which Western institution of higher learning – barring explicit state interference – is nowadays likely to decline such a person admission, regardless of their political motives? In this respect, even Western efforts to contain the spread of terrorism by legal means stop short of examining why terrorists might resort to such extremes. The suspects are tried on the liberal relativist grounds of 'You will not be tolerated, unless you are tolerant'. While this policy may lead to easy convictions, or at least indefinite detainment (in the USA), the principle is itself an affront to the universalist sensibility that the terrorists believe the West itself founded but has now forgotten.

The policy of indefinite tolerance suggests that liberals have a superstitious attachment to their own history, since the promotion of tolerance from a mediating to an ultimate virtue emerged in medieval Christendom as an adaptive response to a political-economic situation more fragmented than in rival Islam, which was seen as the potential beneficiary of any internal dissent among the Christian lands. Indeed, legal notions of political autonomy – including the all-important category of *universitas* – emerged to make a virtue out of a necessity (Fuller, 1997: Chapter 5). Seen in world-historic terms, the intrinsic tolerance of differences and the suspension of the quest for ideological uniformity was always a 'quick fix' that happens to have lasted – with the notable hiatus of the 16th and 17th century European religious wars – for nearly a thousand years (Seabright, 2004). However, the current wave of Islamic fundamentalism is hardly the first acknowledgement of liberalism's culture of 'repressive tolerance'. The Jewish tradition in modern social science – including Marx, Simmel, Freud and later Norbert Elias, Claude Lévi-Strauss and Erving Goffman – has keenly documented the debasement of Christian charity to first chivalry, then courtesy and now 'civility', the species of hypocrisy that results from a refusal to either encourage or recognize difference – not so as to promote a project of universal humanity, but simply to prevent the outbreak of total war (Cuddihy, 1974).

Westerners who find the Islamic fundamentalist response to the current world order objectionable tend to misread its anti-establishmentarian posture as 'other worldly', perhaps because fundamentalists often appropriate practices from a bygone, putatively purer era (Armstrong, 2000). That this view is mistaken became clear from the reaction of Christian fundamentalists in the USA in the hours immediately following the destruction of the World Trade Center. Several evangelical preachers who would otherwise not be associated with radical domestic politics, including Jerry Falwell, interpreted the disaster as a sign of divine disapproval for secular America's self-absorption. But more to the point, the writings of Muhammad Iqbal (1964) and Sayyid Qutb (1990) – the Pakistani and Egyptian heroes of the modern pan-Islamic movement – position Islamic fundamentalists as the natural successors of Trotskyites, still eager to have the secularized monotheistic promise of the Enlightenment fully redeemed, but reaching back beyond Karl Marx to the Qur'an (Horowitz, 2004). A kindred Christian spirit is to found in the 'liberation theology' of Roman Catholic Latin America, which converts Biblical talk of a 'salvation' passively bestowed by God into an active political campaign of universal human entitlement to the means of production (Gutiérrez, 1990).

Fundamentalists set a society's moral benchmark by its treatment of the weak, poor, and infirm. It is here that humanity's connection to God is most sorely tested, as the divine is manifested in its least outwardly attractive and most socially burdensome human form. To be sure, it is here that fundamentalists come closest to the intentions of the original liberal reformers who as children of the Enlightenment called for the political and economic enfranchisement of traditionally disadvantaged social groups. In principle at least, fundamentalists and liberals are agreed in condemning the wastage of human life in the name of sectarian self-advancement. However, liberal societies have usually ended up enhancing the political and economic well-being of their members for reasons unrelated to these original noble sentiments of greater inclusiveness. For every violent overthrow of an *ancien regime* in the name of democracy, there have been ten cases in which the dominant class simply came to realize that it was in their interest to open up the labour market, appeal to more consumers, replenish the pool of future leaders, or simply keep the peace. This strategic concession then set the stage for what by the dawn of the 20th century Georges Sorel had already recognized as the 'fallacy of optimism', which via Robert Michels has come to be seen as the 'co-optation' of the vanguard into the new establishment – long before the project of humanity had reached completion.

Moreover, contemporary Western defences of science tend to shore up liberalism's social complacency. They have a disturbing tendency of dialectically pre-empting the idea that things could be other than they are. It is not that philosophers and sociologists deny that things may improve, but improvement comes only at science's own natural pace, not from a recognition that, say, recent scientific developments have been for the worse. The result is that a superstitious 'trickle-down' science policy governs the relationship between basic and applied research (Fuller, 2000b: Chapter 5). For example, the past quarter-century has been given to fashionable, self-avowed 'realist' philosophical arguments, which follow Hilary Putnam (1975) in claiming that the 'success' of science would be a miracle, were it not getting closer to the truth. Here we might marvel at the enormous questions begged here. What success? What science? What truth? Nevertheless, sociologists have similarly followed Robert Merton (1977) in holding that a principle of 'cumulative advantage' governs scientific achievement, whereby graduates of the best universities tend to make the most substantial contributions, which in turn vindicates their having received the best training. Both Putnam and Merton suggest that access to ultimate reality is tracked by the accumulation of capital, be it defined in strictly economic or more broadly cultural terms.

Thus, we witness a massive shift in the burden of proof to potential critics, as epitomized in the following rhetorical question. Why *would* such a large amount of human and material resources be bound up in the conduct of, say, molecular biology, and why *would* the results of its research have such considerable impact, were it not that molecular biology provides reliable knowledge of the nature of life? Of course, there may be a more direct, and less mystified, connection between massive investment and massive impact than the question suggests – and that the appeal to 'reliable knowledge' as a mediating explanation functions as a self-serving 'god of the gaps'. That is, *any* research programme with a large enough share of the available resources at its disposal might display the same features, left to its own devices in a relatively friendly socio-political environment. In that case, the special epistemic (or spiritual) status retrospectively attributed to research programmes lucky enough to have been given such treatment is mere superstition. Unfortunately, the burden of proof is loaded so that one is made to feel like an ignoramus for even entertaining such contrary thoughts.

From a theological standpoint, the philosophical and sociological defences of science outlined above look like secularized versions of Providence. According to the Anglo-Christian theologian, John Milbank (1990), this is no accident. Milbank regards the emergence of a 'scientific' approach to human affairs as not only the secular displacement of Christian theology, but also the vindication of a particular theological perspective. (Milbank complains only about the former not the latter development.) In most general terms, it marks a decisive shift in Western culture from a focus on *humanity's self-formation* to the *historical formation of humanity*. In the former state, humanity appeases and perhaps even realizes God through good works. Original Sin is reduced to humanity's mirroring of the Creator's own fundamental incompleteness, both of whom are then jointly realized in Creation. In the latter state, humanity is born radically alienated from God, whose perfection contrasts sharply with the radical imperfection that is Original Sin. The extent of our reconciliation to God can only be assessed indirectly, as we act in ways that may eventually be seen as having met with divine approval. In the annals of heresiology, this transition marks the ultimate triumph of St Augustine over his contemporary, Pelagius, the English lawyer who notoriously argued that good works alone were sufficient for salvation (Passmore, 1970: Chapter 5).

Thus, Augustinian doctrines of Grace, Providence, and The Elect metamorphosed into such explanatory staples of the social sciences as the invisible hand, the cunning of reason, and natural selection. Presupposed in each case is significant slippage between intention and consequence, in the midst of which, in more religious times, God had moved in characteristically mysterious (or, in Reinhold Niebuhr's sense, 'ironic') ways. However, common to the religious and secular versions of Augustinianism is the view that individuals should be interpreted as instruments of larger forces – be they theological or sociological – beyond their own or anyone else's control. In that case, divine reconciliation may imply coming to understand one's own fate in the larger scheme of things, that is, to cope with what is ultimately irreversible. Thus, intervention is replaced by contemplation: political action by a depoliticized conception of social science that increasingly verges on subsuming humanity under a karmic pan-naturalism. Nowhere is this trajectory more evident than in the modern history of international development policy.

THIRTEEN

Karma Secularized

The Darwinian Turn in Development Policy

Thanks to Max Weber, the route from Christendom to the Protestant Reformation to the rise of capitalism is now a generally accepted feature of modern European cultural history. In *The Protestant Ethic and the Spirit of Capitalism* (1905), Weber famously argued that the defining principle of capitalism is not rapacious self-interest but the endless pursuit of wealth in order to sublimate one's anxieties about salvation by a fundamentally inscrutable deity. This productive asceticism explains the capitalist's preference for long-term investment over short-term consumption. Indeed, such latter-day devotees of the idea as Friedrich von Hayek and Robert Nozick continued to believe fervidly to the very end of the 20th century that this sensibility would inevitably trickle down to benefit all of humanity. Moreover, had the 'captains of industry' of the past two centuries managed to produce wealth in a way that improved the living conditions of *all* human beings, even at the cost of a greater degradation to the rest of nature, they too would now be treated as many of them wished, namely, secular vehicles of Christ's message. At the very least, they would have met with the approval of Karl Marx (Grundmann, 1991: Chapter 5). Unfortunately, the great capitalists failed to improve the lot of *both* human and natural kind. Consequently, it is easy to forget that these are separate goals that may cut against each other, in which case some hard choices must be made. These choices have been only made harder over the past two centuries, as science – like capitalism – has moved increasingly away from its original monotheistic moorings. The history of human population policy provides a convenient entry point into this topic.

Policymakers first became preoccupied with human population just over 200 years ago, as birth rates started to outpace mortality rates in the West. The trend testified to improved living conditions, but in the absence of any clear plans about what to do with the extra people. At the time this was seen as much an opportunity as a problem. Opinion divided along Christian theological lines. For optimists stood the French Catholic aristocrat Marquis de Condorcet, for the pessimists the English Protestant minister Thomas Malthus.

According to Condorcet, the demographic upturn meant that humanity could finally complete the Biblical mission of exercising dominion over the earth, as the extra population inspired extra ingenuity, along the lines of 'necessity is the mother of invention'. Once population reached a critical mass, the value added by collectivizing effort and redistributing benefits would become evident in a way it had never been before. In this context, the state would first play a proactive, even coercive, role that went beyond the simple protection of individual liberties. But as successive generations of citizens were educated in the project of humanity, such that they spontaneously aspired to the collective interest, the state would gradually wither away. The project of humanity so emblematic of the history of the social sciences emerged from this sensibility.

However, from Malthus' point-of-view, the excess population was a perturbation to be redressed by what inspired Spencer to call the 'survival of the fittest' and Darwin, more broadly, 'natural selection'. Malthus envisaged that the earth has its own sense of equilibrium to which it always eventually returns that keeps population in balance with natural resources. Spencer and Darwin managed to inject a bit of progressivism into this steady state picture by arguing that the surplus population generates a competitive market that tends to favour – that is, enable the reproduction of – those who flourish in an environment that is continually remade by its inhabitants. In practice, these so-called 'fit' creatures are those a given generation would regard as healthiest and most intelligent, and hence in least need of social assistance (Harris, 1968: 121–7).

Until the late 1960s, Condorcet's optimism inspired international development policy. The idea was to grow societies and redistribute their fruits. Malthus-inspired worries about overpopulation were associated with either an active or a passive policy of eugenics, as they typically centred on one type of people (for example, the Slavs) proliferating at the expense of a more favoured type (for example, the Germans). The invidious politics behind such judgements were transparent. The retreat from Condorcet to Malthus came in a one-two punch delivered in 1968. First was Garrett

Hardin's notorious *Science* article, 'The tragedy of the commons', which updated the Malthusian scenario by suggesting that overseas aid had merely delayed the restoration of equilibrium, the only difference now being that the planet would now be left a much resource poorer place once the human excess is finally removed (Hardin, 1968). The second punch was dealt by Paul Ehrlich (1968) in his bestseller, *The Population Bomb*, which coined the expression 'population explosion'. Whereas Hardin the ecologist was content to follow Malthus' original advice and let the invisible hand of death make the earth whole again through the withdrawal of overseas aid, Ehrlich the geneticist advocated a more proactive policy of mass contraception and even sterilization in 'overpopulated' parts of the world, typically Third World nations.

The early 1970s marked a change in mood more favourable to Malthus. It amounted to a pincer attack on the promise of welfarist and socialist regimes, which were subject to diminishing returns on public investment, resulting in greater fiscal burdens. From the high-tech end came the Club of Rome's 1972 scenario-mongering *The Limits to Growth*. From the low-tech end came, the following year, E.F. Schumacher's manifesto of Buddhist economics, *Small is Beautiful*. The two sides gained support with the Arab oil boycott following the 1973 Arab-Israeli war. By the end of the 1970s, developing countries remained politically unstable and economically backward. The gap between the rich and the poor nations – and the rich and the poor inside nations – was starting to widen again. All of this led to an increasingly pessimistic attitude toward the prospects for global development. Biologists started jostling with economists as the gurus of choice, and the field of development was widened to cover ecological stewardship. It became increasingly fashionable to speak of *all* humanity as a blight on the planet. Now both our productive and reproductive capacities had to be curtailed – the former targeting the first and second worlds, the latter the third world. The seepage of Neo-Malthusianism into mainstream development policy was exemplified by the reflections of long-time World Bank president, Robert McNamara, who included population control as part of a package for global prosperity that would otherwise have met with Condorcet's approval (McNamara, 1973).

To be sure, at the time, there were some intelligent attempts to reinvigorate Condorcet's vision within an ecological sensibility. Most notable among them was Barry Commoner's 'critical science', which diagnosed overpopulation and environmental degradation as by-products of persistent inequities in the world's economy, in which high birth rates functioned as insurance against high infant mortality rates in parts of the world where child labour was necessary to sustain families. Commoner retained a positivistic faith in science's ability to extend the carrying capacity of the planet with built environments and synthetic foods, as scientists organized themselves as an enlightened lobby to force politicians to address the larger economic problems. Here Commoner drew on his experience as an organizer and publicist for scientists against the proliferation of nuclear technology in the Cold War (Commoner, 1963). Ravetz (1971) remains the most articulated philosophical and sociological defence of this position, written by a founder of the British Society for Social Responsibility in Science.

The marginalization of the Condorcet vision in the 1970s is symbolized by Peter Singer's re-appropriation of the title of Commoner's most famous book for his own purposes. Whereas Commoner (1971) had spoken of the *closing circle* with respect to humanity's options for survival, Singer (1981) appealed to the *expanding circle*, which extended – or perhaps dissipated – the redistribution of wealth among humans to the redistribution of sentiment across species. What is striking about the recent history of development policy is not the belief that all species are created equal or that humanity is an expendable feature of the cosmos. These ideas have ancient pedigrees. But never before have they been so enthusiastically embraced by self-described political *progressives* in the West. Singer asks us to expand the moral circle to encompass all of nature without ever having properly closed the circle around humanity. Prophets of overpopulation who follow in Malthus' footsteps believe that we never will achieve the original aim, and so our best strategy is to diminish humanity's overall presence on the planet. This strategy of cutting losses simply uses science to mask a loss of political will, thereby turning Occidentalism from a myth to a reality that is rightly contested by both religious and secular peoples everywhere.

That the world includes much more than *Homo sapiens* need not add to the burden of world-weary policymakers. Taking on the entire planet may ironically lighten their load. Thus, ecological outcomes can be defined in terms like lowered carbon dioxide emissions (for example, the Kyoto Protocols) that are removed from politically sensitive zones of engagement, such as income per capita or life expectancy. A market that trades in pollution shares is politically more palatable than a super-state that explicitly redistributes national incomes. Policymakers may believe that ecological and human indicators are somehow connected, but the scientific ambiguities surrounding the connection offer much scope for 'creative implementation' that may end up trading off the interests of humans against those of other creatures or the environment more generally. Consider the 2002 Johannesburg Earth Summit, where agreement was reached on the need to provide the world's poor with clean water *but not water as such*. This seemingly strange result is comprehensible from a ruthless 'logic of capital': if the poor already have access to water, then cleaning it up is an efficient step toward enabling them to participate as workers and consumers. However, for drought-stricken regions, the provision of water would require substantial capital investment, the returns to which would take years to materialize. At the end of this chapter I shall say something similar about the rise of 'corporate environmentalism'.

Perhaps the most influential biologist in these Neo-Malthusian times has been the controversial father of sociobiology, Harvard ant scientist E.O. Wilson, who has been rehabilitated for the current generation as the father of 'biodiversity' (Wilson, 1992). Wilson's doctrine of biodiversity warns of an impending 'era of solitude' in which human beings will be the only species left, unless we change our ways. To be sure, from a strictly Darwinian viewpoint, biodiversity is a strange doctrine, since the regular extinction of species provided Darwin himself with the evidence he needed for natural selection at work. Is Wilson then trying to reverse the course of nature? On the contrary, Wilson wants to introduce a sense of justice into natural selection, which would provide each species an equal opportunity for survival. This is motivated by 'biophilia', an ethics based on the 90+% of genetic overlap among all life forms. The logical conclusion to Wilson's argument is that any anthropocentric development policy is bound to be short-sighted.

As a basis for development policy, biodiversity is remarkably presumptuous. Only some of the available ecological models claim that there has been a recent rise in species extinction rates, and none conclusively demonstrate that human activity has been responsible for any of these purported rises (Lomborg, 2001: Parts II and V). Wilson's most important assumption turns out to be that species will be eliminated as more people come to adopt the lifestyles of the wealthiest nations. Yet, given the recent failure of development policy to narrow the gap between the rich and the poor, it is very unlikely that this will happen in the foreseeable future. In that case, Wilson may be seen as providing a kind of 'sour grapes' explanation for why development policy should not have been so ambitious in the first place. This conclusion has been explicitly drawn by the British political theorist, John Gray (2002), who fancies the scaled-down expectations of the Eastern religions as an antidote to the anthropic hubris of the West's secularized monotheism. Thus, science succeeds by offering solace for failure in the past and diminished expectations in the future.

The karmic spirit runs deep in the Neo-Darwinian synthesis in evolutionary biology. It certainly helps to explain the knee-jerk Darwinian resistance to an idea that seems perfectly acceptable to most Americans, namely, that evolution itself may be a product of a divinely inspired 'intelligent design,' which humans are especially well-placed to fathom, complete, and/or master. But the Neo-Darwinians are not consistently karmic. Otherwise, they would be forced to conclude that their own theory is no more than a locally adaptive chance occurrence that rashly generalizes from an incomplete and unrepresentative fossil record to aeons of natural history. Indeed, this is precisely the critique of the explanatory value of evolutionary theory offered by the dissident 'cladists' who provide the taxonomy of species that evolutionists take as data (Gee, 2000).

As it turns out, Darwinians harbour an anthropic residue. The processes of evolution are conveniently divided, so that room is made for intelligent design, but only once *Homo sapiens* takes control of heretofore species-blind processes. In truly *homo ex machina* fashion, our scientific pursuits over the last 300 years have somehow managed to acquire an unprecedented sense of purpose and progress that has culminated in the Neo-Darwinian synthesis. In philosophical parlance, this position is known as 'convergent scientific realism'. But to those with historical memory, it is simply an updated version of 'perfectionist' natural theology – minus any explicit reference to God (Passmore, 1970). This was certainly the intention of Charles Sanders Peirce, the founder of American pragmatism (Laudan, 1981: Chapter 14).

Not surprisingly, this dualistic treatment of the role of design in nature has exposed Darwinians to embarrassment from, so to speak, 'above' and 'below'. From 'above', academic humanists are increasingly attracted to karmic accounts of the history of science that threaten to deconstruct the Neo-Darwinian double-think that would grant to scientifically inclined humans precisely the purposiveness denied to other life forms and nature as such (Latour, 1993). In this respect, a completely consistent Darwinian would adhere to an epistemology closer to postmodernists who would reduce all universal knowledge claims – including their own – to temporarily effective, self-serving narratives. From 'below', eco-warriors and animal liberationists actively campaign to return Darwin to the karmic fold by putting a halt to experimental genetics research and other displays of 'speciesist hubris' that would place the welfare of humans above that of other creatures. In popular science writing, the karmic roots of contemporary evolutionary biology are alloyed with misdirected rhetoric, which has fuelled the imaginations of readers while diverting them from the overall thrust of the authors' arguments. The authors I have in mind here – E.O. Wilson, Richard Dawkins, and Peter Singer – are listed in increasing order of commitment to the consequences of a karmic view of evolution.

I place Wilson at the low end because he is the popular evolutionist with the most explicit anthropic sensibilities. These may reflect his Baptist roots, which first inspired him to seek order in nature through the study of ant societies, a project that in the mid-1970s he christened 'sociobiology' (Wilson, 1975). Yet, despite having paid his dues to the Neo-Darwinian cause, Wilson was roundly condemned by fellow Darwinians when he tried to renovate the 'unity of science' ideal in his 1998 best-seller, *Consilience* (Wilson, 1998). The very word 'consilience' suffered from religious taint. It was coined by William Whewell, a mid-19th century Cambridge don who sought unity through a combined commitment to geology and holy orders. Today Whewell is mainly remembered (minus his religious interests) as a founder of the historical and philosophical study of science, though in his own day he was best known for championing the inclusion of the experimental sciences in the university curriculum as an aid to natural theology (Fuller, 2000b: Chapter 1). Indeed, he coined the word 'scientist' in English to underscore that contributors to universal systematic knowledge required formal accreditation – at a university like his own. However, Whewell also criticized Darwin's theory of evolution by natural selection for rendering the unity of the natural order more mysterious than ever. I shall return to this criticism – also lodged by John Stuart Mill – toward the end of this chapter.

That Wilson does not share Whewell's doubts about Darwin has not stopped him from carrying some of Whewell's conceptual baggage. This is best exemplified in the title of Wilson's Pulitzer Prize-winning book, *On Human Nature* (Wilson, 1978). The idea of human nature is an anachronism in Neo-Darwinian times. It harks back to Aristotle's doctrine of species essentialism, which historically has provided a strong basis for humans being raised (metaphysically) and raising themselves (morally) above the animals. To be sure, the Aristotelian doctrine has not died a quiet death. We need only consider Chomsky's and Habermas' continuing attempts to accord a privileged status to humans by virtue of our (allegedly) unique species capacity for language. True Darwinians find such appeals quaint but hopelessly outdated, since humans differ in degree, not kind, from other life forms. For them, it is only a matter of time before we discover that the communication systems of other creatures are just as syntactically regular and semantically rich as human language.

Here the history of research into human language sets an illuminating precedent, since it has been only over the past half century that all normal-brained human beings have been themselves accorded equal status as language users. In our post-Chomsky world, it is easy to forget that traditionally languages have been regarded as 'equals' only in the sense of being equally adequate to the environments in which they are regularly used, not equally complex or creative as cognitive instruments. In this respect, even a perspective as seemingly enlightened as the Sapir-Whorf Hypothesis of linguistic relativity implied that the capacity for thought is so tightly bound with the language normally spoken that one could explain people's differential capacities to understand, say, the cosmology underlying the Einsteinian universe in terms of the ease with which it can be articulated in one's native language (Fuller, 1988: Appendix B). The frisson created by this hypothesis was its suggestion that some non-European languages (such as Hopi) may be syntactically better equipped than European ones for articulating such recent conceptual innovations in science as Einstein's cosmology. But at most, this was an argument for the untapped capacity of particular languages to access particular aspects of reality, not for the capacity of all languages to access all of reality.

Making the empirical case for the equality of all human languages required going beyond Chomsky's own application of largely philosophical arguments to the standard grammars of European languages. The ultimate challenge was provided by so-called sub-standard dialects, examples of what the sociolinguist Basil Bernstein had called (originally in reference to British working class speech patterns) 'restricted codes' because of their seemingly limited expressive capacities. Generally speaking, the challenge was met by loosening the concept of syntax so as to incorporate what a more traditionally trained linguist like Chomsky might regard as elements of the environment in which language is used. Thus, attention to the mode and tempo of speech could be shown to provide an additional level of syntactic complexity that might otherwise go unnoticed. This enabled randomly distributed grammatical errors to be reinterpreted as the expression of systematically different norms. Crucial to this transformation in perspective was both a greater appreciation of the paradigmatic situations in which, say, Black American English – now renamed 'Ebonics' – is normally used and more general self-criticism by linguists who had traditionally isolated the cognitive from the social functions of language (Cole, 1996: Chapter 8).

This transformation in the protocols of linguistics research has gradually seeped into animal behaviour studies, especially primatology, leading to a radical reappraisal of the potential for animal communication. The views of a structural anthropologist like Claude Lévi-Strauss have been effectively turned on their head. Instead of regarding social structure as a projection of cognitive structure, it is increasingly common to regard cognitive structure as the internalization – or better still, 'simulation' – of social structure. Apes may be seen as engaging in complex logical operations as they are forced to anticipate the complex contingencies governing their fellow apes' behaviors (Byrne and Whiten, 1987). To be sure, apes still seem to lack the impulse to engage in *pedagogy*. In other words, the apes being simulated do not try to improve the efforts of the apes trying to simulate them – except in laboratory settings that fail to generalize to the native habitat (Premack and Premack, 1994). But this failure to generalize is familiar. It had been invoked by defenders of the Sapir-Whorf hypothesis to show that different human languages convey incommensurable world-views. Universalists observed, in response, that with great study and preferably greater social intercourse, people may come to bridge such differences, if not completely integrate them. Nowadays, carrying this observation to its logical conclusion, Neo-Darwinists shift the burden of proof to those who would *not* see this principle extended to bridge the gap between apes and humans.

More generally, if the Neo-Darwinian synthesis were truly to colonize the popular imagination, the highly charged debates that Wilson and other social and biological scientists have had over the role of 'nurture *versus* nature' in determining our humanity would disappear. Both Wilson and his opponents continue to presuppose the anthropic idea that there is something quite special to explain about human beings, over which a disciplinary turf war is worth fighting (Rose and Rose, 2000). Thus, should we look to genetics or sociology (or theology, for that matter) to explain our linguistic capacity? All sides agree that non-humans exert relatively little control over their fate, but humanity's cumulative achievements provide a *prima facie* case for the formative role of upbringing, experience, and will. However, were it shown that, in some sense, *all* species engage in communication, form societies, and perhaps even harbour spirituality, then the metaphysical point of adjudicating between 'nature' and 'nurture' would start to evaporate. Even the sociologists for whom Wilson normally has nothing but scorn have begun to take the hint. A section on 'Animals and Society' has been recently chartered by the American Sociological Association (Patterson, 2002).

Wilson's original entry into the Neo-Darwinian fold via natural history, rather than genetics may help to explain his anthropic residue, which tends to be stronger in evolutionists whose study of cross-species patterns is focused on behaviour rather than genes. An ant colony looks like an evolutionary prototype for a human society. However, the temptation to treat non-humans as inferior versions of humans weakens once organisms are regarded as simply a string of amino acids rather than individuals, however interdependent, clearly defined to the naked eye (Fuller, 1993: Chapter 3). After all, from a genetic standpoint, there is a 90+% overlap in the constitution of humans and all other animals – 97+% in the case of primates. If our understanding of biodiversity is grounded in these genetic facts, then it is easy to see how Darwinians would come to regard our 'uniqueness' a chimera born of our greater familiarity with humans vis-à-vis other life forms. A goal of biological science, then, would be to redress this imbalance in our knowledge, thereby dispelling the anthropic chimera, which in the karmic tradition would be an instance of *maya*, namely, the illusion of difference that instills feelings of superiority and inferiority, the source of all misery, according to the West's most profound karmic philosopher, Arthur Schopenhauer.

This brings us to the second major source of misdirection, Richard Dawkins, the Oxford zoologist who is perhaps Britain's most famous atheist. Rather than suffering from Wilson's need to sublimate an original religious impulse, Dawkins' problem is simply that he writes too well for his own good, thereby leaving the impression that Darwin is continuous with common sense. Starting with Dawkins (1976), his quarter-century campaigns on behalf of the 'selfish gene' and the 'gene's eye-view of the world' are usually read as overstretched metaphors that have left many readers with the impression that we are genetically programmed to be selfish. But the impression is false. Dawkins' message is much more karmic: individual organisms, including humans, are ultimately vehicles that genes construct to reproduce themselves. Thus, whatever we do – altruistic *or* selfish – is simply a by-product of these larger genetic machinations. The implicit cosmology here is closer to the great Hindu epic, the *Mahabharata*, than anything found in the Bible. In short, as I first remarked in Chapter 10, Dawkins' 'selfish gene' is meant to be taken *literally*.

However, it would be a mistake to lay all the blame for the misdirection caused by the selfish gene metaphor on Dawkins himself. Neo-Darwinian researchers have yet to fully come to grips with the karmic character of their own theory. For example, Dawkins' Oxford mentor, the late W.D. Hamilton, was preoccupied with the explanation of altruistic behaviour, which he regarded as an anomaly for the Neo-Darwinian synthesis (Segerstrale, 2000: Chapter 4). His solution – that altruism results from one organism enabling others of its kin to reproduce their common genes – is among the most elegant in modern theoretical biology. Nevertheless, Hamilton seemed to suppose that ordinary selfish behaviour is more easily explained by the Neo-Darwinian synthesis, when it is not. Strictly speaking, it is a matter of genetic indifference whether particular *organisms* are selfish or altruistic. If organisms were to act 'selfishly' in the sense that matters to their genetic masters, they would try to maximize the reproducibility of their genes in future generations. They would indeed turn themselves into pure gene machines, which – in light of the statistical nature of genetic transmission – would probably increase levels of sexual promiscuity, in the spirit of bet hedging. In the long term, this strategy would blur and ultimately erase kin and other sociologically salient distinctions relevant to the 'I' versus 'thou' and the 'us' versus 'them' mentality characteristic of human orientations to the self. As family lineages and group identities fade, the individual's sense of self would evaporate in classic Buddhist manner.

Of course, much of the original support for Darwin's *Origin of the Species* came from those who, like Herbert Spencer, read it as a naturalized version of Adam Smith's 'invisible hand' argument for the conversion of private vices into public virtue. Smith himself had justified the long-term survival of selfish behaviour in terms of the realization that one's own interests are best served by serving the interests of others. Spencer simply extended Smith's conception of self-interest to an interest in reproducing one's genetic material. But the dreams of eugenicists notwithstanding, nothing in the Neo-Darwinian synthesis suggests that these capitalist calculations are directly inscribed on the genetic code. This harsh reality had been recognized by one of Darwin's original German defenders, August Weismann, who engaged in a heated debate with Spencer in 1893–4 (Richards, 1987: 293–4).

Twenty years before Mendel's mathematical theory of inheritance was widely available, Weismann made a clean theoretical break between Darwin's selectionist and Lamarck's orthogenetic view of evolution, arguing that the 'germ plasm' (namely an organism's genetic potential) is impervious to purely somatic changes (namely 'inscriptions on the body', as anthropologists would say). As Mendel was incorporated into mainstream biology in the early 20th century, Darwin's followers began to differentiate sharply an organism's manifest ('phenotypic') and latent ('genotypic') traits, between which only statistical relations can obtain. Today even Dawkins admits that the most we can affect the course of evolution is by an 'extended phenotype' (a.k.a. culture) that alters the environment in which genes are naturally selected (Dawkins, 1982).

In effect, a parallel sub-universe was created – originally called 'genetics' and now 'genomics' – that is governed by a hand even less visible than Smith's. Long-term genetic survival is not merely a happy knock-on effect of locally advantageous behaviour. Rather, it is the result of factors, of which humans have only limited control and slightly less limited understanding. It is fine for Darwinians to say that rational agents aim to maximize the reproduction of their genes, but they have precious little to say about exactly how this is to be done, especially in relation to what agents would recognize as their self-interest. This sort of 'rationality' amounts to a throw of a dice whose loading can only be guessed. At best, one can play it safe and minimize the worst possible outcomes, say, by neutralizing genes for physical disabilities. This has led even some analytic philosophers to scale down their normative expectations of science's meliorative capacities (Kitcher, 2001). In any case, by the time we get to Dawkins' talk of selfish genes, we have left Adam Smith's defence of rational self-interest in the mists of our Enlightenment past.

We have already encountered the third source of misdirection in Peter Singer's recent attempt to launch a 'Darwinian Left' successor to Marxism, perhaps the most remarkable feat of karmic politics ever (Singer, 1999a). The Darwinian Left largely accepts people as they are but then tries to get them to do good by reinforcing (or 'selecting for') things they naturally do that also happen to benefit their fellows. Such a scaled-down vision of the Left has been traditionally the preserve of the Right: on the basis of pro-perties people have as individuals, the left's ultra-humanist ideals are either unrealizable in principle or already spontaneously realized. Hence the alter-native images of the right's policy horizons are governed by either the harsh hand of natural selection or the benevolent invisible hand of capitalism. Excluded from both alternatives is a constructive role for the products of politics and science – that is, law, medicine and technology – in raising the standard of human achievement by systematically altering the conditions in which humans live and preserving those alterations for the benefit of future generations.

This is not the first time a Darwinian Left has been proposed. Over 30 years ago, at the height of the Cold War, the radical behaviourist B.F. Skinner made just such an appeal in his controversial bestseller, *Beyond Freedom and Dignity*, itself a philosophical elaboration of the principles underlying his fantasy of social engineering, *Walden Two* (Skinner, 1971). Skinner, in his day certainly the most influential academic psychologist and perhaps the most explicit defender of Darwinism in social science, reminds us that Darwinism is a theory of two halves: genetic variation *and* environmental selection. As a good post-Second World War Darwinist, keen to avoid the excesses of Nazi and Soviet eugenics, Skinner 'black boxed' the composition of our brains and genes, assuming that humans differed only according to their 'reinforcement schedules'. Skinner hypothesized that selection pres-sures would outweigh any minor physical or genetic differences among members of a common species. Nevertheless, what in the third quarter century of the 20th century had been regarded as the quintessentially 'Darwinist' point-of-view is nowadays derided by evolutionary psychologists as the 'Standard Social Science Model', consigning Skinner to the ranks of Marxists and relativists, all of whom allegedly have shared a belief in the indefinite plasticity of people (Pinker, 2002: 20).

Even in his own time, Skinner caused concern by stressing the state's relatively easy access to the relevant covert technologies of behaviour modification. He had not discovered the rhetorically palatable term 'incentive' to describe what he was talking about. Consequently, many dismissed him as an aspiring totalitarian. Not surprisingly, at least one evolutionary psychologist has speculated that Skinner's rhetorical failure suggests that we are genetically predisposed to reject the idea that we are victims of manipulation (Pinker, 2002: 169). For his part, Skinner would probably have explained it in terms of the rewards that people living in democracies receive for responding with suspicion to forms of authority to which they have not consented. Moreover, Skinner would have been enough of a scientist to learn from the experience (and thereby display an admirable sense of reflexive consistency that would be loathsome in an evolutionary psychologist who holds that, to a considerable extent, we are programmed to believe as we do).

Here it is worth recalling an unsung virtue of Skinner's ill-fated attempt to align the selection side of Darwinism to social policy: namely, a fundamentally open-minded, albeit scientistically expressed, optimism about the prospects for substantially improving the human condition by rearranging our 'schedules of reinforcement', or what are nowadays called 'smart environments'. He tried to render transparent the contingencies that underwrite human behaviour. What so scandalized the *bien pensant* intellectuals of Skinner's day was not the mere thought that differential access to reinforcement schedules – or 'information asymmetries', as economists like to put it – was thoroughly embedded in the fabric of social life. Much more galling was Skinner's suggestion that we could and should do something about it. Perhaps, then, a deep reason why Skinner's vision failed to take hold was that he would have placed too much responsibility on society for determining the fates of its members, since strictly speaking everyone an individual encounters contributes to the 'environment' that selectively reinforces her behaviour. More comforting to cowards is a Darwinism that front-loads our capacity for action in a genetic potential over which its possessors exert only marginal control.

For his part, Singer knows all about incentives and the socially desirable states that would result from their use. His renovated Darwinian Left fits comfortably in a neo-liberal political environment, where a weakened state is happier to provide incentives to convert private vices into public virtue than to pave the road to hell with good intentions, as Skinner arguably would have had it do. This somewhat cynical characterization is not meant to deny the appropriateness of incentives as vehicles for promoting social welfare. But in the context of Singer's Darwinian Left, they become a 'natural baseline' of human behaviour, whose presence is given a 'deep' (namely genetically entrenched) explanation, which implies that successful legislation amounts to more-or-less clever adaptations to a largely uncontrollable situation. Moreover, Singer's Darwinian Left has a clear sense of where the baseline is, namely, patterns of behaviour that contribute, either positively or negatively, to reproductive fitness. Indeed, in exact opposition to Skinner, Singer treats behaviour as a mediated form of genetic expression.

As a scientific theory of life on earth, Darwinism addresses how species manage to survive as long as they do. However, as a political theory, Darwinism makes species survival the ultimate good, even if this means sacrificing or manipulating individual members of a given species, including our own. Thus, Singer notoriously – albeit consistently – advocates that healthy non-humans should be protected from experimental intervention, while costly medical treatment is withheld from unhealthy humans, especially at the extreme ends of the life cycle. Seen charitably, Singer's Darwinian politics amounts to a second-order application of classical liberalism's imperative that the good society is one where everyone enjoys the most freedom that is jointly realizable. But whereas liberals normally suppose that 'everyone' means every human being (or perhaps every citizen), Singer means every species. Thus, just as the classical liberal requires individual self-restraint in order to enable everyone to enjoy the same degree of freedom, Singer requires species-based restraint – including abortion, euthanasia, and birth control – so that enough members of each species can lead fulfilling lives.

In theory, Singer's Darwinian politics implicitly appeals to the doctrine of 'uniformitarianism', namely, that social policy should be constrained by the principles that are known to have governed nature in the past. Specifically, humans should not attempt to countermand these principles to extend their ecological advantage over other species. An obvious target of this proscription is the use of animals in experiments and treatments for the sole purpose of extending human life. In practice, Darwinian politics would return us to an earlier period in the history of medicine, when the physician's role was to facilitate, not obstruct, nature's course. This might include the withdrawal of treatment in order for the passage from life to death to occur by the path of least resistance. To be sure, the ethical sensibility informing such politics is broadly multicultural, with precedents in Epicureanism and Buddhism, both of which place an overriding value on minimizing individual suffering. However, I do not believe that this sensibility can serve as a springboard for resurrecting a distinctly *leftist* politics.

Singer takes as axiomatic several propositions that connect the ancient Epicurus with the first modern utilitarian, Jeremy Bentham: all sensations are created equal, and they afford either positive or negative utility to their bearer. The bearers experience these sensations as 'pleasure' and 'pain'. Moreover, the bearers themselves entitled to equal treatment as alternative forms assumed by the same fundamental matter. In this context, it is often forgotten just how close Bentham was to Singer's own position. For example, Bentham's quip that human rights are 'nonsense on stilts' was not merely a proto-positivist swipe at metaphysical justifications in politics but a concrete complaint about the role that inflated views of humanity had in the law's failure to recognize cruelty to animals. Bentham went as far as to ask in *Principles of Morals and Legislation* (1789): 'Why should the law refuse its protection to any sensitive being?'

The subsequent apostasy by Bentham's godson, John Stuart Mill, is a perfect example of how one person's 'sensitivity' constitutes another's 'coarseness'. Moral philosophers today generally presume that Mill's anthropic sensibility is an improvement over Bentham's karmic one, if not the final word on ethics. Here Singer may be credited with providing a Benthamite rejoinder to Mill's preference for a dissatisfied Socrates over a satisfied pig by ranking a fully functioning pig over a disabled Socrates (for example, the quadriplegic Stephen Hawking). Singer's answer to Mill is made all the more insidious by its supposed basis on a scientifically improved understanding of life.

When Singer is hailed as a pioneer in ethics, it is usually for his radical redefinition of the *summum bonum* in terms of the alleviation of cosmic suffering, as opposed to the specific improvement of human welfare. For Singer, an increased understanding of biology enables us to anticipate and eliminate potential sources of suffering without adding still more misery to the world. In pre-scientific times, the classic path of least resistance in this sense was suicide. Euthanasia and abortion were always more controversial because they necessarily involve the cooperation of others who may themselves suffer in the process. However, these objections began to lose some of their force, as moral and legal status came to be associated with 'rights' exclusive to individuals. Singer is very much part of that tradition, which tends to downplay the social distribution of pleasure and pain. Thus, Singer's paramount concern is that each individual, regardless of species membership and more specific group ties, be both protected from gratuitous suffering and relieved of any such suffering as efficiently as possible (Singer, 1994).

The advancement of biomedical science plays a curiously inconsistent role in Singer's world-view. It certainly helps reduce the difference in moral worth assigned to humans and other animals by raising our awareness of the levels of sentience and intelligence possessed by animals, not to mention the significant genetic overlap between them and us. However, these insights had been often gained by means that Singer and his fellow animal rights activists now condemn, namely, laboratory experiments that incarcerate animals long enough to inflict pain on them. The irony is compounded by the fact that Singer's high estimation of chimpanzees is heavily based on their sign language performance, even though sign language was itself originally developed to serve the needs of sensorily disabled humans who, if Singer had his way, would have been subject to prenatal termination (cf. Rée, 1999).

Under the circumstances, Singer might not be the biggest defender of extensive public funding for research designed to *overturn* current scientific assumptions, even though (or because?) he is happy to use those assumptions to ground his judgements. Certainly his followers are often of this disposition. Thus, an influential version of 'political correctness' in our times supports the abortion and euthanasia of humans, while at the same time opposing the production and distribution of biomedical technologies that might enhance human lives in ways that would complicate judgements of termination. The opposition to new biotechnologies is officially expressed in terms of possible environmental hazards and genetic monstrosities (as well as a background belief that the earth already houses too many humans to afford a sustainable environment for all life-forms). To be sure, these concerns have some basis in fact, but more tellingly they presuppose an unwillingness to embrace the human introduction of substantial novelty into the world. However, these same people would probably have no qualms about welcoming a recently mutated organism in which no human intervention is implicated.

In short, Singer is fortunate to be living now, for had he lived a century earlier, he would never have supported the research that gives his ethics its scientific veneer. Instead, he would have probably followed in Schopenhauer's footsteps. Singer shares Schopenhauer's pessimistic appraisal of humanity's capacity for moral growth: at our most intelligent, we cause the least pain. Not surprisingly, Schopenhauer was more impressed by the recent German translation of the *Upanishads* than by the directions being taken by 19th century biomedical research. This research, often appearing in the guise of 'positivism', presumed that humans are in a unique position to increase the world's overall good, not merely minimize its worst effects. Specifically, progress is characterized by our collective capacity to adapt to those humans who deviate significantly from physical and moral norms. Unlike Schopenhauer, and Singer after him, the positivists did not regard humanity as an abject condition, but a project in the making.

However, the continuity between positivism and the anthropic religious spirit is easily overlooked. In its day, and especially in the hands of its megalomaniacal founder, Auguste Comte, positivism promised a 'religion of humanity' that openly competed with the Roman Catholic Church (Wernick, 2001). This institutional challenge has left lasting scars, not least the lingering popular impression that science and religion are natural enemies. To be sure, Christians were rankled by positivism's blasphemous conflation of the divine and the human. Nevertheless, with the advantage afforded by hindsight, positivism might be now credited with having taken the anthropic character of Christianity with a seriousness that is lacking in the normative lessons drawn from Darwin by Peter Singer and his followers. Ironically, the great monotheistic religions and their modern secular foils are natural allies against Darwinism's more karmic tendencies.

Positivism extended a message common to Christianity, Judaism, and Islam: that the weakest and most despised of our kind are to be cherished and learned from, not simply eliminated as unfortunate freaks of nature (MacIntyre, 1999). Updating the theodicy of St Irenaeus, the leading early Patristic philosopher, positivists tended to regard these apparently negative turns in the human condition as occasions of, in Mill's words, 'constructive unhappiness' designed to spur humanity as a whole to a higher level of being. This sensibility informed a wide range of 19th century cultural innovations. In politics, it motivated Mill's liberal defence of minority dissent. In a rapidly democratizing political scene, the endangered 'freaks of nature' extended beyond physically challenged individuals who might be seen as a 'burden' on the able-bodied. They also included social and intellectual non-conformists who add friction to the smooth – and hence mindless – reproduction of the social order. Since only a swing in popular opinion potentially determines whether deviants are regarded as geniuses or 'enemies of the people', as Ibsen would say, they were all equally in need of special protection and cultivation.

In medicine, positivism was influential in focusing the physician's charge specifically on the preservation of human life, instead of the facilitation of 'nature's course', which had allowed a good bedside manner to slip into acts of euthanasia. Here the French tradition of clinical medicine from Xavier Bichat, who merited a prominent place in Comte's calendar of positivist saints, to Claude Bernard inspired a redefinition of death as the exhaustion of life, which may be forestalled through organized scientific resistance (Albury, 1993). Moreover, the positivist legacy lurks in Singer's own project of expanding the moral order to encompass all animals. 'Animal rights' are modelled on the extension of civil rights to groups who traditionally did not own property, especially women and workers. Here positivists championed alternative indicators of competence, which by the second half of the 19th century had led to the implementation of literacy tests and the development of sign language as means for enlarging the sphere of civil society (Rée, 1999).

Interestingly, positivists have always regarded Darwinism with ambivalence. They embraced the theory only insofar as it encouraged humans to improve their condition. Thus, positivists have been keen on projects of education, subsidization, rehabilitation – and, yes, behaviour modification and genetic manipulation. This multifacetedness was epitomized in the career of Karl Pearson, the founder of applied statistics and the first self-declared positivist to hold an academic chair in Britain. Moreover, positivists have been mindful of the lessons to be drawn from genetic mutations, the Darwinian basis for new varieties and even species of organisms. If it only takes the right environmental conditions for these improbable beings to reproduce themselves, then why cannot these conditions be humanly created and thereby potentially enhance the overall state of humanity? Modern biomedical research owes much to this sentiment.

What positivists found unacceptable in Darwinism was any karmic suggestion that organisms can do little to alter their fit to the environment – the very idea that we are born to our fate. Perhaps this shows that the positivists were beholden to an outdated view of evolution that owed more to the utopian biologist Lamarck than Darwin himself. Once again John Stuart Mill sets a perceptive precedent. Mill was among the critics of Darwin's *Origin of the Species* when it was first published in 1859. He faulted the book for overemphasizing the contingently diverse character of nature, about which humans can do very little but observe and adapt to its passage. As a liberal with strong welfarist tendencies, Mill was sensitive to *Origin*'s immediate adoption by defenders of *laissez-faire* social and economic policies, who could now boast that Nature itself demonstrated the futility of subsidizing those who persistently fail to survive by their own means. Let us recall that the intellectual lineage from Thomas Malthus to Charles Murray runs right through Charles Darwin.

But Mill's proposed philosophical antidote turned out, for most Christians of the day, to be just as bad as the disease it purported to cure (Sell, 1997). In the first place, Mill wanted to jettison the traditional distinction between 'nature' and 'artifice' that Darwin reinforced with a vengeance. For Mill, God and humans are both creative beings, and what is normally called 'nature' is simply the raw material of their joint creation. A unified world-view, the goal of modern science, does not aim to represent the original divine plan. Rather, according to Mill, it is the human completion of the project begun by God. Implied here was the idea that God is all good but not all powerful. Thus, what humans experience as ignorance and pain are ultimately invitations to bring God's work to fruition. They are most certainly *not* direct expressions of divine wishes or insurmountable barriers to human progress – two common meanings of 'nature' that Mill thought Darwinism would bolster.

As Comte's most sympathetic British reader, Mill was regarded by the Christians of his day as trying to implant the positivist religion of humanity on British soil. But now that positivism no longer poses a credible threat to Christianity, we might be better placed to appreciate what had attracted Mill to Comte's weakened deity. The virtue that Comte himself stressed was that his vision of God is not reducible to sheer power-worship. Here Comte meant to oppose the tendency of autocrats, both before and after the French Revolution, to justify their policies by appeals to divine omnipotence and omniscience. Today a similar sense of power-worship is most likely to flow from science, especially when our current scientific understanding is frozen into the metaphysical ground on which life and death judgements are made. Indeed, what both Comte and Mill would find most distressing in Singer's 'scientifically informed' preference for a healthy pig over a congenitally diseased human is its *finality*: Singer assumes such an elevated view of what we now know that we are effectively discouraged from finding out more – especially if it might eventuate in a reversal of current preferences.

The main problem is that the maximization of minimum suffering – Singer's version of a global utilitarian ethic – sets too low a standard for moral progress, one that is easily met by a society that is unwilling to adjust its members' normal patterns of behaviour to accommodate the existence of newcomers who are not well adapted to the society's default environments. Thus, arguments for abortion may mask a society's unwillingness to assume responsibility for raising a child who the parents do not want. (However, I suspect that the 'pro-life' opponents to abortion are equally disingenuous, since they rarely imagine that the aborted foetus might have been disabled, had it been brought to term.) Similar glosses explain the unspoken attractiveness of euthanasia and, at the most general level, birth control in third world countries. If the rest of humanity really had an interest in preserving the lives of these people (and proto-people), it would make room for them, even if it meant a major redistribution of wealth and power. The ease with which 'minimum suffering' is nowadays operationalized in terms of 'not living' presumes that making room for awkward others is more a personal and societal inconvenience than a spur to the political imagination. This sense of inconvenience may even be mutual on the part of the awkward others, especially the disabled who, as in France, may be permitted to sue their parents for abrogating their 'right not to be born' (Henley, 2002).

The careful reader familiar with the writings of Singer and other supporters of animal rights and a global ecological ethic will notice an ironic dimension to my argument. After all, do not Singer and his ilk make analogous pleas for humans to make room for the awkward others in the animal kingdom who cannot fend for themselves in the manner expected by able-bodied adult humans? Of course. Nevertheless, such irony should alert us to two issues:

First, the terms for expressing human sympathy with animals and the natural environment – for example, legal protection in the form of 'rights' and a liberalized view of self-expression – are modelled on historic movements to empower disabled and disadvantaged humans. For example, property ownership was traditionally required for suffrage because it clearly demonstrated social competence. The modern history of democracy has been about identifying alternative means for demonstrating the same thing, given the elite nature of property ownership. Something similar may be said about the democratization of criteria for what counts as 'rational' or 'intelligent' behaviour. Today one need not express these qualities in purely mathematical or even verbal terms: certain practical skills may count as well. Singer would simply liberalize these criteria a bit more to correspond to what we know – and continue to learn – about the mental life of animals. One shudders to think how Singer would have regarded the birth of blind and deaf humans before the invention of Braille, hearing aids and other techniques enabled these people to contribute creatively to modern society. Yet, it is unlikely that the Darwinian Left would be able to mount such an intuitively strong challenge to anthropocentrism today, had these humanistically inspired political and scientific precedents not occurred.

Secondly, even though their campaign for animal rights is modelled on human rights campaigns, Singer and other environmental activists presuppose a long-term tradeoff between extending the domains of human and non-human nature. But then what is the status of species that have become populous because of their utility for the human condition? There would probably be many fewer farm animals and pets today, if humans did not systematically cultivate them. Perhaps the lucky few would have led better lives, but equally without human intervention entire species might have become extinct. To be sure, these are speculative matters, about which reasonable people may disagree. Nevertheless, the intuitive plausibility of Singer's position relies on a clear view that animal husbandry and pet ownership have been systematically disadvantageous to the animals concerned because the animals are removed from their natural environments. By the same logic, one might argue that capitalism should not have happened at all because it forced the vast majority of people to alter radically their lives and habitats, with many suffering in the process. Of course, some environmentalists wish to pursue this analogy. Nevertheless, it would have been alien to Karl Marx, who regarded capitalism as having laid down the material conditions for socialism.

The above considerations lead me to propose a basic condition for any leftist political project: *that the empowerment of nature is not permitted to preempt the empowerment of humanity.* This injunction is not meant to deny the importance of animals or the natural environment. Normatively, it is meant to set clear policy priorities. Empirically, the injunction issues a reality check on our current place in political history. I fear that the Darwinian Left presumes that all of humanity already enjoys – or at least aspires to enjoy – the lifestyle of those people who live in the upper middle reaches of the developed world. In short, the Darwinian Left's moral compass is fixed on avoiding a dystopian future that presupposes that *Homo sapiens* is materially more advanced than it really is. Thus, instead of continuing to reduce the difference between the material conditions of the rich and the poor, the Darwinian Left would shift our policy focus to improving the lot of the planet's non-human inhabitants – even if this delays, if not derails, the completion of the left's original humanistic project.

My fears along these lines are based on the emergence of *corporate environmentalism*, whereby big business has come to realize that waste management, pollution prevention and animal conservation may combine with the usual exploitation of human labour to form an ideologically convenient policy of 'total quality environmental management' (Hoffman, 1997). Despite their reputation as inveterate risk-seekers, competing multinationals ever in search of new profits find it in their mutual interest to pool risks by maintaining stewardship over the natural resources from which they would like to benefit indefinitely. After all, just one disaster like the 1984 Union Carbide plant explosion in Bhopal, India, can jeopardize the future of an entire industry in a large region. However, the 'precautionary' measures taken by firms to prevent and contain ecological disasters rarely extend to issues of social equity such as increased life expectancy, quality of life and worker rights for the locals. Progress in these areas is harder to quantify and

FOURTEEN

Might we become Nazis in Paradise?

In the coming years, citizens will increasingly find themselves in conflict with their own states, as personal lifestyle and research choices run up against larger public interest issues. In these domestic clashes, the state – as informed and legitimated by the social sciences – may remain the last court of appeal for humanity 'as such' against the inconstancy of individuals and groups. In the preceding chapter, we saw that the idea of the state as the institutional vehicle for consolidating human dominion over nature lay behind Condorcet's historic alternative to Malthus, whereby the proliferation of humans stimulates the production of artifice to overcome the insufficiency of nature (Rothschild, 2001). A similarly optimistic view of population growth may be found not only among Condorcet's positivistic followers, but also Hegel and Marx, as well as such latter-day theologically inspired scientists as the Jesuit paleontologist Pierre Teilhard de Chardin, who discovered the skull of one the earliest hominids ('Peking Man'), and the Russian Orthodox geneticist Theodosius Dobzhansky, who helped to forge natural history and experimental genetics into today's Neo-Darwinian synthesis (Wagar, 1967: 72–82; Dobzhansky, 1967).

It is worth underscoring that karmic threats to the anthropic vision come from the heartland of science itself. Singer's attempt to peg animal rights to sentience and intelligence has yet to be generally seen as a threat to the value of human life only because our understanding of animals is sufficiently limited that cross-species attributions of feeling and thought remain relatively restricted. However, with advances in ethology, sociobiology and most recently evolutionary psychology, an increasing number of animals turn out to be increasingly sentient and intelligent. Moreover, this curious development cannot be explained simply in terms of wanton anthropomorphism. Two rather different things seem to be working in consort. First, animals are being studied more closely than in the past. This has involved both improved research methodology and an increased level of sympathy. But it is unclear that the two can be neatly separated: the former may be a self-reinforcing product of the latter (Crist, 1999). Secondly, our conceptions of sentience and intelligence have become more abstract, perhaps even alienated, as scientists develop more powerful computer models of sensory perception and problem-solving. Even when these models do not figure explicitly in biological research, their general presence has helped to attenuate the intuitive tendency to judge animals by anthropic standards.

Darwinians generally do not issue judgements on nature's normative trajectory, but when they venture into this traditional ground of natural theology, they speak against the anthropic vision. A natural entry point is E.O. Wilson's concept of biodiversity, mentioned earlier. Wilson follows the trail of population theorists from Malthus to Paul Ehrlich, who have assumed that a normatively desirable natural order is to be had by maximizing the range of species, even if it requires the curtailment of spontaneous reproductive tendencies (Schwartzman, 1995). In its extreme form, the underlying principle is that the life of any individual is never equal to that of an entire species, whatever the species. Informing this intuition is the spin given to what ecologists call 'Rapoport's Rule', according to which less biodiverse environments (typically temperate climates) tend to be inhabited by species, such as cockroaches and humans, which can also survive in many different environments, and hence have the potential to crowd out local species (Eldredge, 1998). In other words, in Nature's economy, there seems to be a tradeoff between the proliferation of individuals and species. The only remaining question, then, is just how much human intervention is needed – such as the enforced contraception, sterilization, or termination of individuals – for the right balance to be struck. Here Malthus and Ehrlich occupy, respectively, *laissez-faire* and *dirigiste* poles, with Wilson himself somewhere in the middle.

An exceptionally pessimistic version of this sensibility is Stephen Jay Gould's bestseller, *Wonderful Life* (Gould, 1989). Gould argues that the contemporary focus on biodiversity is too little too late. Gould takes the regulative ideal of Nature to involve the inclusion of the widest possible disparity in the basic blueprints for life, from which a diverse range of species may then be constructed. From that standpoint, the Cambrian Era best approximated this ideal. The last 500 million years has been marked by a steady decline, which has only accelerated with the introduction of *Homo sapiens*. Nevertheless, according to Gould, this decline is not merely ignored but often mistaken for genuine progress, as apparent 'direction' in nature is acquired by gradually narrowing Nature's capacity for self-expression. It is worth remarking that Gould clearly conceives of these blueprints in morphological rather than strictly genetic terms, since the 'disparity' he values is probably the product of marginal differences in DNA. Here Gould harks back to a normative sensibility whose natural home is pre-Darwinian but post-Christian, a secularized recognition that we live in a 'fallen' state of nature: say, natural history, circa 1750 to 1850. In this respect, Gould is more Cuvier the catastrophist than Lamarck the meliorist. But why should the human trajectory be judged in terms of Nature's overall expressive capacities? And even if this standard is appropriate, why cannot the human contribution be seen as providing a direction to Nature that it would otherwise lack?

The latter is precisely how positivists would read the situation. For Comte or Mill, God experiments by creating alternative life forms without knowing or controlling their fates. Progress, then, consists in the conversion of inter-species differences into intra-species ones as the plan comes to be realized. This is what economists call the 'internalization of externalities'. It is perhaps best understood as a crude account of the history of technology: humans note that the much differently designed birds have the desirable capacity to fly. Humans then proceed to reproduce that capacity in their own terms – via aviation technology – and thereafter regularly compete with, often eliminating, the birds in the skies. Moreover, recourse to aviation becomes a multi-purpose status marker amongst humans. In this example, the tradeoff between scientific progress as the vanguard of humanity and an intrinsic concern for the natural environment is very clear. In the positivist mind, a robust belief in the inheritance of acquired traits was joined to a Biblically inspired view of humanity as Nature's domesticator. Sometimes this perspective was even interpreted to mean that animals themselves could be turned into humans, as in the 'missing link' arguments made by the 18th century Scottish jurist Lord Monboddo, who held that with the right care and training orang-utans could become citizens (Ingold, 1994).

The surface absurdity of Monboddo's project should be judged against the policy implications associated with treating humans as just another part of the biological continuum. In his own day, Monboddo railed against the complacent racism (a.k.a. 'benign neglect') promoted by one of his law clerks, David Hume, who treated humanity's various habitats, however rich or poor, as 'natural' and hence best left undisturbed, which may imply (as we saw in Chapter 9) that historically slave-holding societies should be left in that state. As Darwinian natural selection forged tighter links with population genetics in the first half of the 20th century, species boundaries became so blurred that certain 'race scientists', following the lead of Ernst Haeckel, argued that given their ratio of achievement to potential, higher order apes and African humans may need to reverse positions in the evolutionary hierarchy (Proctor, 1988: Chapter 1). In sum, the removal of naturalized species distinctions opens the door to the normative transposition of individuals across what now appear to be merely conventional species markers.

This relativization of species categories against a naturalized monistic metaphysics has arresting political consequences. However, I should observe at the outset that not all of them bring us closer to Nazism. In particular, a version of Haeckel's argument is often used to counter claims that there is a statistically significant difference in the average intelligence of, say, Whites and Blacks or men and women. Lewontin (1972) famously demonstrated that the variation of test scores *among* members of a given race or gender is considerably wider than the difference *between* the average members of the races or genders. Here too the policy advice involves the normative transposition of individuals, but with consequences normally seen as politically progressive. Thus, instead of privileging men over women or Whites over Blacks *per se*, many members of the former group would be replaced by those of the latter in relevant posts. Of course, the key difference between the context of Haeckel's and Lewontin's arguments is that whereas Lewontin reasonably presumes a common standard (namely the same IQ test) in terms of which all individuals may be evaluated, Haeckel and his fellow race scientists never overcame the ultimate barrier to cross-species comparisons, namely, the need for a common standard of performance in terms of which members of two or more species might be compared.

Nevertheless, this did not stop race scientists from presupposing analogues of such cross-species standards. For example, shortly after the end of the First World War and the death of his great rival Max Weber, Werner Sombart argued that Jews resembled cockroaches for reasons akin to Rapoport's Rule. Read as a normative principle, the Rule cast aspersions on highly mobile and multiply adaptive creatures, since their survival was at the expense at other creatures sharing the same environment. The ability of such flexible creatures to extract much benefit from more locally embedded ones while contributing little in return marks them as 'parasites'. In the specific case of Jews, their capacity for abstract thought proceeded through the alienation of local forms of knowledge that was then resold to the locals as scientific expertise. Parasitism thus functioned as a racialized theory of surplus value

(Stehr and Weinstein, 1999). Some of the more extreme 'deep ecology' literature that celebrates biodiversity may be understood as an extension of this 'Higher Anti-Semitism' to all of *Homo sapiens*, resulting in a kind of zoocentric misanthropy (Franklin, 1999: 197–9). Moreover, the connection between deep ecology and race science is not accidental. They were two sides of the Nazi quest for a 'master lifestyle' suitable to a 'master race', namely, care for the environment and care for the organism.

The ecologically destabilizing effects of overpopulation were mirrored at the individual level by the lethal overproduction of cells that defined *cancer*, research into which Germany was the world's leader from Rudolf Virchow's formal identification of the disease in the 1860s as the ultimate enemy of modern industrial society to the Second World War (Proctor, 1999: Chapter 1). The source of both the macro- and the micro- 'problem' was the attempt to replace nature by artifice in the modalities of human existence, ranging from the design of homes, factories and public spaces to the manufacture of food and other consumer goods. From this sensibility came an alternative regulative ideal of scientific medicine to the indefinite postponement of death favoured by the positivistic apotheosis of humanity. The alternative invested the analogy between cancer and overpopulation with causal significance. Thus, the extended life-spans afforded by positivistic medical innovations – that often carried the cost of chronic dependency on drugs and institutional supervision – were seen as themselves carcinogenic on the eco-system as a whole. In that case, the job of medicine was to be an agent of natural selection. It should contain and, where possible, reverse the cancer spreading agents. In practice, this meant stricter policies on hospitalization and medication and more liberal policies on contraception, abortion and euthanasia. The name used for this version of Darwinian medicine was *racial hygiene*, whose German professional society in 1930 – three years before Hitler came to power – boasted a membership of 1300 academics, many holding chairs in medical faculties (Proctor, 1988). Of course, the rise of Nazism gave further momentum to racial hygiene, but the fact that it flourished long before Hitler underscores its continuity with the normal development of biomedical science. A scientifically updated version of 'Darwinian medicine' is Neese and Williams (1995).

Racial hygiene was first proposed as a new science in 1895 by Alfred Ploetz, whose development of the subject was recognized with a nomination for the 1936 Nobel Prize in Medicine. Nevertheless, the 2002 edition of the *Encyclopaedia Britannica* does not feature an entry on Ploetz, and racial hygiene appears only in connection with the life of Auschwitz's 'angel of death', Josef Mengele, as if the science had been a creation of the Nazi

concentration camps. (This is yet another case of political correctness sacrificing historical salience to simplify the normative task at hand.) For most
of his career, Ploetz saw himself as a man of the left, just like the British biometricians in the line of Galton and Pearson – including George Bernard
Shaw, the world's foremost playwright in the first half of the 20th century.
Certainly, in the century's early years, the biometricians and the racial
hygienists understood each other as operating in complementary fields: the
former studied tendencies in entire populations, while the latter studied the
characteristics of individuals.

Ploetz's leftist credentials should be seen in the spirit in which we still
regard ecologists as being on the left. He saw the looming social problems presented by both overpopulation and cancer as the result of the undue influence
of *chemistry* on Germany's world-historic horizons: on the one hand, the drive
to create new drugs, especially vaccines, undermined mortality rates that
maintained a population in equilibrium with its environment. On the other
hand, the desire to transcend the limits of the environment, as evidenced in
the production of synthetic foods, fabrics and metals, generated new mal-
adies ranging from allergies to mental disorders, as well as increased the
spread of cancer. Germany's chemists, the envy of the world in the early 20th
century, were typically liberal imperialists of a positivistic disposition who
enthusiastically supported the Kaiser's cause in the First World War – to disastrous consequences (Fuller, 2000b: Chapter 2). Racial hygiene acquired
both political and scientific momentum after the war as part of the holistic
backlash against what was seen as the unduly 'materialistic' and 'deterministic'
world-view that had come to corrupt modern science, symbolized by the
military deployment of poison gas (Herf, 1984).

Those who observe a debate from afar – from a foreign country but also
from the future – tend to underestimate the issues at stake because the very
terms of the debate are so alien from what the observers are used to.
Germany's importation of evolutionary and genetic doctrines from Britain
is a good case in point. The secret to Germany's scientific ascendancy in the
19th century – in physics, chemistry and biology – was its institutionalization of British ideas as research programmes and ultimately academic disciplines. The point is easily obscured in national stereotypes of the British as
'practical' and Germans as 'theoretical'. It would be more correct to say that
the Germans took British ideas more seriously than the British themselves
were inclined to do. Moreover, this Anglo-German intellectual trafficking
was often accompanied by a harmonization of perspectives that the British
had held in tension. Thus, in the case of racial hygiene, Ploetz read Huxley's
1893 Romanes Lecture, 'Evolution and Ethics', as less a critique than an

extension of Herbert Spencer's evolutionary ethics. In particular, Ploetz interpreted Huxley's self-appointed task of humanity to reverse 'natural- ized' societal tendencies as a call for humans to remove the last vestiges of pre-scientific obstacles to the workings of natural selection. He had got Huxley exactly backward.

Ploetz's signature contribution to racial hygiene was the concept of *counter-selection* for all the attempts by the nation-state to reverse the work- ings of natural selection. Following Spencer, Ploetz regarded *welfare* and *warfare* as two sides of the same counter-selectionist coin, which 'sociology' would undermine so as to facilitate the workings of natural selection. Racial hygiene was thus positioned to be the policy science for Spencer's sociology. The obsession with keeping people fit for as long as possible in Bismarck's Germany reflected a nation-state ready to go to war at any moment to defend its interests, both at home and abroad. This obsession was manifested in the first social security scheme, a national healthcare system and a uni- versal education provision: the three bulwarks of the modern welfare state. A particular source of Ploetz's scorn was the drive to mass immunization against contagious diseases, whereby a war on nature was illegitimately con- ducted as part of a war against another nation-state. Robert Koch's work on the anthrax vaccine to protect German troops in the Franco-Prussian War was very much in living memory. If there is to be universal education, then according Ploetz it should enable people to accommodate to the contin- gencies of nature rather than cultivate ideas worth defending under any circumstance, a sensibility that the German university had nurtured in the 19th century, with its studied reclamation of the Greek origins of 'Western civilization' (Fuller, 2000b: Chapter 1).

In an argument reminiscent of pacifist critiques of the 'irrationality' of Cold War nuclear strategy of 'mutually assured destruction', racial hygien- ists reasoned that there would be no need to extend people's lives artifi- cially, were we not so often trying to kill each other. According to this logic, people were being bred not for survival but destruction – a complete per- version of natural selection. On these grounds, Spencer had rejected all forms of militarism, including those associated with Britain's imperialist ambitions. (Here he broke most sharply with fellow Victorian liberals Mill and Huxley.) The German racial hygienists followed suit. With cold consis- tency, they held that so-called 'diseases' like tuberculosis are really full- fledged organisms existing symbiotically with *Homo sapiens* as a selection filter for discriminating the fit from the unfit members of our species.

From this mentality came the 'deep' solution proposed by the Nazis and extended by self-described 'deep ecologists' for the wanton proliferation and extension of human life: we humans must abandon our species-based hubris and identify more fully with nature. It was against this background belief that the Nazis pioneered anti-pollution legislation, 'organic' foods, and other ecologically friendly social policies that are today associated with the prosperous and enlightened lifestyles practiced by the *bien pensant* of California. The US historian Robert Proctor has identified an important moment in the passage from Germany to America. Rachel Carson, whose 1962 bestseller *The Silent Spring*, launched American eco-evangelism, cited the father of US occupational and environmental cancer research, Wilhelm Hueper as her inspiration. As it happens, once Hitler came to power in 1933, Hueper, then chief pathologist at the University of Pennsylvania School of Medicine, unsuccessfully sought a professorship in his native Germany under what had become – for him – ideologically sympathetic conditions (Proctor, 1995: 36–53; Proctor, 1999: 13–15). Of course, this does not mean that all ecologists are Nazis in waiting. Yet, it would be hard to find a Nazi who did not share a broad range of Green sensibilities. Indeed, one of Hitler's first pieces of legislation when he came to power in 1933 was to prohibit vivisection on the grounds of 'the unbearable torture and suffering in animal experiments'. He threatened the livelihoods of laboratory scientists who would treat animals 'as inanimate property'. A cartoon of the day even depicts Hermann Göring enjoying the 'Heil!' salute from animals newly liberated from their cages (Proctor, 1999: 129).

I raise these uncomfortable facts to counteract the tendency to identify Nazism too closely with the Holocaust, as if it were the ultimate self-realization of Nazi ideology. The implicit association has led to the censorship of Neo-Nazi parties around the world today – unfairly in the view of both Nazi supporters and some liberals, such as myself, who would prefer to deal with their knowledge claims more openly. With a little historical distance and sociological insight, we should now be able to conclude that the Holocaust was an extreme outcome *even within Nazism's own terms* that need not have happened. Moreover, by fixating so strongly on the actual events surrounding the Holocaust, we may have unwittingly permitted the underlying cognitive and affective tendencies to flourish in other guises. This implication of claiming the 'unprecedented' nature of the Holocaust has not been sufficiently stressed (cf. Baehr, 2002b). Indeed, it is surprising that Neo-Nazis have not followed the example of Hitler confidant, the architect Albert Speer, who suggested that the Holocaust reflected Hitler's deteriorated judgement from which the movement as a whole should be dissociated. (The prospect of rational Nazis who forsake a misguided leader to conserve the ideal for a future embodiment is the real provocation posed in the recent German film, *Der Untergang*, much more than its alleged 'humanization' of Hitler.) That Neo-Nazis tend to either deny or valorize the Holocaust – in both cases presuming Hitler's infallibility – suggests that their attitude toward history is just as superstitious as that of their demonizing opponents. It would be a shame if we can aspire to no better even in our imperfect world.

In the rest of this chapter I shall argue that had Hitler not pursued the Holocaust, Nazism might well have eventuated in a Green paradise that would have been more in keeping with racial hygienist ideal of *non-violent (or diffuse) genocide*, the exact translation of 'natural selection' into the language of contemporary political discourse.

For starters, it will not do simply to claim that the Holocaust resulted from science having lost a clear external value orientation or become fused with the state without the mediation of civil society, as maintained, respectively, by Adorno and Horkheimer (1972) and Bauman (1989). It is telling that these social theorists, who are inclined to trace Nazi excesses to an unrestrained scientific impulse, typically presuppose a simplistic understanding of the history of science, one whose narrative flow is governed by an internal logic, which may result in progress or regress, depending on the social policies to which it is attached. It is precisely this simplistic vision of science as a 'self-organizing system' that has attracted social scientists so uncritically to Kuhn's (1970) theory of scientific change, even though *at most* it captured about 300 years of the history of physics (Fuller, 2000b: Chapter 5). What the vision crucially omits is that, at any point in its history, science – like any other major social institution – has pursued multiple trajectories simultaneously, typically drawing on the same intellectual and material resources, though some trajectories have clearly done a better job than others in laying legitimate claim to those resources. So-called Nazi science was not a perversion of science or a failure of society to provide adequate checks on science. *It was our common scientific legacy taken in a direction that was always there to be explored and, as we have seen, had been already explored and – most importantly – will be increasingly explored in the future.*

From this perspective, the fixation on the Holocaust as the epitome of Nazism – or worse still, the unchecked scientific world-view – blinds us to the real spiritual continuities between Nazism, ecologism and the karmic sensibility that define a deep strain in human history. (The place to start to recapture these continuities is Oswald Spengler's classic post mortem reflections on the First World War, *The Decline of the West*, which so influenced Hitler and Heidegger.) This point can perhaps be made most vividly by setting out in a few paragraphs what science would look like today had Hitler managed to negotiate a peace with the Allies early in the Second World War that entailed recognition of the legitimacy of the Nazi regime and its conquests. This exercise involves *counterfactual historiography*, which is widely used in economic history and offers a methodologically principled take on the 'alternate history' scenarios popular in science fiction literature (Elster, 1979: Chapter 6).

In bluntest terms, had the Nazis 'won' the Second World War, sub-atomic physics and nuclear energy would not have dominated the science and technology agenda for the next half-century. They would have remained the stuff of science fiction. Instead ecological concerns that have only come to the fore with the end of the Cold War would have continuously led research and policy. Ideas such as biodiversity, the precautionary principle and animal rights would not now be utopian principles backed by voluntary practices and sporadic shows of force. Rather, they would form the conceptual basis of a politically correct Social Darwinism, a biosocial science that updates the tenets of racial hygiene in aid of a sustainable global environment.

My counterfactual history of Nazi science rests on two assumptions. The first pertains to the method of counterfactual history itself. To avoid evaporating into pure fiction, all alternate histories must be potentially present in the actual history as 'paths not taken'. Moreover, we should aim to change as little of the past as possible when inserting the counterfactual. In other words, we should find the latest point in the actual history when the future could have gone in the hypothesized direction (Tetlock and Belkin, 1996: 23–5). Thus, how far back must we rewind the history of Nazi Germany to get to the latest point when Hitler could have done otherwise and turned out victorious – or at least not vanquished? My answer is early 1941, when Hitler could have decided to conquer the Middle East's oil fields instead of invading Russia (Keegan, 1999). Even had this not been entirely successful, Hitler would have probably ended up controlling enough of Europe's energy supplies to force a stalemate, ending the war, say, three years earlier. It would have prevented most – if not all – of the Holocaust, which some maintain was inspired by the cosmic approval that Hitler read into his early Russian victories (Browning, 2003). Moreover, an early end to the war would have halted the race to build the atomic bomb, which the Nazis undertook only in grudging response to the Allies' Manhattan Project (Cornwell, 2003: Chapters 22–4).

Of course, in this alternate world, Nazi-inspired science would have become normalized, which raises my second assumption. Because it is hard to believe that we could benefit from unequivocally evil actions, we need to reduce what social psychologists call 'cognitive dissonance'. Thus, had we been heir to a Nazi victory, Nazi science would now appear in a more positive light. Even in the actual world, where the Nazis appear as history's ultimate villains, they clearly remain part of 'us' as members of the collective project of humanity. This is why public remembrance of the Holocaust has been such a high-maintenance activity (Novick, 1999; Finkelstein, 2000). Our sense of ourselves as heading to somewhere better depends on our finding something redeemable even in the most heinous acts. This may be especially true in matters of science, which by definition is the common possession of humanity. It helps to explain how Nazi scientists were so easily welcomed in Allied countries after the war. Since we cannot bear to see ourselves – especially our scientific selves – in Nazi evil, the urge to forget and repress, if not mitigate and excuse, runs very strong. *If the Holocaust has been a unique event in human history, its uniqueness lies not in what actually took place but in the effort subsequently expended to ensure that it is neither forgotten nor forgiven.* Thus, 'six million' as the number of Jews killed in the Holocaust is much better known than 'fifty million' as the number of people killed in the Second World War as a whole. Without questioning the value of all this collective memory work, it may nevertheless have served to obscure the lingering Nazi sensibilities in our supposedly anti-Nazi world.

Suppose a 1941 peace treaty allowed Hitler to retain his European (and Asian) conquests. Nazi economists, acutely aware of Germany's poor natural resources, advocated a re-agrarianization of conquered industrial nations to prevent them from becoming competitors (Neumann, 1944: 327–37). Command over at least some Middle East oil would have also allowed for Nazi control over the pace of competition among the remaining free nations. This strategy would have enjoyed ideological support from racial hygiene, a science whose prominence predates Hitler's rise and declined only with his fall. It took the Earth's point-of-view, nowadays popularized as 'Gaia', with deadly seriousness. Recall that racial hygienists held that global misery results from misguided human attempts to reverse the effects of natural selection.

Emblematic of such counter-selection was the development of vaccines to immunize populations against diseases that would otherwise normally claim some part. Racial hygienists sharply distinguished between *therapeutic* and *prosthetic* uses of medicine: For them vaccines did not restore the body to a natural state; rather they artificially enhanced the body. That vaccine research had been historically driven by the mixing of peoples caused by imperial expansion led racial hygienists to conclude that only states with stable homogeneous populations could survive naturally. The implications for medical research and policy would be clear. Vaccines would be omitted from what we now call 'preventive medicine', a field in which the Nazis were otherwise major pioneers (Proctor, 1999). Nevertheless, Nazi research into the health effects of radiation, asbestos, lead, cadmium, mercury, alcohol and tobacco would have advanced more rapidly. The Nazis would have also mandated the production of organic foods, outlawed vivisection and encouraged vegetarianism and natural healing. Moreover, the eco-friendly Nazis' sensitivity to the scarcity of the world's oil supply would have sparked an early scientific interest in curtailing carbon dioxide emissions from cars and shifting to alternative energy sources. In short, the late 1940s would have seen scientifically informed policies that only began to be broached in the late 1960s.

Of course, there would have also been compulsory sterilization and permissible euthanasia. All of this would be done to reverse the damage caused to the ecosystem by those late 19th century enemies of biodiversity, Louis Pasteur and Robert Koch, who failed to grasp that a disease like tuberculosis was nature's way of culling an unsustainable human population. Over time, as balance was restored to nature, sterilization and euthanasia might no longer be required. All of these developments would presuppose a state-enforced corporate environmentalism that reached an early accommodation between big business and ecological values. In the process, however, the value of human life would have become negotiable. Those who raised principled objections to the natural selection of *Homo sapiens* would be consigned to the political and scientific margins. The 'centre' would be preoccupied by differences over whether we should play an active or passive role in the culling of the species: surgical removal or benign neglect?

The Nazis would have pioneered the first manned space missions, courtesy of Werner von Braun, who had already been working on them for the Nazis before he defected to the Americans. They would have realized that sending surplus people into space might enable them both to test the limits of their most advanced physical sciences – astrophysics and aeronautics – and to expand the Reich's carrying capacity to other planets or orbiting space stations. The latter would come to be seen as a humane yet scientifically informed alternative to culling. As for nuclear physics, since the Nazis would submit much of the ecosystem to direct political control, there would be little need to countenance substantial non-natural energy sources. Indeed, the very idea of smashing atoms to release untold energy would be linked to the 2 August 1939 letter from the émigré Jew Albert Einstein encouraging FDR to build the atomic bomb, which postwar Nazis would use to stoke the flames of anti-Semitism. After all, Einstein was wrong to have thought that the Nazis were likely to build such a bomb. While they had mastered some (but by no means all) of the relevant scientific principles, there was little ideological enthusiasm for applying them. Thus, the Jews would continue to be demonized, but now for having recommended a bomb that once detonated would have brought about a different but equally lethal 'final solution' – as it turns out, the very one the Americans used against Japan in the actual world to end the Second World War.

Conclusion

Is there no Escape from Human Nature?

The past quarter century has witnessed a revival of the classical interdiscipli-
nary and international conversation over 'human nature' that became dor-
mant in the third quarter of the 20th century with the rise of the welfare
state. It is now hard to believe the confidence of anthropologists like Ashley
Montagu (1945) and my old teacher, Marvin Harris (1968), who however
much they disagreed with each other – Montagu's genial scepticism was too
rationalist and idealist for Harris's more explicitly ecological and materialist
approach – were united in championing 'nurture' over 'nature'. The increasing
attention given to cognitive neuroscience, behavioural genetics, evolutionary
psychology and, of course, sociobiology since 1975 would have struck them
as a barbarous regression, one that specifically overestimated the similarities
between Spencer and Darwin. They were inclined to dismiss the very idea
of human nature as an illusory phenomenon in search of an impossible explanation – perhaps even an atavism of a pre-scientific world-view. A vestige of
this Enlightenment sensibility remains in the pious incantation that race is
a 'myth' or 'superstition' – though the old chant does not quite fit with
today's increasing emphasis on 'ethnicity' and 'genetic diversity' as markers
of social identity.

  More typical of our times is the following remark by the developmental psycholinguist and self-styled evolutionary psychologist Steven Pinker:

> Moral and legal proscriptions are not the only way to reduce discrimi-
> nation in the face of possible group differences. The more information
> we have about the qualifications of an individual, the less impact a

race-wide or sex-wide average would have in any statistical decision concerning that person. The best cure for discrimination, then, is more accurate and more extensive testing of mental abilities, because it would provide so much predictive information about an individual that no one would be tempted to factor in race or gender. (Pinker, 2002: 147)

Pinker quickly adds in parentheses: 'This, however, is an idea with no political future'. Unless Pinker is a master of irony, he greatly underestimates the ease with which his observation could be adopted by policymakers. Indicative of the early 21st century *Zeitgeist* is that racism and sexism are seen as problematic not because they are discriminatory but because they don't discriminate well enough. One thus needs more finely grained indicators that will ultimately replace judgements of surface anatomy with readings of a mapped genome. The biologization of social policy doesn't disappear: it simply intensifies. Of course, discrimination is central to the allocation of resources associated with distributive justice. In that context, the allocations are made to compensate for deficiencies seen as the products of past injustices, so as to achieve a rough sense of the relevant sorts of 'equality' among individuals in society. Unfortunately, Pinker also believes that the factors configuring our brains and genes may lie outside our control, regardless of how deeply we understand them. Indeed, his willingness to sever the Enlightenment link between knowledge and power extends to claiming that we may need to admit a scientific basis for what humanists have traditionally called 'fate' (377–9). Whatever his intentions, Pinker's message is bound to be music to the ears of those who doubt the need for additional political reforms that might compel a greater sense of social responsibility.

It is a conceit among today's Darwinists that people generally recoil from the idea that our capacity for change is genetically constrained. Actually, only those imbued with the spirit of social science recoil. Everyone else is relieved. Coping with the inevitable is much less troublesome than contesting the available. *Pace* Lepenies (1988), it is unlikely that the social sciences ever intended, let alone succeeded, to bridge the 'two cultures problem' between the humanities and natural sciences. More likely they *created* it. Certainly, the social sciences have contributed to severing the good will that had traditionally existed between the natural sciences and the humanities by exemplifying the qualities that each culture most disliked in the other, perhaps by each reminding the other of how it has failed to better the human condition. Thus, after encountering the social sciences, natural scientists became more vocal in their disdain for humanistic woolly-mindedness (a.k.a. 'contextualism'), while humanists bemoaned the philistinism of natural scientists (a.k.a. 'reductionism'). In both cases, the proximal targets were usually social scientists.

If one wishes to trace the 20th century history of the *entente cordiale* between the humanities and the natural sciences that tactfully excludes the social sciences, one could start with the 'Great Books' and 'Classics of Western Civilization' curricula that surfaced on US campuses after the First World War. The German scientific community's explicit backing of the war plus the success of Lenin's Marx-inspired Russian Revolution conjured up the spectre of a 'social science' that mixed the worst elements of the humanities and the natural sciences to produce an ideologically repressive war machine. Offering immunity against this prospect was University of Chicago President Robert Maynard Hutchins, who believed all knowledge could be unified under a Neo-Aristotelian world-view enhanced by Darwin – but not Marx, Weber or Durkheim. Nowadays this tradition (minus Aristotle) is continued on the website, www.edge.org, maintained by literary agent to the scientific stars, John Brockman, under the rubric 'third culture'. In this context, social scientists are portrayed as too parochial, ideological, incompetent or incomprehensible to enter into such civilized conversation – though occasionally we manage to come up with some interesting data that demand a 'deeper' explanation than we can muster.

Unsurprisingly, then, the purveyors of the new sciences of human nature, as synthesized in, say, Wilson (1998) and Pinker (2002), notwithstanding their intriguing research findings, display an almost studied ignorance of the social sciences. Moreover, when they try to come to terms with social science's explanatory (as opposed to descriptive) side, they quickly revert to philosophical views – such as Hobbes' or Rousseau's – that predate the actual emergence of social science and consequently are not centred in the social institutions and organizations that characterize the modern world. Rather, these seminal but empirically outdated philosophical positions are generalized as a 'blank slate' approach to the human condition, which is then made the basis of the so-called Standard Social Science Model (SSSM) that would explain the full range of human behaviour in terms of corresponding differences in learning and context. It is remarkable that book reviewers and cultural commentators have not made more of this simple but devastating observation. Still more remarkable is how rarely we social scientists have done so. Such silence allows us to be defined by our opponents, as if we tacitly conceded their criticism, thereby positioning ourselves as theologians did to the onslaught of Darwin's defenders over a century earlier.

Ultimately social scientists are excluded from the great conversation over human nature because they take the subject too seriously. The intriguing hypotheses advanced by Brockman's 'third culture' are little more than pleasant parlour games – and the stuff of bestsellers – until they are tried out on flesh-and-blood people, as opposed to the bits of us that most resemble the bits of other animals. This means taking problems of *method* more seriously than, say, Wilson or Pinker is inclined to do. Shall we conduct experiments or ethnographies? Will this research be funded by business or government? Whose consent shall we need to secure and under what terms? Whom shall we believe when testimony conflicts with theory and observation? To whom will our research be made available and are we liable for any adverse applications? These questions form the matrix in which the social sciences have developed over the last two centuries. Moreover the field's track record is much better than our detractors claim, especially when seen over the long haul and extended to include the social formations that social science has helped to create and maintain, as well as describe and explain. (Perhaps we need to update Deutsch et al., 1986?) To be sure, bitter experience has shown that social scientists have often got it wrong. However, this is something to learn from, not to avoid by retreating to thought experiments about humanity in 'the state of nature' or treating the human genome like an astrologer's star chart. Without a strong social scientific presence in the human nature debates, these pre-modern modes of thought may well be reinvented as our own.

Human nature seems to burn anyone who dares come near it. This book has been largely concerned with social scientists, whose *raison d'être* has been to marginalize, if not outright eliminate, human nature in the name of research programmes and policy horizons aimed at extricating us from our animal roots if not quite turning us into gods. In return, human nature has wreaked its revenge, or at least is credited with having thwarted our ambitions by posing various biologically based barriers. Today these barriers appear quite formidable because greater scientific understanding of our biological makeup has coincided with the increased devolution of societal decision-making. Now suppose we were to conclude that social science is incapable of meeting these challenges. It still would not follow that human nature can be absorbed into sociobiology or evolutionary psychology. For the more human nature is blended into the sort of ecumenical natural science promoted by Brockman's 'third culture', the harder it becomes to distinguish the specifically human from the generically natural. This is because human nature is itself a conceptual throwback from a pre-Darwinian past, when organic species were held to possess essential qualities. Human nature really does not belong in a properly Darwinized world.

The debate between 'nurture' and 'nature' historically turned on how an individual acquires the properties that make them who they are: in philosophical terms, *a priori* or *a posteriori*; in sociological terms, inheritance or achievement. However, according to the Neo-Darwinian synthesis, species are *not* essences. You are a human simply by virtue of your capacity to enter a relationship that produces more humans – that is, you can perform what biologists define as 'being human'. To be sure, this capacity is causally underwritten by a possible range of amino acids strung along your genome, but there is no consensus over where to draw the line between a 'human' and a 'non-human' genomic string. Moreover, allowances are made for the obvious cases when individuals function as humans in every sense *except* that they cannot procreate. Ultimately, then, your humanity rests on an evolutionary biologist's ability to find a place for you somewhere in the genealogical narrative entitled '*Homo sapiens*'. In this important sense, human nature in modern evolutionary biology is an indeterminate concept subject to ongoing social construction by the self-appointed experts. (I say 'self-appointed' only because it is unclear when biologists were formally delegated with the task of defining the human.) This is a point that deserves greater publicity and reflection in secular scientific culture. So far only monotheistic religious leaders and theologians have fully appreciated its import.

Steven Pinker, nowadays the public face of evolutionary psychology, provides a vivid, albeit unwitting, demonstration of the point. Pinker (2002) contains an Appendix that lists over 400 'human universals', that is, behavioural tendencies and mental and physical capacities that have been observed in all human cultures studied. The list is presented as the best scientific guess at the constitution of human nature. Let us grant Pinker at the outset that his list puts paid to relativists who hold that people vary radically across cultures. This still leaves a problem. The list contains very many properties that humans share with many other animals: 'age statuses', 'classification of colours', 'memory', 'pain', 'rhythm', 'sex statuses', etc. Perhaps Pinker would respond that *only* humans possess *all* 400+ properties. A glance at the list suggests this might be true *today*. The first two items certainly look very 'human': 'abstraction in speech and thought', 'actions under self-control distinguished from actions not under control'. However, Pinker can hardly take comfort from such cases, since much of the excitement surrounding evolutionary psychology concerns precisely the prospect of discovering animal, especially primate, versions – and perhaps even roots – of traits traditionally seen as exclusively human. To a devotee of the programme, those exceptional items on Pinker's list are simply clever experiments waiting to be conducted that will reveal hidden analogues, if not common causal mechanisms, between ourselves and the rest of nature. Moreover, the devotees have reason for their enthusiasm, given the history of animal behaviour studies since Darwin's day. Indeed, the increasing respectability accorded to Peter Singer's call to expand the circle of moral concern across species is one by-product of our ability now to see qualities in animals that in the past we could only perceive in humans.

Put harshly but not inaccurately, the new sciences of human nature are dedicated to reabsorbing the human into the natural. They are 'natural sciences' in the strictest sense, whose corresponding world-view is more 'karmic' than 'anthropic', in the terms introduced in Part Three of this book. But will these new sciences succeed? Taking the long view once again helps. The recent breakthroughs and speculations surrounding the sciences of human nature concern virtually every part of the Neo-Darwinian synthesis. Not only has the evidential base of natural history improved, but also the human genome has now been mapped. Assuming the persistence of neo-liberalism, whereby no state agency is sufficiently powerful to control the flow and use of this knowledge, the relevant historical comparator becomes the Protestant Reformation, in which the Renaissance's recovery of the original classical – including Biblical – languages, was complemented by the transla-tion and mass dissemination of the classics in the 'vulgar' modern European languages, as symbolized by the printing press. In that case, Craig Venter may turn out to be our Johannes Gutenberg.

The 'Book of Nature' that Galileo aspired to map in mathematical terms is now the 'Book of Life' mapped as biochemical sequences of amino acids (Kay, 2000). Given this analogy, we should understand today's leading popu-larizers of the biologistic world-view – including Wilson, Dawkins, and Pinker – as latter-day descendants of Desiderius Eramsus who have mastered the ancient languages but continue to believe that the spread of Christianity in the vulgar tongues will not dislocate people's fundamental belief in the unity of humanity under a common God ministered, in this case, by state-sponsored Neo-Darwinism rather than the Roman Catholic Church. However, if noth-ing else, history has taught that greater access to a code eventuates in a wider range of messages. Thus, widespread access to the map of the human genome in a time of weak states – let alone states incapable of enforcing international law – is likely to lead to consequences unintended and perhaps even unwanted by those present at the original mapping. Consider the proliferation of Protestant denominations in the wake of the Reformation, which emerged from the interpretive ambiguities revealed in the Bible's original languages. These are like today's proposals to distinguish human and non-human on bases other than the default patterns of biological reproduction. The relevant analogue is that arguments about, say, how we incorporate the disabled, the animal or the android into 'society' will be conducted along lines similar to debates about divine properties or the requisites for salvation in the 16th and 17th centuries. Corresponding to the internecine textual debates that in the past had resulted in civil war will be (hopefully) public discussion and, when necessary, civil disobedience that eventuates in electoral resolution that stops short of civil war.

My general point here is twofold. The first is a recognition that we have always wanted to be human. The second is that barring the establishment of some global regulatory regime, we may come to treat 'human' as we currently treat 'Christian', that is, a universal project with which those potentially implicated may not wish to be associated. It may be, as I believe, that to be human is to be difficult. Since animals by definition adapt to circumstances, humans have always been reluctant to identify themselves with their biology. The history of Western philosophy and theology bears witness to this fact. All of the objects nominated as essential to our realization as human beings – reason, truth, justice, goodness, beauty – have been traditionally defined without reference to what cognitive neuroscientists nowadays call a 'wetware constraint'. From Plato through the medievals to Descartes and the Enlightenment, there has been considerable speculation and complaint about the restrictions our animal nature places on our capacity to achieve humanly desirable ends. The more Gnostic of these thinkers concocted strategies to enable humans to liberate their divine spirit from their material containers. Secular versions of these strategies are emblematic of the modern era. Two exemplary projects stand out: the construction of rational machines that avoid the friction of the passions and the design of revolutionary politics that escape the fetters of tradition.

My point here is less to valorize these projects than to present the problem their existence poses to the new sciences of human nature. *Just because humanity was discovered by a creature with a certain physical constitution, why should we suppose that this constitution is required for humanity to be fully realized?* Suddenly those preoccupied with the biological basis of humanity look rather like purists in political theory who believe that democracy is possible only in societies having the physical parameters of classical Athens. Both appear to rely on a superstitious understanding of history: that is, things are essentially as they began – the *arché* of archaeology.

But how does this point bear specifically on the future of social science? An interesting feature of the trajectory of human progress is that it corresponds not merely to increased production but more importantly to *productivity*. Progress has not simply been a matter of enabling more people to enjoy benefits previously limited to the wealthy. Rather, it has entailed periodic changes in the *sources* of power and value, as new things – typically of less material substance – come to set the standard of a high quality human existence. Much of the sociological literature on 'symbolism' should be understood in this light. This point may be interpreted as an indefinite extension of the value of *efficiency*. Yet, the spiritual character of efficiency is rarely noted. The desire to get 'something for nothing', the ultimate expression of efficiency, secularizes creation *ex nihilo* in Western monotheism (cf. Gouldner, 1973: 269–99). Depending on whether humans are regarded as pale imitations of the Creator or the actual achievers of Creation, this viewpoint has appeared as blasphemous or revelatory.

The history of chemistry as an autonomous discipline – that is, *not* as something that exists before or after physics – provides the most reliable narrative thread for this tradition. It includes medieval alchemists like Roger Bacon, Enlightenment natural philosophers like Joseph Priestley, as well as ergonomists like Andrew Ure and Wilhelm Ostwald (Rabinbach, 1990). All preached a gospel of asceticism that went beyond the alleviation of suffering in the short term (as in the Eastern religions) to the promotion of welfare in the long term. Sociologically speaking, efficiency emerges as a dynamic principle under conditions of 'scarcity' in its most abstract sense – when more people are formally entitled to the valued goods than are materially available. In that case, society seeks substitutes, which at first may consist of cheaper synthetic versions but over time raise questions about the exact nature of the value served by the good – and whether some entirely different, less material good might not suffice instead. The replacement of the struggle for survival with the struggle for recognition, raised in Chapter 9, is the philosophical expression of this development.

Economic revolutions are not alone in being driven by entrepreneurs with a visionary sense of efficiency. The same tendency is more generally implicated in the social and political spheres. Today the possession of money and literacy enables forms of power that 200 years ago could only be secured by property ownership and religious sanction. Carrying this line of thought to its logical conclusion, the German sociologist Nico Stehr (2001) has recently suggested that the world's increasingly paperless knowledge-based economy permits an optimistic forecast that we may still square the circle of an ecologically sustainable yet increasingly wealthy world. Knowledge that required leisured wealth two centuries ago and a university degree a century ago is now readily available with the click of a mouse on the internet: Fewer resources are required to get comparable results – or so it seems. Arguably this view underestimates the vast, perhaps even increasing, numbers of humans still living in conditions of bare subsistence and the historical trend for new forms of technology – now computer-based – to reconstitute, if not exactly reproduce, class distinctions. Nevertheless, Stehr's reasoning points to the larger truth that standards of humanity have tended to shift to enable more members of *Homo sapiens* to meet them. However, the fugitive, perhaps de-materializing, and in any case increasingly efficient nature of these democratic standards calls into question the exact locus of our humanity (Fuller, 2002a: Chapter 3). It is epitomized in a question that is bound to loom large as the century wears on: *What is distinctly human that must be retained across episodes of social reproduction?* This should be the fundamental question of social science in the new century.

Certainly the material baseline of humanity, an inalienable right to bodily integrity, has received a one-two punch from biotechnology. In this book I have concentrated on the first punch served by Singer's Darwinian Left, which observes that the 90+% genetic overlap between humans and most animals shifts the burden to those who would pursue a project of humanity distinct from that of animal welfare more generally. However, the second punch is rather alien to Singer's world-view but bears on Stehr's more Gnostic vision of a de-materialized knowledge economy. It is the *cyborg vision* that regards carbon-based organs and organisms as potentially replaced by or combined with silicon-based ones – without loss of value. It covers the gamut from prosthetic extensions of human life, including the implantation of computer chips and the nanotechnology of 'smart molecules', to full-fledged computerized automata with human-like interfaces, or 'androids'. The cyborg enthusiast thus asks, 'Why privilege pure carbon-based creatures, as Singer still does, rather than a cyborg hybrid whose internal and external operation performs most of the same functions that have traditionally qualified entities for moral concern and political rights?' To be sure, the reproduction of human wetware in all its exactitude may provide an aesthetic or engineering challenge, but if semi-siliconized cyborgs excel at qualities – such as scientific or artistic achievement – that have been traditionally considered definitive of humanity, why can't they be simply identified as members of the human community? (Indeed, why can't they be considered *superior* to 'disabled' humans?)

Once so informed by a cyborg sensibility, the new developments in biotechnology and nanotechnology may unwittingly tip the balance in favour of social constructivism over evolutionary psychology as a framework for explaining the human condition. This prospect has been long recognized within science and technology studies (Haraway, 1990), and android ethics has already received some serious philosophical attention (Ford et al., 1995). It reflects the founding moment in the history of artificial intelligence research, the development of the so-called Turing Test, which marked the realization that the capacity for thought is no more than the ability (of a man, woman or machine) to pass as a thinker – an insight that should bring a smile to eth-nomethodological lips (cf. Fuller and Collier, 2004: Chapter 5). However, because so much of the cyborg discussion draws inspiration from science fiction writers like Karel Čapek, Isaac Asimov and William Gibson, there has been an unfortunate tendency to invoke the rhetoric of 'posthumanity' to describe this development, which leaves the misleading impression that it constitutes a break with historic pro-human sensibilities (cf. Hayles, 1999). This overlooks the original inspiration that the sociological imagination received from what Hobbes called the 'artificial person' – the legal category of *universitas* or corporation – an entity brought into being to pursue ends of a distinctly 'human' character that transcend the personal interests of the particular individuals who happen to constitute it at any given moment. The *universitas* is the social entity that makes the sharpest break with humanity's biological origins, while retaining the capacity to meet the cyborgian challenge that we 'incorporate' in new ways. It has the potential to reinvent humanity for a social science worthy of the 21st century.

Glossary

Anthropic world-view: The world-view common to the great monotheistic religions – Judaism, Christianity, Islam – and secular humanism, all of which identify humans as the 'measure of all things'. Generally speaking, monotheism has been more egalitarian than humanism, as the former values individual humans intrinsically by virtue of their common divine ancestry, whereas the latter has often distinguished between 'the best' and 'the rest', as if only some humans ever fully realize their *humanity*. For contrast, see *karmic world-view*.

Beveridge, William (1879–1963): Political economist and director of the LSE who, as a member of Winston Churchill's wartime cabinet, designed Britain's *welfare state* as an instance of applied 'social biology'.

Bioliberalism: The emerging dominant ideology of our time, characterized by a politically devolved *eugenics* sensibility, in which decisions concerning the design, commercialization and termination of life are taken with minimal state intervention. Bioliberalism indirectly promotes the *karmic world-view* by easing the passage of humans in and out of existence, that is, the casualization of the human condition. It may be seen as the natural outcome of *neo-liberalism* when the biomedical industries are the ascendent mode of production.

Biology: The science of life, first named by Lamarck in 1810, having been central to Aristotle's science but marginal to Newton's. It regained respectability in the modern era from two countervailing strands of secularism that recognized (1) the finality of death – the discovery of the fossil record, which implied a natural history of extinct organisms; (2) the extension of survival – the advancement of medicine beyond the prevention of harm and suffering to the enhancement of human life.

Bioprospecting: The physical extraction, chemical synthesis and commercialization of the genetic material of plants and animals, including humans. Bioprospecting is increasingly central to the pharmaceutical and biotechnology industries, where it has spearheaded the literal conversion of life into intellectual property, effectively rendering racism profitable in the global marketplace. See *genetic diversity*.

British sociological tradition: The national tradition in which the relationship between *sociology* and *socialism* was most tightly forged. Its most significant achievement was the *welfare state*, the intellectual legacy of which remains in departments of 'Sociology and Social Policy'. The tradition's signature figures, *Hobhouse* and *Beveridge*, provided idealist and positivist reconstructions of the concept of social progress in response to Darwinian evolutionary theory.

Comte, Auguste (1798–1857): The founder of both *positivism* and *sociology*, which he regarded as aspects of a common social movement designed to modernize society by replacing theology with science as the cornerstone of education. Sociology was meant to be the ultimate positive science, comprehending all previous sciences and showing the way to a progressive future.

Condorcet, Marquis de (1743–94): Quintessential *Enlightenment* source of modern social science who believed that growing human societies and redistributing the surplus of their collective production would eliminate poverty. He was also the seminal theorist of voting as a method for democratic decision-making.

Corporate environmentalism: A business strategy that aims at maximizing profits with minimum damage to the natural environment typically by continuing to exploit human labour. It provides a vivid example of the trade-off between 'Red' and 'Green' political values.

Counterfactual historiography: A kind of writing made possible once the contingency of history is taken seriously. It requires understanding history in prospect (namely as decisions available to the agents in their day) rather than in retrospect. The trick is to locate in the actual history the moment when things could have plausibly taken a course other than they did, resulting in some specified alternate outcome, such as (discussed in the text) a Nazi victory in the Second World War.

Darwinian Left: *Singer's* attempt to have Darwin replace Marx as the scientific basis for progressive politics in the 21st century. It would extend the left's constituency to cover all of nature, while de-centring its traditionally human focus. In a world of scarce resources, it would thus increase equality across species and diminish it within species to produce an ecologically sustainable polity.

Durkheim, Émile (1858–1917): The person who finally institutionalized *Comte's* vision of sociology. Unsurprisingly it coincided with the *secularization* of the French educational system in the Third Republic.

Enlightenment: The 18th century European cultural movement most responsible for *secularizing* the *anthropic world-view*, whose main 19th century legacies included *positivism* and *sociology*. Its association of human emancipation with the spread of science came under increasing attack in the 20th century, in light of the two world wars, culminating in *postmodernism*.

Eugenics: A term coined by Darwin's nephew, Francis Galton, for the policy of selectively breeding the best traits of humanity for purposes of raising the overall level of social welfare. Originally presented as part of scientific *socialism*, albeit before the advent of modern genetics. Nowadays *bioliberalism* continues a scientifically updated and politically devolved version of the same policy. See *racial hygiene*.

Evolutionary psychology: The laboratory and field study of animals, especially primates, for clues to understanding and explaining human behavioural dispositions. Essentially an updated version of *sociobiology*, it has rekindled interest in *human nature*.

Foucault, Michel (1926–84): Totemic postmodern theorist whose emphasis on the transience of *humanity* as a scientific and political object unwittingly contributed to the decline of *sociology's* salience.

Fundamentalism: Nowadays portrayed as a politically reactionary movement, especially within Christianity and Islam, but better seen more broadly as a monotheistic backlash to secularism based on identifying the divine with the weakest of those created in the image and likeness of God, itself the theological basis for modern *socialism*. See *Occidentalism*.

Genetic diversity: A politically correct term, associated with geneticist Luigi Cavalli-Sforza, for the fine-grained racism that is enabled by a wide range of biotechnology-based research. *Bioprospecting* promotes genetic diversity by encouraging inbreeding in populations bearing rare genomic sequences.

Hobbes, Thomas (1588–1679): English philosopher whose classic *Leviathan* (1651) is the founding modern philosophical reflection on science and politics. Hobbes promoted a contractual view of society that systematically redistributes power to escape the *struggle for survival*. Hobbes controversially held that redistribution requires a corporate super-agent (see *universitas*). One of Hobbes' translators, the legal scholar Ferdinand Tönnies, established sociology in Germany.

Hobhouse, Leonard Trelawny (1864–1929): The LSE's first sociology professor, whose attempts to reconcile German idealism with evolutionary theory led to an emphasis on rights and citizenship that came to character-ize the distinct British contribution to sociology.

Humanity: The 'human' as a collective project undertaken by *Homo sapiens* to transcend its animal nature (a.k.a. *human nature*), including one histori-cally associated with social scientific inquiry and leftist politics since the *Enlightenment*. See *universitas*.

Human nature: An ancient concept that defines the 'human' in terms of certain genetic properties of *Homo sapiens* that may be promoted or inhibited by the environment. Marginalized by much of social science, the concept has enjoyed a revival under *evolutionary psychology* and *sociobiology*. See *third culture*.

Huxley, Thomas Henry (1825–95): Contrary to his popular image as 'Darwin's bulldog', Huxley's medical background instilled nagging doubts about the anti-humanistic implications of evolutionary theory. He formally broke with more die-hard evolutionists like *Spencer* in his 1893 Romanes Lecture, 'Evolution and Ethics'.

Karmic world-view: The world-view common to the great Eastern pan- and poly-theistic religions and the *neo-Darwinian synthesis*. It stresses the massive genetic overlap in organic species deriving from a generic life force. It reduces the supposed 'uniqueness' of *humanity* to marginal inter-species differences that are not necessarily valuable in themselves. *Huxley* first drew attention to the scientific significance of this world-view when pondering Darwinism's implications for the 'meaning of life'.

London School of Economics (or LSE): Perhaps the world's foremost higher education institution dedicated to the social sciences, founded in 1895 by the 'Fabians', liberal intellectuals sympathetic to both *socialism* and *eugenics*. It is the spiritual home of the *British sociological tradition*.

Malthus, Thomas (1766–1834): Classical political economist whose observations about human population cycles provided the basis for Darwin's theory of natural selection and lurks behind much of today's ecological pessimism, if not fatalism.

Marx, Karl (1818–83): *Socialism*'s greatest theorist and publicist, who remains capitalism's ablest diagnostician. With socialism's decline, Marx's original intellectual struggles – especially between a humanist individualism and a materialist collectivism – have come to be reified as a theoretical debating point in *sociology*.

Mill, John Stuart (1806–73): Underrated founder of social science who first promoted *Comte* in Britain and reconciled *utilitarianism* with the *anthropic world-view*.

Neo-Darwinian synthesis: The integration of lab-based and field-based biological research ranging from molecular genetics to ecology under an updated version of Darwin's theory of evolution. The synthesis, which provides the explanatory framework for contemporary *biology*, dates only from the 1930s.

Neo-Liberalism: Liberalism seen from the historical perspective of *socialism* as a failed project rather than an attractive prospect. The political analogue of *postmodernism*, in which the *Enlightenment* corresponds to socialism. Margaret Thatcher and her guru Friedrich von Hayek are associated with its ascendancy. See *Vienna circles*.

Occidentalism: A pejorative for the decadent form of Western liberal 'tolerance' that devolves such global problems as poverty and inequality to matters of individual or sub-national discretion, such that letting people die is always better than forcing others to ensure their survival. The term acquired salience after 11 September 2001, when it became the ideological target of Islamic *fundamentalism*.

Orientalism: A pejorative for the decadence of Asia that acquired currency in the early 19th century as Europe began to overtake China, India and especially the Islamic world in global economic and cultural significance. As Edward Said observed in a 1978 book by this name, Islam in particular came to represent for Europeans all they loathed and feared in themselves, given the common ancestry of Christian and Muslim cultures.

Parsons, Talcott (1902–79): The world's leading sociologist in the third quarter of the 20th century whose 'structural-functionalism' was intended as a metatheory for all the social sciences based on a conception of society tailored to the *welfare state*. He was largely responsible for presenting *Durkheim* and *Weber* as participants in a common disciplinary project.

Positivism: *Comte*'s name for both the scientific method and the principle of universal governance, which was to assume the institutional form of the Roman Catholic Church in realizing the *Enlightenment*'s project of *humanity*. Under the influence of *Mill*, positivism took on a more Protestant inflection with stronger ties to liberalism. Nevertheless much of the old Comtean zeal remained in 20th century logical positivism's call for the unity of the sciences. See *Vienna circles*.

Postmodernism: A broad-gauged movement of largely French provenance predicated on the failure of the *Enlightenment*, which it diagnoses as either having self-destructed or simply been illusory all along. Postmodernism began to gain currency in the late 1970s with the decline of *socialism*. See *Foucault*.

Racial hygiene: Nowadays seen as the quintessential 'Nazi science', it had originated in late 19th century German medical schools, where it was treated as a rival to the emerging science of *sociology*. Much of German sociology's interest in *Hobbes*' 'artificial' conception of society was constructed in opposition to racial hygiene's appeal to *Spencer*'s more 'natural' conception.

Schutz, Alfred (1899–1959): The self-styled phenomenological sociologist who provides the missing link between the Austrian school of economics and the 'social construction of reality', a politically correct expression for capitalism's invisible hand when invoked as a surrogate for macro-social entities. See *Vienna circles*.

Secularization: The decentralization of the production and distribution of knowledge, be it religious or scientific. The first wave of secularization followed the Protestant Reformation, when the Roman Catholic Church lost its state-backed monopoly in northern European countries. We are now witnessing the second wave, as nation-states devolve their stakes in the funding and authorization of science. Secularization typically results in a sensitization of knowledge producers to market conditions, what to an onlooker might appear to be a 'relativization' of knowledge interests.

Singer, Peter (1946–): The leading theorist of 'animal liberation' (the title of his first major book) and devotee of *utilitarianism*. The originator of the *Darwinian Left*, Singer is perhaps the world's leading public philosopher at the dawn of the 21st century.

Socialism: The political movement most explicitly associated with the project of *humanity*, a dialectical synthesis of early 19th century liberal and conservative responses to the emergence of industrial capitalism, as epitomized in the Marxist slogan, 'From each according to their ability to each according to their need'. The most successful version of socialism has been the *welfare state*.

Sociobiology: The title of a controversial 1975 book by Harvard ant specialist E.O. Wilson that began the recent natural scientific backlash against *sociology*. Originally demonized as providing ideological cover for *eugenics*, it is now treated respectfully as the forerunner of *evolutionary psychology*.

Sociology: *Comte*'s name for the empirically informed normative discipline designed to realize the project of *humanity* as the culminating stage in the history of science.

Spencer, Herbert (1820–1903): Self-styled 'Social Darwinist' and adopted father of *racial hygiene*, whose theory of evolution predated Darwin's and drew on many of the same sources, especially *Malthus*. Responsible for popularizing the word 'sociology' in Britain, which for him ranged over spontaneously self-organizing associations across all forms and levels of life.

Standard Social Science Model (or SSSM): A caricature of the social sciences invoked by *sociobiology* and *evolutionary psychology* in both popular and scientific settings. Social scientists are depicted as ignoring universal, especially genetic, factors in favour of explaining all human traits in terms of environmental differences. This stereotype purports to capture the fundamental error common to historicists, relativists and behaviourists. SSSM's most disturbing feature is its very status as an object of ridicule, rather than a reasonable research strategy for further elaboration and improvement.

Struggle for Survival *vs* Recognition: A distinction associated with Francis Fukuyama, which captures the difference in existential horizons between the concepts of *human nature* and *humanity.* In terms of philosophical lineage, the former is associated with *Hobbes*, the latter Hegel.

Sympathy: A term associated originally with Adam Smith for those whose predicament we can understand. In *utilitarianism*, it defines the circle of moral concern. The open question is the principle by which sympathy is established, especially whether knowing more about someone increases one's sympathy – or rather, 'familiarity breeds contempt'. On the latter basis, some animals may appear more sympathetic than some humans.

Third Culture: Originally, a term for the social sciences as the dialectical synthesis of the humanities and natural sciences but now increasingly used to refer to the reconciliation of the humanities and the natural sciences – to the exclusion of the social sciences – in a common inquiry into *human nature.*

Universitas: The Latin word for 'corporation', a 12th century Roman legal innovation that enabled the creation of such 'artificial persons' as city-states, churches, guilds, monasteries and, of course, universities. All of these entities share a non-hereditary, typically elected, mode of succession that enjoys legal protection in perpetuity because they are dedicated to ends that transcend the interests of its current members. The nation-state has been the dominant *universitas* of the modern era. Business firms, what are today normally called 'corporations', are relative latecomers to this status. The distinctness of *sociology* lies in its focus on *universitates* as the unique expression of *humanity.* See *Hobbes.*

Utilitarianism: The signature British contribution to modern ethics, epitomized in Jeremy Bentham's slogan 'The greatest good for the greatest number'. It also captures the principle of distributive justice that underlies the *welfare state*. The open question is the range of beings whose 'greatest good' is of concern – all living humans, all able-bodied humans, all sentient creatures and/or future generations? *Mill* and *Singer* represent contrasting answers.

Vienna circles: In the decade before Hitler's rise to power, two intellectual circles flourished in Vienna, the disapora from which seeded the golden years of social science methodology. The more famous logical *positivist* circle – including Wittgenstein, Carnap and Popper – had a generally socialist, macro-social, quantitative orientation. The less famous circle of 'Austrian economists' – including Mises, Hayek and *Schutz* – tended to be liberal, micro-social, and qualitative. Both claimed the legacy of the *Enlightenment*, the former more French the latter more Scottish.

Weber, Max (1864–1920): German social scientist grounded in law and political economy who gradually saw himself as a 'sociologist', especially after the First World War, when he helped to draft Germany's first republican constitution. Notable for having anticipated the de-humanizing effects of the spread of natural scientific thought in the wider culture, though without succumbing to antiscientism.

Welfare state: The original 'third way' between capitalism and socialism, philosophically rooted in *Mill*'s version of *utilitarianism*, whereby the principle of diminishing marginal utility is deployed to redistribute incomes so as to ensure the most freedom compatible with the least inequality. However, the concrete welfare state began as a piece of Bismarckian *Realpolitik*, introduced to immunize German workers against more *Marx*-inspired forms of revolutionary socialism. It reached its heyday in the third quarter of the 20th century and has since then declined, reflecting the state's fiscal burdens and loss of ideological salience.

Westermarck, Edward (1862–1939): The LSE's first anthropologist, whose work seems to conform to the *Standard Social Science Model* caricature, except that Westermarck universalized cultural relativism to make it continuous with evolutionary adaptationism. Thus, he anticipates today's convergence of *postmodernism* and the *Neo-Darwinian synthesis*.

References

Adorno, T. and Horkheimer, M. (1972) *The Dialectic of Enlightenment*. (orig. 1943). New York: Continuum.

Ainslie, G. (2001) *Breakdown of Will*. Cambridge: Cambridge University Press.

Albury, R. (1993) 'Ideas of life and death', in W.F. Bynum and R. Porter (eds), *Companion Encyclopedia of the History of Medicine*. London: Routledge. Chapter 13.

Allen, G. (1998) 'Modern biological determinism', in M. Fortun and E. Mendelsohn (eds), *The Practices of Human Genetics*. Dordrecht: Kluwer.

Amin, S. (1991) 'The ancient world-system versus the modern capitalist world-system', *Review*, 14: 349–86.

Anderson, B. (1983) *Imagined Communities*. London: Verso.

Appignanesi, L. and Forrester, J. (2000) *Freud's Women*. 2nd edn (orig. 1992). Harmondsworth, UK: Penguin.

Archer, M. and Tritter, J. (eds) (2000) *Rational Choice Theory: Resisting Colonization*. London: Routledge.

Armstrong, K. (2000) *The Battle for God: Fundamentalism in Judaism, Christianity and Islam*. London: HarperCollins.

Atran, S. (2002) *In Gods We Trust*. Oxford: Oxford University Press.

Baehr, P. (1998) *Caesar and the Fading of the Roman World: A Study in Republicanism and Caesarism*. New Brunswick, NJ: Transaction.

Baehr, P. (2002a) *Founders, Classics, and Canons: Modern Disputes over the Origins and Appraisals of Sociology's Heritage*. New Brunswick, NJ: Transaction.

Baehr, P. (2002b) 'Identifying the unprecedented: Hannah Arendt, totalitarianism and the critique of sociology', *American Sociological Review*, 67: 804–32

Barkow, J., Cosmides, L. and Tooby, J. (eds) (1992) *The Adapted Mind: Evolutionary Psychology and the Generation of Culture*. Oxford: Oxford University Press.

Barnes, C. and Mercer, G. (2003) *Disability*. Cambridge: Polity Press.

Barron, C. (ed.) (2003) 'A strong distinction between humans and non-humans is no longer required for research purposes: a debate between Bruno Latour and Steve Fuller', *History of the Human Sciences*, 16: 77–100.

Bauman, Z. (1989) *Modernity and the Holocaust.* Cambridge, UK: Polity Press.

Beck, U. (1992) *The Risk Society.* London: Sage.

Berger, P. and Luckmann, P. (1967) *The Social Construction of Reality.* Garden City, NY: Doubleday.

Berman, H. (1983) *Law and Revolution.* Cambridge, MA: Harvard University Press.

Bernal, M. (1987) *Black Athena.* New Brunswick, NJ: Rutgers University Press.

Bhaskar, R. (1979) *The Possibility of Naturalism.* Brighton: Harvester.

Blackmore, S. (1998) *The Meme Machine.* Oxford: Oxford University Press.

Bloor, D. (1979) 'Polyhedra and the abominations of Leviticus', *British Journal for the History of Science*, 13: 254–72.

Boas, F. (1921) *Ethnology of the Kwakiutl.* Report 35. Washington, DC: Smithsonian Institution, Bureau of Ethnology.

Botwinick, A. (1990) *Skepticism and Political Participation.* Philadelphia: Temple University Press.

Brandon, R. and Burian, R. (eds) (1984) *Genes, Organisms and Populations.* Cambridge, MA: MIT Press.

Brockman, J. (1995) *The Third Culture.* New York: Simon and Schuster.

Brooke, J.H. (1991) *Science and Religion.* Cambridge, UK: Cambridge University Press.

Brown, D.E. (1988) *Hierarchy, History and Human Nature: The Social Origins of Historical Consciousness.* Tucson: University of Arizona Press.

Brown, M.F. (2003) *Who Owns Native Culture?* Cambridge, MA: Harvard University Press.

Browning, C. (2003) *The Origins of the Final Solution.* London: Heinemann.

Buruma, I. and Margalit, A. (2004) *Occidentalism: A Short History of Anti-Westernism.* London: Grove Atlantic.

Butler, J. (1990) *Gender Trouble.* London: Routledge.

Byrne, R. and Whiten, A. (eds) (1987) *Machiavellian Intelligence.* Oxford: Oxford University Press.

Canguilhem, G. (1989) *The Normal and the Pathological.* Cambridge, MA: MIT Press.

Cassirer, E. (1923) *Substance and Function.* (orig. 1910). La Salle, IL: Open Court.

Castells, M. (1998) *The Power of Identity.* Oxford: Blackwell.

Cavalli-Sforza, L. (2000) *Genes, Peoples, and Languages.* New York: Farrar, Straus and Giroux.

Ceccarelli, L. (2001) *Shaping Science with Rhetoric: The Cases of Dobzhansky, Schrödinger, and Wilson.* Chicago: University of Chicago Press.

Charry, E.Z. (1987) 'A Step toward ecumenical Esperanto', in L. Swidler (ed.), *Toward a Universal Theology of Religion.* Maryknoll, NY: Orbis.

Clarke, J.J. (1997) *Oriental Enlightenment.* London: Routledge.

Cole, M. (1996) *Cultural Psychology*. Cambridge, MA: Harvard University Press.

Collini, S. (1979) *Liberalism and Sociology: L.T. Hobhouse and Political Argument in England 1880–1914*. Cambridge, UK: Cambridge University Press.

Collins, R. (1998) *The Sociology of Philosophies*. Cambridge, MA: Harvard University Press.

Commoner, B. (1963) *Science and Survival*. New York: Viking.

Commoner, B. (1971) *The Closing Circle: Nature, Man, and Technology*. New York: Alfred Knopf.

Conant, J.B. (1959) *The American High School Today*. New York: McGraw Hill.

Connolly, K. (2002) 'German animals given legal rights', *Guardian* (London), 22 June.

Cornwell, J. (2003) *Hitler's Scientists*. New York: Viking.

Crist, E. (1999) *Images of Animals*. Philadelphia: Temple University Press.

Croskery, P. (1989) 'The intellectual property literature: a structured approach', in V. Weil and J. Snapper (eds), *Owning Scientific and Technical Information*. New Brunswick, NJ: Rutgers University Press. pp. 268–81.

Cuddihy, J.M. (1974) *The Ordeal of Civility: Freud, Marx, Levi-Strauss and the Jewish Struggle with Modernity*. New York: Basic Books.

Dahrendorf, R. (1995) *LSE: A History of the London School of Economics 1895–1995*. Oxford: Oxford University Press.

Dasgupta, P. and David, P. (1994) 'Toward a new economics of science', *Research Policy*, 23: 487–521.

Dawkins, R. (1976) *The Selfish Gene*. Oxford: Oxford University Press.

Dawkins, R. (1982) *The Extended Phenotype*. Oxford: Oxford University Press.

Dawkins, R. (2001) 'The word made flesh', *Guardian* (London), 27 December.

Degler, C. (1991) *In Search of Human Nature*. Oxford: Oxford University Press.

Deleuze, G. (1994) *Difference and Repetition*. (orig. 1968). New York: Columbia University Press.

Descombes, V. (1980) *Contemporary French Philosophy*. Cambridge, UK: Cambridge University Press.

Deutsch, K., Markovits, A. and Platt, J. (eds) (1986) *Advances in the Social Sciences, 1900–1980*. Lanham, MD: University Press of America.

Dickens, P. (2000) *Social Darwinism*. Milton Keynes: Open Unversity Press.

Dobzhansky, T. (1967) *The Biology of Ultimate Concern*. New York: New American Library.

Dupré, J. (1993) *The Disorder of Things*. Cambridge, MA: Harvard University Press.

Dworkin, R. (2000) *Sovereign Virtue: The Theory and Practice of Equality*. Cambridge, MA: Harvard University Press.

Ebenstein, A. (2001) *Friedrich Hayek: A Biography*. Chicago: University of Chicago Press.

Ehrlich, P. (1968) *The Population Bomb*. New York: Buccaneer.

Eldredge, Niles (1998) *Life in the Balance: Humanity and the Biodiversity Crisis*. Princeton: Princeton University Press.

Elster, J. (1979) *Logic and Society*. Chichester, UK: John Wiley and Sons.

Elster, J. (1983) *Sour Grapes*. Cambridge: Cambridge University Press.

Elster, J. (1999) *Alchemies of the Mind*. Cambridge, UK: Cambridge University Press.

Evans, G. (2003) *A Brief History of Heresy*. Oxford: Blackwell.

Finkelstein, N. (2000) *The Holocaust Industry*. London: Verso.

Fleishacker, S. (2004) *A Short History of Distributive Justice*. Cambridge: Harvard University Press.

Fodor, J. (1981) *Representations*. Cambridge, MA: MIT Press.

Fodor, J. (1983) *The Modularity of Mind*. Cambridge, MA: MIT Press.

Ford, K., Glymour, C. and Hayes, P. (ed.) (1995) *Android Epistemology*. Cambridge, MA: MIT Press.

Foucault, M. (1970) *The Order of Things*. New York: Random House.

Foucault, M. (1975) *The Archaeology of Knowledge*. New York: Harper and Row.

Franklin, A. (1999) *Animals and Modern Cultures: A Sociology of Human–Animal Relations in Modernity*. London: Sage.

Fraser, N. (1997) *Justice Interruptus: Critical Reflections on the 'Postsocialist' Condition*. London: Routledge.

Fuchs, S. (2000) *Against Essentialism*. Cambridge, MA: Harvard University Press.

Fukuyama, F. (1992) *The End of History and the Last Man*. New York: Free Press.

Fuller, S. (1985) 'Bounded Rationality in Law and Science' Ph.D. dissertation, University of Pittsburgh.

Fuller, S. (1988) *Social Epistemology*. Bloomington: Indiana University Press.

Fuller, S. (1993) *Philosophy of Science and Its Discontents*, 2nd edn (orig. 1989). New York: Guilford Press.

Fuller, S. (1995) 'Review of Anthony Giddens, "Beyond Left and Right"', *Sociology*, May.

Fuller, S. (1996) 'Recent work in social epistemology', *American Philosophical Quarterly*, 33: 149–66.

Fuller, S. (1997) *Science*. Milton Keynes, UK: Open University Press.

Fuller, S. (1998a) 'Divining the future of social theory', *European Journal of Social Theory*, 1: 107–26.

Fuller, S. (1998b) 'From content to context: a social epistemology of the structure-agency craze', in A. Sica (ed.), *What Is Social Theory?*, Oxford: Blackwell. pp. 92–177.

Fuller, S. (1999) 'Making the university fit for critical intellectuals: recovering from the ravages of the postmodern condition', *British Educational Research Journal*, 25: 583–95.

Fuller, S. (2000a) *The Governance of Science*. Milton Keynes, UK: Open University Press.

Fuller, S. (2000b) *Thomas Kuhn: A Philosophical History for Our Times*. Chicago: University of Chicago Press.

Fuller, S. (2001a) 'Positivism, history of', In Neil Smelser and Paul Baltes (eds), *The International Encyclopedia of Social and Behavioral Sciences*. Oxford: Pergamon, pp. 11821–27.

Fuller, S. (2001b) 'Looking for sociology after 11 September', *Sociological Research On-Line*, 6, 3, http://www.socresonline.org.uk/6/3/fuller.html

Fuller, S. (2002a) *Knowledge Management Foundations*. Woburn, MA: Butterworth-Heinemann.

Fuller, S. (2002b) 'Demystifying gnostic scientism', *Rhetoric and Public Affairs*, 5: 718–29.

Fuller, S. (2002c) 'Will sociology find some new concepts before the US finds Osama bin Laden?', *Sociological Research On-Line*, 6, 4. http://www.socresonline.org.uk/6/4/fuller.html

Fuller, S. (2003a) *Kuhn vs. Popper: The Struggle for the Soul of Science*. Cambridge, UK: Iconbooks.

Fuller, S. (2003b) 'In search of vehicles for knowledge governance: on the need for institutions that creatively destroy social capital', in Nico Stehr (ed.), *The Governance of Knowledge*. New Brunswick: Transaction. Chapter 3.

Fuller, S. (2004) 'Intellectuals: an endangered species in the 21st century?', *Economy and Society*, 33: 463–83.

Fuller, S. (2005) *The Intellectual*. Cambridge, UK: Iconbooks.

Fuller, S. and Collier, J. (2004) *Philosophy, Rhetoric, and the End of Knowledge: A New Beginning for Science and Technology Studies*. 2nd edn (orig. 1993). Mahwah, NJ: Lawrence Erlbaum Associates.

Galbraith, J.K. (1967) *The New Industrial State*. Boston: Houghton Mifflin.

Gane, M. (1988) *On Durkheim's Rules of the Sociological Method*. London: Routledge.

Gee, H. (2000) *In Search of Deep Time*. London: HarperCollins.

Gellner, E. (1989) *Plough, Sword, and Book*. Chicago: University of Chicago Press.

Geras, N. (1998) *The Contract of Mutual Indifference*. London: Verso.

Gerschenkron, A. (1962) *Economic Backwardness in Historical Perspective*. Cambridge: Harvard University Press.

Gibbons, M., Limoges, C., Nowotny, H., Schwartzmann, S., Scott, P. and Trow, M. (1994) *The New Production of Knowledge*. London: Sage.

Giddens, A. (1976) *New Rules of the Sociological Method*. London: Hutchinson.

Giddens, A. (1979) *The Central Problems of Social Theory*. London: Macmillan.

Giddens, A. (1990) *The Consequences of Modernity*. Palo Alto: Stanford University Press.

Giddens, A. (1991) *Sociology*. Cambridge, UK: Polity Press.

Giddens, A. (1994) *Beyond Left and Right*. Cambridge: Polity Press.

Glover, J. (1984) *What Sort of People Should there Be? Genetic Engineering, Brain Control and their Impact on Our Future World*. Harmondsworth, UK: Penguin.

Gould, S.J. (1977) *Ontogeny and Phylogeny*. Cambridge, MA: Harvard University Press.

Gould, S.J. (1989) *Wonderful Life: The Burgess Shale and the Nature of History*. New York: W.W. Norton.

Gouldner, A. (1970) *The Coming Crisis in Western Sociology*. New York: Basic Books.

Gouldner, A. (1973) *For Sociology: Renewal and Critique in Sociology Today*. New York: Basic Books.

Granstrand, O. (1999) *The Economics and Management of Intellectual Property*. Cheltenham, UK: Edward Elgar.

Gray, J. (2002) *Straw Dogs: Thoughts on Humans and Other Animals*. London: Granta.

Greek, C.R. and J.W. Greek (2002) *Specious Science: How Genetics and Evolution Reveal Why Medical Research on Animals Harms Humans*. New York: Continuum.

Griffiths, P. (1997) 'The human genome diversity project and indigenous peoples', *Newsletter of the Otago Branch of the Royal Society of New Zealand (Inc.)*, May. pp. 1–2.

Grundmann, R. (1991) *Marxism and Ecology*. Oxford: Oxford University Press.

Grundmann, R. and Stehr, N. (2001) 'Why is Werner Sombart not part of the core of classical sociology?', *Journal of Classical Sociology*, 1: 257–87.

Gutiérrez, G. (1990) *The Truth Shall Make You Free*. Maryknoll, NY: Orbis.

Hacohen, M. (2000) *Karl Popper, The Formative Years 1902–1945*. Cambridge, UK: Cambridge University Press.

Hall, J.R. (1999) *Cultures of Inquiry: From Epistemology to Discourse in Sociohistorical Research*. Cambridge, UK: Cambridge University Press.

Halsey, A.H. (2004) *A History of Sociology in Britain*. Oxford: Oxford University Press.

Hammond, K. and Stewart, T. (eds) (2001) *The Essential Brunswik*. Oxford: Oxford University Press.

Haraway, D. (1990) *Simians, Cyborgs, and Women*. London: Free Association Books.

Hardin, G. (1959) *Nature and Man's Fate*. New York: New American Library.

Hardin, G. (1968) 'The tragedy of the commons', *Science*, 162: 1243–8.

Hardt, M. and Negri, A. (2000) *Empire*. Cambridge, MA: Harvard University Press.

Harré, R. (1984) *Social Being*. Oxford: Blackwell.

Harris, M. (1968) *The Rise of Anthropological Theory*. New York: Thomas Crowell.

Hayek, F. (1948) *Individualism and Economic Order*. Chicago: University of Chicago Press.

Hayles, K. (1999) *How We Became Posthuman*. Chicago: University of Chicago Press.

Henley, J. (2002) 'France limits the right of those born disabled to sue doctors', *Guardian* (London), 11 January.

Herf, J. (1984) *Reactionary Modernism*. Cambridge, UK: Cambridge University Press.

Herrnstein, R. and Murray, C. (1994) *The Bell Curve: Intelligence and Class Structure in American Life*. New York: Free Press.

Hildebrandt, M. (2004) 'Privacy and identity', in E. Claes, A. Duff, S. Gutwirth (eds), *Privacy and Criminal Law*. Antwerp: Intersentia.

Hirsch, F. (1976) *Social Limits to Growth*. London: Routledge and Kegan Paul.

Hirst, P.Q. (1975) *Durkheim, Bernard, and Epistemology*. London: Routledge and Kegan Paul.

Hoffman, A. (1997) *From Heresy to Dogma: An Institutional History of Corporate Environmentalism*. San Francisco: Lexington Books.

Hofstadter, R. (1955) *Social Darwinism in American Thought, 1860–1915*. Boston: Beacon Press.

Horgan, J. (1996) *The End of Science*. Lexington MA: Addison-Wesley.

Horowitz, D. (2004) *Unholy Alliance: Islamic Fundamentalism and the American Left*. Chicago: Regnery.

Howe, H. and Lyne, J. (1992) 'Gene talk', *Social Epistemology*, 6: 109–63. http://www.edge.org

Huntington, S. (1996) *The Clash of Civilizations and the Remaking of World Order*. New York: Simon and Schuster.

Huxley, T.H. (1893) 'Evolution and ethics', (The Romanes Lecture). http://aleph0.clarku.edu/huxley/CE9/E-E.html

Ingold, T. (1994) 'Humanity and animality', in T. Ingold, (ed.), *Companion Encyclopedia of Anthropology*. London: Routledge. Chapter 2.

Iqbal, M. (1964) *Thoughts and Reflections of Iqbal*, ed. S. Vahid. Lahore, Pakistan: Ashraf.

Jacques, R. (1996) *Manufacturing the Employee*. London: Sage.

Jevons, W.S. (2001) 'Of economy of fuel', *Organization and Environment*, 14: 99–104. (orig. 1865).

Kay, L. (2000) *Who Wrote the Book of Life? A History of the Genetic Code*. Cambridge, MA: MIT Press.

Keegan, J. (1999) 'How Hitler could have won the war', in R. Cowley (ed.), *What If?* London: Macmillan. pp. 295–305.

Kent, R. (1981) *A History of British Empirical Sociology*. Aldershot, UK: Gower.

King, D. (1999) *In the Name of Liberalism: Illiberal Social Policy in the United States and Britain*. Oxford: Oxford University Press.

Kitchener, R. (1986) *Piaget's Theory of Knowledge*. New Haven: Yale University Press.

Kitcher, P. (2001) *Science, Truth, and Democracy*. Oxford: Oxford University Press.

Knorr-Cetina, K. (1999) *Epistemic Cultures*. Cambridge, MA: Harvard University Press.

Knorr-Cetina, K. and Bruegger, U. (2002) 'Traders' engagement with markets: a post-social relationship', *Theory, Culture and Society*, 19 (5/6): 161–85.

Koegler, H. and Stueber, K. (eds) (2000) *Empathy and Agency: The Problem of Understanding in the Human Sciences*. Boulder: Westview Press.

Kuhn, T.S. (1970) *The Structure of Scientific Revolutions*. 2nd edn (orig. 1962). Chicago: University of Chicago Press.

La Follette, H. and Shanks, N. (1997) *Brute Science: Dilemmas of Animal Experimentation*. London: Routledge.

Lasch, C. (1995) *The Revolt of the Elites and the Betrayal of Democracy*. New York: Norton.

Latour, B. (1993) *We Have Never Been Modern*. Cambridge, MA: Harvard University Press.

Latour, B. (1996) *Aramis, or the Love of Technology*. Cambridge, MA: Harvard University Press.

Latour, B. (2000) 'E-mail Exchanges', in S. Strum and L.M. Fedigan (eds), *Primate Encounters: Models of Science, Gender and Society*. Chicago: University of Chicago Press. pp. 312–15.

Latour, B. (2002) *War of the Worlds: How about Peace?* Chicago: Prickly Paradigm Press.

Latour, B. (2004) *The Politics of Nature*. Cambridge, MA: Harvard University Press.

Laudan, L. (1981) *Science and Hypothesis*. Dordrecht: Kluwer.

Lawler, S. (2005) 'Rules of engagement: habitus, power and resistance', in L. Adkins and B. Skeggs (eds), *Feminism after Bourdieu*. Oxford: Blackwell.

Lepenies, W. (1988) *Between Literature and Science*. Cambridge: Cambridge University Press.

Lessig, L. (2001) *The Future of Ideas: The Fate of the Commons in a Connected World*. New York: Random House.

Levine, D.N. (1995) *Visions of the Sociological Tradition*. Chicago: University of Chicago Press.

Lewontin, R. (1972) 'The apportionment of human diversity', *Evolutionary Biology* 6: 381–98.

Lewontin, R. (1993) *Biology as Ideology*. New York: HarperCollins.

Lilla, M. (2001) *The Reckless Mind: Intellectuals in Politics*. New York: New York Review of Books.

Livingstone, D. (1984) *Darwin's Forgotten Defenders: The Encounter between Evangelical Theology and Evolutionary Thought*. Grand Rapids: William Eerdmans.

Lomborg, B. (2001) *The Sceptical Environmentalist*. Cambridge, UK: Cambridge University Press.

Lorenz, K. (1977[1963]) *On Aggression*. New York: Bantam.

Lukes, S. (1996) *The Curious Enlightenment of Professor Caritat: A Comedy of Ideas*. London: Verso.

Lyotard, J.-F. (1983) *The Postmodern Condition*. (orig. 1979). Minneapolis: University of Minnesota Press.

MacIntyre, A. (1994) *Marxism and Christianity*. 2nd edn (orig. 1968). London: Duckworth.

MacIntyre, A. (1999) *Dependent Rational Animals*. London: Duckworth.

Mandelbaum, M. (1987) *Purpose and Necessity in Social Theory*. Baltimore: Johns Hopkins University Press.

Martin, D. (1978) *A General Theory of Secularisation*. Oxford: Blackwell.

März, E. (1991) *Joseph Schumpeter: Scholar, Teacher and Politician*. New Haven: Yale University Press.

Mauss, M. (1954) *The Gift: Forms and Functions of Exchange in Archaic Societies*. London: Cohen and West.

McNamara, R. (1973) *One Hundred Countries, Two Billion People*. New York: Praeger.

Meek, J. (2002) 'Cancer gene tests "will destroy private health"', *Guardian* (London), 5 August.

Merton, R.K. (1977) *The Sociology of Science*. Chicago: University of Chicago Press.

Merz, J.T. (1904) *A History of European Thought in the Nineteenth Century*, Vol. 2 London: Blackwood and Sons.

Milbank, J. (1990) *Theology and Social Theory: Beyond Secular Reason*. Oxford: Blackwell.

Montagu, A. (1945) *Man's Most Dangerous Myth: The Concept of Race*. New York: Columbia University Press.

Murray, C. (2003) *Human Accomplishment*. New York: HarperCollins.

Mykitiuk, R. (2003) 'Public bodies, private parts: genetics in a post-Keynesian Era' in B. Cossman and J. Fudge (eds), *Privatization, Law and the Challenge to Feminism*. Toronto: University of Toronto Press.

Nanda, M. (2003) *Prophets Facing Backward: Critiques of Science and the Making of Hindu Nationalism in India*. New Brunswick, NJ: Rutgers University Press.

Neese, R.M. and Williams, G.C. (1995) *Evolution and Healing*. London: Weidenfeld and Nicolson.

Neumann, F. (1944) *Behemoth: The Structure and Practice of National Socialism: 1933–1944*. Oxford: Oxford University Press.

Novick, P. (1999) *The Holocaust in American Life*. New York: Basic Books.

Nowotny, H., Scott, P. and Gibbons, M. (2000) *Re-thinking Science*. Oxford: Polity.

Nussbaum, M. (2001) 'Disabled lives: who Cares?', *The New York Review of Books*, 11 January.

Offer, J. (1999) 'Spencer's future of welfare: a vision eclipsed', *Sociological Review*, 47: 136–62.

Packard, V. (1957) *Hidden Persuaders*. New York: Pocket Books.

Parsons, T. (1937) *The Structure of Social Action*. New York: Harper and Row.

Parsons, T. (1951) *The Social System*. New York: Basic Books.

Passmore, J. (1970) *The Perfectibility of Man*. London: Duckworth.

Patterson, K. (2002) 'The petting order: sociologists look at roles humans assign animals', *Dallas Morning News*, 13 April.

Paul, D. (1998) *The Politics of Heredity*. Albany: SUNY Press.

Peukert, D. (1993) *The Weimar Republic*. Harmondsworth, UK: Penguin.

Pinker, S. (2002) *The Blank Slate: The Modern Denial of Human Nature*. New York: Viking.

Platt, J. (1996) *A History of Sociological Research Methods in America*. Cambridge, UK: Cambridge University Press.

Plender, J. (2001) 'Walking with animals, learning new tricks', *Financial Times* (London), 17/18 March.

Polanyi, K. (1944) *The Great Transformation*. Boston: Beacon Press.

Polanyi, M. (1957) *Personal Knowledge*. Chicago: University of Chicago Press.

Popper, K. (1957) *The Poverty of Historicism*. New York: Harper and Row.

Premack, D. and Premack, A.J. (1994) 'Why animals have neither culture nor history', in T. Ingold (ed.), *Companion Encyclopedia of Anthropology*. London: Routledge. Chapter 13.

Prendergast, C. (1986) 'Alfred Schutz and the Austrian School of Economics', *American Journal of Sociology*, 92: 1–26.

Price, C. (1993) *Time, Discounting, and Value*. Oxford: Blackwell.

Proctor, R. (1988) *Racial Hygiene: Medicine under the Nazis*. Cambridge, MA: Harvard University Press.

Proctor, R. (1991) *Value-Free Science? Purity and Power in Modern Knowledge*. Cambridge, MA: Harvard University Press.

Proctor, R. (1995) *Cancer Wars: How Politics Shapes What We Know and Don't Know about Cancer*. New York: Basic Books.

Proctor, R. (1999) *The Nazi War on Cancer.* Princeton: Princeton University Press.

Putnam, H. (1975) *Mind, Language and Reality.* Cambridge, UK: Cambridge University Press.

Qutb, S. (1990) 'That hidden schizophrenia', in P. Griffiths (ed.), *Christianity through Non-Christian Eyes.* Maryknoll, NY: Orbis.

Rabinbach, A. (1990) *The Human Motor: Energy, Fatigue, and the Origins of Modernity.* New York: Basic Books.

Rabinow, P. (1997) *Essays on the Anthropology of Reason.* Princeton: Princeton University Press.

Radick, G. (2005) 'Other histories, other biologies', in A. O'Hear (ed.), *Philosophy, Biology and Life.* Cambridge, UK: Cambridge University Press.

Rapoport, A. (1994) 'Spatial organization and the built environment', in T. Ingold (ed.), *Companion Encyclopedia of Anthropology.* London: Routledge. pp. 460–502.

Ravetz, J. (1971) *Scientific Knowledge and Its Social Problems.* Oxford: Oxford University Press.

Rawls, J. (1971) *A Theory of Justice.* Cambridge, MA: Harvard University Press.

Rée, J. (1999) *I See a Voice: A Philosophical History of Language, Deafness and the Senses.* London: HarperCollins.

Reisch, G. (2005) *How the Cold War Transformed Philosophy of Science.* Cambridge, UK: Cambridge University Press.

Richards, R. (1987) *Darwin and the Emergence of Evolutionary Theories of Mind and Behavior.* Chicago: University of Chicago Press.

Rifkin, J. (1998) *The Biotech Century.* New York: J.P. Tarcher.

Rifkin, J. (2001) 'This is the age of biology', *Guardian* (London), 28 July.

Rose, H. and Rose, S. (eds) (2000) *Alas Poor Darwin: Arguments against Evolutionary Psychology.* London: Jonathan Cape.

Rose, N. (1999) *Powers of Freedom: Reframing Political Thought.* Cambridge, UK: Cambridge University Press.

Rosenberg, A. (1994) *Instrumental Biology or the Disunity of Science.* Chicago: University of Chicago Press.

Rostow, W.W. (1960) *The Stages of Economic Growth: A Non-Communist Manifesto.* Cambridge, UK: Cambridge University Press.

Rothschild, E. (2001) *Economic Sentiments: Adam Smith, Condorcet, and the Enlightenment.* Cambridge, MA: Harvard University Press.

Rueschemeyer, D. and van Rossum, R. (1996) 'The "Verein für Sozialpolitik" and the Fabian Society: a study in the sociology of policy-relevant knowledge', in D. Rueschemeyer and T. Skocpol (eds), *States, Social Knowledge and the Origins of Modern Social Policies.* Princeton: Princeton University Press. pp. 117–62.

Runciman, W.G. (1998) *The Social Animal.* London: HarperCollins.

Ruse, M. (1979) *The Darwinian Revolution.* Chicago: University of Chicago Press.

Sachs, J. (2005) *The End of Poverty: How We Can Make It Happen in Our Lifetime.* London: Penguin.

Said, E. (1978) *Orientalism*. New York: Random House.

Santayana, G. (1905) *Reason and Commonsense*. New York: Scribners.

Sardar, Z. (1989) *Explorations in Islamic Science*. London: Mansell.

Scheuerman, W. (1994) *Between the Norm and the Exception*. Cambridge: MIT Press.

Schluchter, W. (2000) 'Psychophysics and Culture', in Stephen Turner (ed.), *The Cambridge Companion to Max Weber*. Cambridge, UK: Cambridge University Press. pp. 59–82.

Schmitt, C. (1996) *The Concept of the Political*. (orig. 1932). Chicago: University of Chicago Press.

Schnaedelbach, H. (1984) *Philosophy in Germany, 1831–1933*. Cambridge: Cambridge University Press.

Schumpeter, J. (1934) *The Theory of Economic Development*. Cambridge, MA: Harvard University Press.

Schumpeter, J. (1942) *Capitalism, Socialism, and Democracy*. New York: Harper and Row.

Schutz, A. (1964) 'The well-informed citizen: an essay in the distribution of knowledge', *Collected Papers*, Volume II. (orig. 1932). The Hague: Martinus Nijhoff. pp. 120–34.

Schwartz, J. (1999) 'For sale in Iceland: a nation's genetic code. Deal with research firm highlights conflicting views of progress, privacy and ethics', *The Washington Post*, 12 January.

Schwartzman, P. (1995) 'The population growth debate in the public sphere', *Social Epistemology*, 9: 289–310.

Seabright, P. (2004) *The Company of Strangers: A Natural History of Economic Life*. New Haven, CT: Yale University Press.

Searle, J. (1996) *The Construction of Social Reality*. Harmondsworth, UK: Penguin.

Segerstrale, U. (2000) *Defenders of the Truth*. Oxford: Oxford University Press.

Sell, A. (ed.) (1997) *Mill and Religion: Contemporary Responses to Three Essays on Religion*. Bristol, UK: Thoemmes Press.

Simon, H. (1977) *The Sciences of the Artificial*. Cambridge, MA: MIT Press.

Singer, P. (1975) *Animal Liberation*. New York: Random House.

Singer, P. (1981) *The Expanding Circle: Ethics and Sociobiology*. New York: Farrar, Strauss and Giroux.

Singer, P. (1994) *Rethinking Life and Death*. Melbourne: Text Publishing Company.

Singer, P. (1999a) *A Darwinian Left: Politics, Evolution and Cooperation*. London: Weidenfeld and Nicolson.

Singer, P. (1999b) 'A response', in D. Jamieson (ed.), *Singer and his Critics*. Oxford: Blackwell: pp. 269–335.

Skeggs, B. (1997) *Formations of Class and Gender*. London: Sage.

Skinner, B.F. (1971) *Beyond Freedom and Dignity*. New York: Alfred Knopf.

Smith, B. (1994) *Austrian Philosophy: The Legacy of Franz Brentano*. La Salle: Open Court Press.

Sokal, A. and Bricmont, J. (1998) *Intellectual Impostures*. London: Phaidon.

Solomon, R. (1999) 'Peter Singer's expanding circle: compassion and the liberation of ethics', in D. Jamieson (ed.), *Singer and his Critics*. Oxford: Blackwell. pp. 64–85.

Sorokin, P. (1928) *Contemporary Sociological Theories*. New York: Harper and Row.

Stark, R. (2003) *For the Glory of God*. Princeton: Princeton University Press.

Stehr, N. (2001) 'Economy and ecology in an era of knowledge-based economies', *Current Sociology*, 49: 67–90.

Stehr, N. and Weinstein, J. (1999) 'The power of knowledge: race science, race hygiene, and the holocaust', *Social Epistemology*, 13: 3–36.

Steiner, H. (1998) 'Silver spoons and golden genes: talent differentials and distributive justice', in J. Burley (ed.), *The Genetic Revolution and Human Rights*. Oxford: Oxford University Press. pp. 133–50.

Tamas, G.M. (2000) 'On post-fascism', *Boston Review*, 25 (3).

Tetlock, P. and Belkin, A. (eds) (1996) *Counterfactual Thought Experiments in World Politics*. Princeton: Princeton University Press.

Titmuss, R. (1970) *The Gift Relationship: From Human Blood to Social Policy*. London: Allen and Unwin.

Toulmin, S. (2003) *Return to Reason*. Cambridge, MA: Harvard University Press.

Trivers, R. (1971) 'The evolution of reciprocal altruism', *Quarterly Review of Biology* 46: 35–57.

Turner, B.S. (1984) *The Body and Society*. London: Sage.

Urry, J. (2000) *Sociology without Societies*. London: Routledge.

Urry, J. (2002) 'Mobility and Proximity', *Sociology* 36: 255–74.

Veblen, T. (1904) *The Theory of Business Enterprise*. New York: Scribners.

Wagar, W.W. (1967) *The City of Man*. Boston: Houghton Mifflin.

Wallerstein, I. (1996) *Open the Social Sciences*. Cambridge, UK: Cambridge University Press.

Watson, S. (1998) 'The Neurobiology of Sorcery: Deleuze and Guattari's Brain', *Body and Society*, 4 (4): 23–45.

Wernick, A. (2001) *Auguste Comte and the Religion of Humanity*. Cambridge, UK: Cambridge University Press.

Wheen, F. (2004) *How Mumbo-Jumbo Conquered the World: A Short History of Modern Delusions*. London: HarperCollins.

Whiteside, K. (2002) *Divided Natures: French Contributions to Political Ecology*. Cambridge, MA: MIT Press.

Wilson, E.O. (1975) *Sociobiology: The New Synthesis*. Cambridge, MA: Harvard University Press.

Wilson, E.O. (1978) *On Human Nature*. Cambridge, MA: Harvard University Press.

Wilson, E.O. (1992) *The Diversity of Life*. Cambridge, MA: Harvard University Press.

Wilson, E.O. (1998) *Consilience: The Unity of Knowledge*. New York: Alfred Knopf.

Winch, P. (1958) *The Idea of a Social Science*. London: Routledge and Kegan Paul.

Wise, S. (1999) *Rattling the Cage*. Cambridge, MA: Harvard University Press.

York, R., Rosa, E. and Dietz, T. (2003) 'Footprints on the earth: the environmental consequences of modernity', *American Sociological Review*, 68: 279–300.

Young, R. (1985) *Darwin's Metaphor*. Cambridge, UK: Cambridge University Press.

Zahavi, A. and Zahavi, A. (1997) *The Handicap Principle: A Missing Piece of Darwin's Puzzle*. Oxford: Oxford University Press.

Index

Simmel, Georg 81, 86–8, 157
Singer, Peter 5, 29, 49, 61, 101, 107–9, 111,
    113–15, 121–3, 125–8, 141–3, 156,
    164, 166, 172–7, 179–81, 183, 201,
    204, 208, 212, 214; *see also*
    Darwinian Left
Skinner, B.F. 172–4
Smith, Adam 25, 37, 63, 68, 70,
    75, 171–2, 213
Social Darwinism 44, 61, 192, 212;
    see also Darwinism
Social epistemology 2, 26
Socialism 3–5, 12–13, 16–17, 20–22, 25,
    28, 31–3, 35–44, 48–50, 52, 54, 57–9,
    63–4, 74, 80–2, 108, 111, 147, 153,
    163, 181, 207–12, 214;
    see also Marxism
Sociobiology 5, 29, 81, 84–5, 97, 100, 134,
    165, 167, 183, 196, 199, 208–9,
    212–13; *see also* Evolutionary
    psychology, Wilson
Soviet Union 30–1, 80, 172
Spencer, Herbert 28, 35, 44–5, 48, 58,
    61, 80, 102, 141–2, 147, 156, 162,
    171, 189, 196, 209, 211–12
Stalin, Joseph 21, 45, 82
Standard Social Science Model (SSSM)
    76, 84, 172, 198, 213–14
Structural-functionalism vii, 13, 16,
    88–9, 211; *see also* Merton, Parsons
Sympathy 5, 118–20, 180, 184, 213

Tarde, Gabriel 20–1, 98
Taxation 7, 34, 39–40, 44, 46, 50,
    56, 61, 71, 117, 124, 152

Thatcher, Margaret 11–12, 16, 36,
    41, 46, 210
Third Culture 11–12, 198–9, 209, 213
Toennies, Ferdinand 41–2, 66,
    74, 100, 209

Universitas 6, 42, 75, 157, 205
Utilitarianism 34, 37–8, 58, 104, 110,
    119, 122, 127, 174, 179, 210, 212–14;
    see also Bentham, Mill, Singer
Urry, John 12, 63–6

Veblen, Thorstein 68, 70, 111
Vienna Circle 16–17, 83, 210–12, 214;
    see also Positivism

Wallerstein, Immanuel viii, 13, 15,
    74, 82, 137
Weber, Max 2, 11, 13–15, 17, 42, 48,
    60, 65, 74, 79–84, 89, 111, 128,
    135, 161, 186, 198, 211, 214
Welfare 4, 17–18, 24–5, 27, 29, 31, 33, 37,
    40–1, 44, 50, 54–61, 71, 80, 83, 124–5,
    141–2, 145, 148, 150, 155, 166, 173,
    175, 189, 203–4, 208; *see also*
    Welfare state
Welfare state 3–4, 13, 16–18, 27–8, 32, 39,
    42–4, 46–8, 51, 59, 117, 189, 196,
    205, 207, 211–12, 214
Westermarck, Edward viii, 81, 84–6, 214
Wilson, E.O. 81–2, 85, 92, 95, 165–7,
    169–70, 184, 198–9, 212;
    see also Sociobiology
World War I: *see* First World War
World War II: *see* Second World War

26555237R00134

Printed in Great Britain
by Amazon